CHURCHILL

Man of the Century

CHURCHILL

Man of the Century

Christian Graf von Krockow

Translated by Helmut Bögler

LONDON
HOUSE

First published in 1999 by
Hoffmann und Campe Verlag, Hamburg

This edition published in 2000 by
LONDON HOUSE
114 New Cavendish Street
London W1M 7FD

00-01

A catalogue record for this book
is available from The British Library

ISBN 1 902809 43 2

Designed and typeset by Roger Chesneau

Printed and bound in Great Britain

Contents

Prologue

This book is about Winston Spencer Churchill, his life and his work as a statesman. It portrays him as the key figure of an era, as the exemplary counter-player of tyranny.

This may appear to be unusual. From a continental, and particularly a German, perspective, the history of the twentieth century is characterised by two radical movements, Marxism and Communism on the one hand and Fascism and National Socialism on the other. According to their claims, they were pursuing two sharply contradictory objectives—here the imposition of the 'classless society', there the rule of the 'master race'. In practice, however, there were similarities, not to say corresponding factors. Both movements attempted to eliminate history with its traditional systems, concepts and values, to level it as on a building site, so to speak, in order to erect the new, and now ultimate, on the ruins of the existing. The consequences were the unleashing of a boundless tyranny with millions upon millions of victims.

This also included adulation: the leaders of the movements—Lenin, Stalin, Adolf Hitler—were admired, adored, almost elevated to gods as the leaders to salvation and redemption. In the end, however, came failure—the horror-filled failure of the Third Reich in 1945, the shameful failure of the Soviet empire around 1990.

The spiritual conflict, the intellectual debate of the twentieth century in continental Europe, was also influenced by the two radical movements, be it as a protagonist or as an anti-Communist or an anti-Fascist. The same is true for the writing of history. Should we, for example, talk about a German 'special way' and insist on the uniqueness of the event—particularly with reference to the holocaust—or should we talk about a European civil war, in which Hitler's tyranny was only the counter to the challenge of Communism? How can the seducibility of the masses and the complicity of the intellectuals be explained? In these or similar terms are the questions worded which, by now, are mixed with something close to perplexity, because what has been argued about for so long and so passionately has suddenly become meaningless.

But, at the turn of the century, this is precisely what should give us cause fundamentally to revise our look back at the century behind us, because our debate and our historic perspective, with whatever pros or cons, are tinged by something embarrassingly provincial. The alternative to Communism was not Fascism, nor *vice versa*. The true opposites to both movements were the liberal Western democracies, first and foremost those of Great Britain and the United States of America. And the exemplary counter-player to Hitler was not Stalin but Winston Churchill. In this he was not only the man who blocked Hitler's way to 'final victory' in the West, but also the strict anti-Communist for whom only half the job had been done in 1945. From then on, and with the power of America, the Cold War was waged in his sense until the final collapse of Communism.

Why then has Churchill—at least in the narrow, Continental view—only been perceived as a colourful figure at best, and not recognized as the exemplary counter-player? Apparently for the very reason that he rejected, even despised, all teachings of salvation and redemption, and only took them seriously as forces of destruction and military threats. He did not believe that old Adam could be remoulded into the new Communist man, or into a hero, and a healthy scepticism towards radical world improvement was his credo. (Beneath this scepticism, however, lies the conviction from the Christian heritage, that in this world salvation cannot be achieved by human endeavour alone.) Between him and those intellectuals who can become enthusiastic about philosophical systems, designs for the future or delusions, light years then lay, and still do today. What was important for him was what he portrayed in historic contemplation, in literary works of note such as his great Marlborough biography, his history of the English-speaking peoples and his reports on the two world wars.

Churchill was a conservative born and bred—in the sense that he wanted to save from the attack of the levellers of history what to him appeared to be worth preserving, from parliamentary democracy to liberty and law and all the way to the British Commonwealth. The errors are included: in Churchill the modern and persevering are mixed with the outdated and outlived.

These errors do not detract from the standing of the counter-player: they confirm it. They show that among men there is no such thing as infallibility — and that where infallibility is claimed, we are led not to salvation but into disaster. If you like, this is the message contained in the horrors of the twentieth century which can lead us into the future and guard us against the temptations awaiting us there.

A final word on the book: it follows its model in that it recounts instead of speculating. It is intended to provide views of the life of the man who actually did play a key rôle if we wish to understand the history of the twentieth century, instead of only constantly voicing our indignation in hindsight as know-alls.

The Shudders of Childhood and Youth

Children need love, the tender care of their parents, if they are to grow up healthy and happy. This, so it would appear, is a cast-iron rule, proven by our knowledge of man, and to no small degree by horror stories—that children, for example, suffer and can go wrong if their parents separate. Looked at more closely, however, this dictum is only the rather recent discovery or invention of a society which is influenced by bourgeois concepts—or, to put it into more modern terms, by the middle classes.

In any event, within the older systems things are quite different. There children are only small, unfortunately as yet unfinished adults whom one drives by strictness, and also by beatings, to grow up and become useful as quickly as possible. In the poor, hard-working lower classes of farmers, craftsmen and day labourers—in other words, among the large majority of the population—children have to work in the house, in the garden and the stables, in the fields and with the livestock, at the spinning wheel and at the loom just as soon as they are able. From earliest childhood to old age life is imprinted by the biblical curse: 'Thou shall eat thy bread in the sweat of thy brow until thou returneth to the earth from which thou hast come.' And if you stay half-way healthy and can eat your fill, that is already a great deal.

Among the European upper classes, at the courts and among the nobility, things are different, yet still quite similar. While one does not need to work like the common people, one is still so variously occupied that there is no time left for the children. This is particularly true for the select families, only a few hundred in total, who have ruled Great Britain since time immemorial. Social gatherings and conversation, status and intrigues within one's own élite circle, hunting and riding, politics and sports—there is always something to do. Consequently the saying is: 'The English do not suckle their young'—they leave that to wet-nurses, nurses and governesses, and finally to a strict upbringing in famous schools such as Harrow or Eton.

Winston Churchill's childhood illustrates what we are talking about. He was born on 30 November 1874 in Blenheim, in the house of his grandfather, the 7th Duke of Marlborough. No, not in the house, in the palace of Blenheim, which testifies to the hereditary estate, the almost immeasurable wealth the first bearer of the name accumulated at the turn of the seventeenth and eighteenth centuries. But since, according to English law, only the first-born son inherits the title and the fortune, as a younger son the father is only Lord Randolph and his son simply Winston Churchill.

To pause here for a moment: the strict laws of inheritance of British nobility create a different situation from that on the Continent—not a closed caste but an open upper class. The younger children step down into the middle class, and in the opposite direction social risers can be rewarded for their achievements by being decorated with resounding titles without any danger of an inflation of the nobility.[1] The only split is a political one: their lordships take their seats in the Upper House without having to stand for election. In exchange they are excluded from the Lower House. In order not to lose his seat there, many a person has declined his elevation to a lordship or—as in Churchill's case after 1945—to a dukedom.

Winston's mother, Jennie Jerome, in whose veins, it was alleged, there flowed a proportion of Indian blood, was the daughter of an American social riser and broker in New York. Lord Randolph saw her, fell in love and pushed through the marriage, much to the consternation of the ducal family. But, as a dazzling beauty, she was soon beseiged by admirers and began to enjoy the life of an aristocrat in full measure. She did not want to give up social gatherings and dancing even after her pregnancy was far advanced. But the uncouth child was impatient, and the contractions suddenly set in. Through the endless corridors of the palace Jennie just managed to reach the powder room where she gave birth to Winston in a precipitate delivery, seven weeks too early. As quickly as possible, she then again went back to her pleasures.

In his memoirs of his youth Churchill wrote:

My mother always seemed to me a fairy princess . . . Lord D'Abernon has described her . . . in words for which I am grateful.

. . . 'I have the clearest recollection of seeing her for the first time. It was at the Vice-Regal Lodge at Dublin. She stood on one side to the left of the entrance. The Viceroy [Churchill's grandfather, Marlborough] was on a dais at the farther end of the room surrounded by a brilliant staff, but eyes were not turned on him or his consort, but on a dark, lithe figure standing somewhat apart and appearing to be of a different texture to those around her, radiant, translucent, intense. A diamond star in her hair, her favourite ornament—its lustre dimmed by the flashing glory of her eyes. More of the panther than of the woman in her look, but with a cultivated intelligence unknown to the jungle. Her courage not less great than that of her husband—fit mother for the descendants of the great Duke. With all these attributes of brilliancy, such kindliness and high spirits that she was universally popular. Her desire to please, her delight in life, and the genuine wish that all should share her joyous faith in it, made her the centre of a devoted circle.'[2]

'My mother', Churchill continues, 'made the same brilliant impression upon my childhood's eye. She shone for me like the Evening Star. I loved her dearly—but at a distance.' Yes, from as far away as a star, basically unreachable. Incidentally, after Lord Randolph's death Jennie re-married twice, first an officer who was twenty years her junior and of whom it was said that he was the most handsome man of his times. Jennie simply wanted to go on shining socially instead of sinking into widowhood. She died in 1921.

There is much more to be told about the father than the mother. In his youth he was what we today would call a playboy, and the scandals were not long in coming. In a series of interlinked affairs it even came to the point where the Prince of Wales—later King Edward VII—challenged Lord Randolph to a duel. The Lord replied that he would fight any second, but not the future king. The Prince in his turn declared that he would no longer enter any house in which the Churchills were received. The wise old Prime Minister Benjamin Disraeli finally found a way out. He sent the Duke of Marlborough to Dublin as Viceroy—and Lord Randolph, after his father as private secretary, into Irish exile to cool down, so to speak. And so it came to pass that the earliest childhood memories of little Winston stem from Ireland.

In the meantime the father discovered his political ambitions. He became a party man—a Conservative of course—and soon moved up to a leadership position. 'Tory Democracy' was his rousing slogan. He recognised that the Whigs hardly represented more than a limited middle class, and that one could gain the support of the working masses—who had now achieved the right to vote—for the Conservative camp if one only approached them in the right way—in other words, demagogically—in their own world. He was a radical in the cloak of a conservative, a rousing speaker who attacked his opponents in rude terms never before heard. This made him highly suspect to his own party colleagues as well. Lord Salisbury, the party leader, said: 'Randolph and the Mahdi [the leader of a fanatical religious revolt in the Sudan] occupy my attention in about equal amounts. The Mahdi acts mad, but is really quite clear in his head. With Randolph it is the opposite way around.'

Possibly only Gladstone, the Liberal Prime Minister, would have been a match for Randolph. His demagogy consisted of always highly moral sermons underlaid with sobriety. (When Gladstone fell tears flowed copiously among his ministers, yet Gladstone himself subsequently only mocked this 'tearful Cabinet meeting'.) But by now Gladstone was an old man, and in the General Election of 1886 he was beaten — thanks to Randolph Churchill. What could Salisbury do except appoint the victor as Chancellor of the Exchequer and Minister for the House of Commons? And how long was it going to be before Churchill inherited the office of Prime Minister from Salisbury?

The appointment took place in August 1886 — and only months later Lord Randolph was politically dead. And for a trivial reason: because the Minister for War demanded — as usual — more money than he was willing to approve, he tendered his resignation, and Salisbury seized the opportunity to banish his rival to the wilderness. People then said that the self-opinionated Randolph had committed the most sensational political suicide of the century.

Or was there more behind it — something worse than that? 'The man is insane,' Queen Victoria said. And in fact there were already indications of the paralytic collapse which took place a few years later and let Lord Randolph die in darkness at only 45 years of age.

The son admired the father, but, like the mother, as an unreachably distant and then rapidly sinking star. Winston Churchill always treasured the few occasions of a personal encounter with his father as precious memories, and later he dedicated a great biography to him.

But what was left for the child? Where did little Winston find his hold? First and foremost with his nurse, Mrs Everest. She, and she alone, gave him security, tenderness, love. When she died in 1895, the young lieutenant of Hussars cried at her grave. But, unfortunately, besides Mrs Everest the dark figure of a governess soon appeared, for whom the issue was not love but learning. And then the horror of school! The mother took the seven-year-old to the boarding school selected for him, St George's in Ascot,[3] and what then took place there has been described by no one more forcefully than Churchill himself:

When the last sound of my mother's departing wheels had died away, the Head-master invited me to hand over any money I had in my possession . . . Then we quitted the Headmaster's parlour and the comfortable private side of the house and entered the more bleak apartments reserved for the instruction and accom-modation of the pupils. I was taken into a Form Room and told to sit at a desk. All the other boys were out of doors, and I was alone with the Form Master. He produced a thin greeny-brown-covered book filled with words in different types of print.

'You have never done any Latin before, have you?' he said.

'No, sir.'

'This is a Latin grammar.' He opened it at a well-thumbed page. 'You must learn this,' he said, pointing to a number of words in a frame of lines. 'I will come back in half an hour and see what you know.'

Behold me then on a gloomy evening, with an aching heart, seated in front of the First Declension.

Mensa	a table
Mensa	O table
Mensam	a table
Mensae	of a table
Mensae	to or for a table
Mensa	by, with or from a table

What on earth did it mean? Where was the sense in it? It seemed absolute rig-marole to me. However, there was one thing I could always do: I could learn by heart. And I thereupon proceeded, as far as my private sorrows would allow, to memorize the acrostic-looking task which had been set me.

In due course the Master returned.

'Have you learnt it?' he asked.

'I think I can *say* it, sir,' I replied; and I gabbled it off.

He seemed so satisfied with this that I was emboldened to ask a question.

'What does it mean, sir?'

'It means what it says. Mensa, a table. Mensa is a noun of the First Declension. There are five declensions. You have learnt the singular of the First Declension.'

'But,' I repeated, 'what does it mean?'

'Mensa means a table,' he answered.

'Then why does mensa also mean O table,' I enquired, 'and what does O table mean?'

'Mensa, O table, is the vocative case,' he replied

'But why O table?' I persisted in genuine curiosity.

'O table, —you would use that in addressing a table, in invoking a table.' And then seeing he was not carrying me with him, 'You would use it in speaking to a table.'

'But I never do,' I blurted out in honest amazement.

'If you are impertinent you will be punished, and punished, let me tell you, very severely,' was his conclusive rejoinder.

Such was my first introduction to the Classics from which, I have been told, many of our cleverest men have derived so much solace and profit.

The Form Master's observations about punishment were by no means without their warrant at St James's School. Flogging with the birch in accordance with the Eton fashion was a great feature in its curriculum. But I am sure no Eton boy, and certainly no Harrow boy of my day, ever received such a cruel flogging as this Headmaster was accustomed to inflict upon the little boys who were in his care and power. They exceeded in severity anything that would be tolerated in any of the Reformatories under the Home Office. My reading in later life has supplied me with some possible explanations of his temperament. Two or three times a month the whole school was marshalled in the Library, and one or more delinquents were haled [*sic*] off to an adjoining apartment by the two head boys, and there flogged until they bled freely, while the rest sat quaking, listening to their screams . . .

How I hated this school, and what a life of anxiety I lived there for more than two years. I made very little progress at my lessons, and none at all at games. I counted the days and the hours to the end of every term, when I should return home from this hateful servitude . . . The greatest pleasure I had in those days was reading. When I was nine and a half my father gave me *Treasure Island,* and I remember the delight with which I devoured it. My teachers saw me at once backward and precocious, reading books beyond my years and yet at the bottom of the Form. They were offended. They had large resources of compulsion at their disposal, but I was stubborn. Where my reason, imagination or interest were not engaged, I would not or I could not learn. In all of twelve years I was at school no one ever succeeded in making me write a Latin verse or learn any Greek except the alphabet . . .[4]

Terrible stories about the childhoods of men who became famous later are anything but rare. One need only recall Frederick the Great. Or Bismarck. The latter recalled that the school to which his ambitious mother sent the six-year-old appeared 'like a prison' to him, and that he constantly cried out of longing for the security of home. But the *Plamannsche Anstalt* in Berlin had been founded in the spirit of the reformatory teachings of Pestalozzi and its methods of education were certainly light years ahead of those of St

George's in Ascot, even though Churchill attended school sixty years later than Bismarck. (It would be interesting, and certainly not to the detriment of Prussia, to compare the systems of education in the nineteenth century. That, however, is another topic.)

After the summer holidays in 1884, Winston was sent to a different school in Brighton. It was less exclusive than the one in Ascot, but milder, and was run by two elderly spinsters. Churchill himself said that he had fallen ill and that the change of school took place to enable him to regain his strength in the sea air. What is more probable is that Mrs Everest, the much-loved nurse, discovered the marks of his beatings and protested to the mother.[5] In Brighton the boy even made some progress, in French for example, in history, in learning poetry by rote and 'especially' in riding and swimming.

But, of course, the stay with the Misses Thompson in Brighton only served as a preparation for the really important school at Harrow. He was accepted there in the spring of 1888, and stayed until 1892. In actual fact his grades were not good enough for acceptance, which was probably only due to the position and influence of his family. And there were constant problems with failure and staying down. Churchill never became an even half-way decent scholar. He only excelled here and there, in fencing, for example, as in polo later on as a lieutenant of Hussars. This was certainly not unimportant, because sports play an incomparably greater rôle at British boarding schools than gymnastics play in German *Gymnasien*. Much later, however, as an old man, Churchill's alleged reply to the question on the key to remaining healthy was: 'No sports!' But this does not in any way apply to his youth, even though he never wanted to become an all-round athlete, and never did.

For the scholar at Harrow the question of what he was going to do in life became ever more pressing. With regret and a dash of contempt about which he made no bones at all, Lord Randolph came to the conclusion that his son was probably only good for a military career. This 'only' provokes a comparison. The Prussian-German army of the *Kaiser*'s Empire enjoyed the highest status; the man in uniform was worth far more than a civilian. And if one was not able to pursue the career of a serving officer, one had at least to become a lieutenant or captain in the reserves. Then one could, as a professor at a *Gymnasium* for example, put on a uniform on Sedan Day and give a patriotic speech in the school auditorium. Even Chancellor Bismarck preferred to appear before the *Reichstag* in uniform.[6]

It would have been unthinkable for a British Prime Minister to show himself in the Commons in such a martial guise. While the small professional army was not without lustre, it only offered the sons of the upper class a secondary career possibility. One could join the Civil Service, and the Empire offered many enticing positions. But one could above all embark on a political career, be it as a Whig or a Tory, assume one's seat in the Lords or the Commons and hope to be called into the Cabinet.

An officer, then — and in the cavalry instead of the infantry. While this required money for the maintenance of horses, it required less knowledge. One still had to pass exams, however, in order to be accepted as a cadet. Harrow offered preparatory courses for this, yet Churchill failed twice and finally only achieved his objective with the help of a sort of 'cramming course'. One is reminded of Theodor Fontane's latter-day novel *Der Stechlin*, in which it says about the hero:

> Having preferred from youth to be in the saddle rather than with his books, he only steered his way successfully through the cadet exam after two failures, and immediately thereafter joined the Brandenburg Cuirassiers, with whom his father had, of course, already served.

This 'of course' is exactly what does not apply in Britain. Such a tradition is far more likely to exist with regard to the seat in Parliament.

Unfortunately, the cadet school at Sandhurst, which Churchill attended in 1893 and 1894, was first of all a school. One had to gain knowledge in many subjects and then, difficult enough, prove that one had done so in order to collect the 'points' which in their sum led to the desired commission as a lieutenant.

Taken altogether, Churchill was certainly not without talents. For the rest of his life he proved that he was quick on the uptake. Time and again, and sometimes in desperately complicated situations, he found his way about and proved himself in new assignments. He read and wrote an incredible amount. As a speaker and writer he developed a mastery of the language which can stand any comparison, even with the greatest minds of his age. But, for all this, he needed more than the powers of his intellect, a deeper drive — his personal interest, curiosity, a passion which came from the heart. And he found none of this at school. His very first school day at St George's and the *mensa* declension had already sealed him off against any compulsion to learn imposed from the outside. The only thing still left was revolt — a never-ending rebellion against overpowering circumstances.

Sometimes, it appears, this revolt turned into desperation and came very close to the abyss of the death wish. Once, in the sea air of Brighton, the boy fell so mortally ill with pneumonia that the doctors hardly believed they could save him. 'We are still fighting the battle for your son,' went a letter the doctor wrote to Lord Randolph on 15 March 1886. Another time, in January 1893, he deliberately jumped off a thirty-foot high bridge and injured himself badly.

Churchill wrote in his memoirs:

My stay at the Royal Military College formed an intermediate period in my life. It brought to a close nearly 12 years of school. Thirty-six terms each of many weeks (interspersed with all-too-short holidays) during the whole of which I had enjoyed few gleams of success, in which I had hardly ever been asked to learn anything which seemed of the slightest use or interest, or allowed to play any game which was amusing. In retrospect these years form not only the least agreeable, but the only barren and unhappy period of my life. I was happy as a child with my toys in my nursery. I have been happier every year since I became a man. But this interlude of school makes a sombre grey patch upon the chart of my journey. It was an unending spell of worries that did not then seem petty, and of toil uncheered by fruition; a time of discomfort, restriction and purposeless monotony.[7]

But perhaps we can also draw a hidden yet positive balance besides the obvious disaster. Because Winston Churchill closed himself off from all attempts at education so determinedly and persistently that turning him into a well-polished gentleman — so boring and so bored inside his armour of good manners — failed, he was able to build up within himself a power for achieving the extraordinary which was soon to amaze and astonish his contemporaries. In Churchill's own words:

Solitary trees, if they grow at all, grow strong: and a boy deprived of a father's care often developes [sic], if he escape the perils of youth, an independence and vigour of thought which may restore in after life the heavy loss of early days.[8]

Life as an Adventure

. . . But the years 1895 to 1900 . . . exceed in vividness, variety and exertion anything I have known . . .

When I look back upon them I cannot but return my sincere thanks to the high gods for the gift of existence. All the days were good and each day better than the other. Ups and downs, risks and journeys, but always the sense of motion, and the illusion of hope. Come on now, all you young men, all over the world! . . . You have not an hour to lose. You must take your places in life's fighting line. Twenty to twenty-five! These are the years! Don't be content with things as they are. 'The earth is yours and the fulness thereof.' Enter upon your inheritance, accept your responsibilities! Raise the glorious flag again, advance them upon the new enemies, who constantly gather upon the front of the human army, and have only to be assaulted to be overthrown. Don't take No for an answer. Never submit to failure. Do not be fobbed off with mere personal success or acceptance. You will make all kinds of mistakes; but as long as you are generous and true, and also fierce, you cannot hurt the world or even seriously distress her. She was made to be wooed and won by youth . . .[1]

This is what Churchill writes when looking back at his own youth. And, indeed, when we recall the contrary, often desperate schoolboy, one can hardly believe that the man between twenty and twenty-five is the same person. The dull caterpillar has turned into a butterfly, the failer and repeater has already become an author, and a successful one at that, who has made a small fortune—and a sort of national hero whose name is on everyone's lips.

How can this metamorphosis be explained? Probably by the fact that now the lessons are no longer being set by others without insight. Therefore Churchill is able to unfold his dammed-up lust for knowledge, his passion for the new and unknown almost explosively. Or does his liberation from his father play a rôle here, who from his distance and estrangement still let him feel his disapproval, not to say contempt, clearly enough? Lord Randolph died in January 1895, exactly in keeping with the new stage in his son's life. The veneration Churchill felt for his father certainly also included a burden, a ban, a form of paralysis. The great biography of Lord Randolph which Churchill wrote soon afterwards must therefore certainly be seen psychologically in its duality: like so many books of note, together with the care and love it contains it also contains the dissolution which is accomplished in the work of the author.

Churchill's appeal to the youth of the world also reflects his own attitude, of course, and an almost 'un-British' behaviour, which was soon to cause offence. As one of his biographers has stated, it was deplored when young people displayed their obstinacy: 'In reality, Youth is deemed a regrettable interlude, to be borne with appropriate patience and modesty; Ambition is tolerable only if it is decently concealed.'[2]

This disguise was initially still provided by the uniform of a lieutenant of the 4th Hussars at Aldershot, whom Churchill joined in March 1895. Within the circle of officers he found, if not friendship, then at least comradeship. One could ride and play polo to one's heart's content. The love of riding probably indicates a mother fixation: among the earliest memories of little Winston belongs that of Lady Jennie returning from the hunt, 'marvellously bespattered with mud'. And even the mature man still maintained his love of polo: he played his last game at the age of 52.

There was only one thing that worried the young people: where, then, could one prove oneself and gain fame? The last British entanglement in a European conflict lay far in the past. It had occurred during the Crimean War between 1853 and 1856, and it was a foregone conclusion that such a barbarity would never occur again, at least not with British participation.[3] By now there were grey-haired colonels and generals who had never heard a shot fired in anger. The only places something might still be hoped for, if at all, were far away on the fringes of civilisation.

A part of the British Army was always on service in India, and in 1896 came the turn of the 4th Hussars to be transferred there. Because the stay was to last for several years, generous furloughs were granted beforehand. Churchill took advantage of these to go to Cuba via New York. Here, at least, there was a sort of war going on, the only one to be found – a revolt by the population against Spanish colonial rule.[4] In order to finance his trip, Churchill made a deal with the *Daily Graphic*: he reported from Cuba, and, even in this first proof of his writing ability, his colourful portrayals attracted attention.

During the intermediate stay in America he discovered 'a great, crude, strong, young people'. It appeared, he noted, 'like a boisterous healthy boy among enervated but well bred ladies and gentlemen'.[5] Another of those encapsulated self-descriptions: was he not half-American himself? Later on, in good old England, some people called him just that, but it was meant derogatorily. He viewed this fact as something to be proud of. When, during the Second World War, American aid to Great Britain became a matter of survival, he deliberately harked back to it.

In Cuba Churchill accompanied the Spanish troops in their marches up and down through the territories of the rebels, and on 1 December 1895 he experienced his baptism of fire:

> ... the day was hot, and my companion and I persuaded a couple of officers on the Staff to come with us and bathe in the river. The water was delightful, being warm and clear, and the spot very beautiful. We were dressing on the bank when, suddenly, we heard a shot fired. Another and another followed; then came a volley. The bullets whistled over our heads. ...

During the night one tore a hole through the tent, and the next day the 'Battle of La Reforma' took place. The expenditure of ammunition was copious, the result meagre, the track of the rebels losing itself in the wilderness.[6]

Garrison duty in Indian Bangalore, which began in the autumn of 1896, bored the lieutenant. While the British officers led the lives of lords and there was much free time, what was there to fill it with except sleeping, drinking and playing cards? Churchill turned to reading, almost insatiably, in order to make up for the education his contemporaries were acquiring as students at Oxford or Cambridge. His mother was constantly besieged for more books. Included in the curriculum were the historians Edward Gibbon (1737–1794), famous for his *Decline and Fall of the Roman Empire*, and Thomas Macauley (1800–1859) whose *History of England From the Accession of James II* brought Churchill closer to his ancestor Marlborough. Besides these there were *Hansard*, the collection of speeches in Parliament, and the *Annual Register*, the chronicle of current events.

But onward, ever onward — the Bible, Charles Darwin, in the end even Arthur Schopenhauer. His principal work, *Die Welt als Wille und Vorstellung*

(The World as Will and Concept), underlaid with pessimism, influenced many, from Richard Wagner and Friedrich Nietzsche to Thomas Mann. And also a young Englishman in Bangalore. More clearly a part of his fundamental feeling became that he was living in an age of decline which could only be faced in heroic and tragic rebellion, as its counterpart, always washed by disaster, threatened by downfall. It is no coincidence that the final volume of Churchill's history of the Second World War is entitled *Triumph and Tragedy*.[7]

Churchill not only read, he wrote a novel — *Savrola: A Tale of the Revolution in Laurania*. In his memoirs of his youth he writes:

> . . . I chose as a theme a revolt in some imaginary Balkan or South American republic, and traced the fortunes of a liberal leader who overthrew an arbitrary Government only to be swallowed up by a socialist revolution. My brother officers were much amused by the story as it developed and made various suggestions for stimulating the love interest which I was not able to accept. But we had plenty of fighting and politics, interspersed with such philosophizings as I was capable of . . . The novel was finished in about two months. It was eventually published in *Macmillan's Magazine* under the title of *Savrola*, and being subsequently reprinted in various editions, yielded in all over several years about seven hundred pounds. I have consistently urged my friends to abstain from reading it.[8]

Naturally memories of Cuba come in, and whoever is so inclined may discover something of a prophecy — namely the hero of the story as a sort of young Fidel Castro, who dreams of liberation but who then, after his victory, falls into dogmatic ossification by which he knocks himself aside. But there is little real-life experience; instead, characters come from the Procrustean bed of ideas, not from flesh and blood, a child of the intellect. No, we are not dealing with an early, even if still immature stroke of genius. And Churchill quickly realised that writing novels was not his cup of tea, and never attempted a second one. But he was soon to discover a broad field which challenged his real talent and his mastery.

In north-west India, on the ever-restless frontier with Afghanistan, there was yet another revolt, and Churchill succeeded in leaving his troop in order to be on the spot as a reporter. He experienced the marches, the attacks, the killings; he ran into real danger and proved his courage. Out of his experiences came the book *The Story of the Malakand Field Force*, which appeared in 1898. It attracted attention, became a success and made the author well known.

But what next? Far more exciting things than those in India were going on in the Sudan, deep in the south up the River Nile. There, in 1881, Mohammed Ahmed had risen against Anglo-Egyptian rule as the leader of a religious movement. His adherents revered him as the Mahdi, as the god-sent founder of eternal peace — which, it goes without saying, first had to be established by means of war. After four years, in 1885, the Mahdi's troops took the capital of Khartoum and killed the British governor General Gordon. Now, however, in 1898, Lord Kitchener was leading civilisation's campaign of revenge. Churchill wanted to be an eye-witness at any price, and he succeeded in obtaining leave from India.

Unfortunately Lord Kitchener had already heard of the mercurial and therefore (in his eyes) highly unsoldierly lieutenant, and did not wish to have him along at any price. Churchill had to call upon all of his connections, particularly those of his mother, and in the end even Prime Minister Lord Salisbury, in order to achieve his objective. He arrived just in time to take part on 2 September 1898 in the decisive battle at Omdurman, and in the last cavalry charge in British history.

Modern military technology head on against the Middle Ages, the enemy drawn up as walls:

> I saw the full blast of Death strike this human wall. Down went their standards by dozens and their men by hundreds. Wide gaps and shapeless heaps appeared in their array. One saw them jumping and tumbling under the shrapnel bursts; but none turned back. Line after line they all streamed over the shoulder and advanced towards our zeriba . . .[9]

And then the attack:

> Once again I was on the hard, crisp desert, my horse at a trot. I had the impression of scattered Dervishes running to and fro in all directions. Straight before me a man threw himself on the ground. The reader must remember that I had been trained as a cavalry soldier to believe that if ever cavalry broke into a mass of infantry, the latter would be at their mercy. My first idea therefore was that the man was terrified. But simultaneously I saw the gleam of his curved sword as he drew it back for a ham-stringing cut. I had room and time enough to turn my pony out of his reach, and leaning over on the off side I fired two shots into him at about three yards. As I straightened myself in the saddle, I saw before me another figure with uplifted sword. I raised my pistol and fired. So close were we that the pistol itself actually struck him. Man and sword disappeared below and behind me. On my left, ten yards away, was an Arab horseman in a bright-coloured tunic and steel helmet, with chain-mail hangings. I fired at him. He turned aside. I pulled my horse into a walk and looked round again.[10]

With the battle of annihilation of Omdurman the campaign came to an end for all practical purposes. What followed for Churchill was the work of the writer. But this time he proceeded far more thoroughly than he had with his report from northern India. He read all the documents he could find. His *Historical Account of the Reconquest of the Soudan*, which appeared in two volumes in 1899 under the title *The River War*, attracted far more attention than his story about the Malakand Field Force. First of all, it was a highly colourful, truly masterly portrayal. Secondly, the author permitted his sympathy for the foe to shine through. And thirdly, he shunned neither political, nor military, nor personal criticism. What, for example, was the reader to think when he learned that the famous Kitchener had a drinking vessel made for himself out of the Mahdi's skull, while at the same time the care of the wounded was in a sorry state? The ironic knight's gambits which history loves, incidentally, brought about the fact that Kitchener and Churchill later sat together as ministers in the same War Cabinet.

On 7 November 1899 the *Daily Mail* wrote in its review of the book:

> Mr. Winston Spencer Churchill is an astonishing young man, and his *River War* an astonishing triumph. It is well-written, impartial, and convincing, and it is hardly conceivable that anyone else could have written this book. Of course, it also has its faults. For example, it is far too long.

This fault is actually there, incidentally, also as a pointer for the future. Churchill's writing is like a storm flood which breaches all the dykes and flows far into the hinterland. His accounts of the First and Second World War are works of four volumes each. Even if one thinks one knows the history of these wars, one still reads the accounts with bated breath, because they are captivatingly told. Nevertheless, one constantly skips over the endlessly inserted documents which would have found a better place in an appendix or a supplementary volume.

To give a further example: for his Marlborough biography the author agreed a book of about 200,000 words with the publisher. In the end a collossal baroque painting was created with more than five times the number. *My Early Life: A Roving Commission* is an exception, perhaps because it is a secondary, casual work. Concerning it, long-time Prime Minister Stanley Baldwin noted quite rightly: 'It is a remarkable work, which I read with enjoyment. I constantly thought, "My goodness" — or something along those lines — "is this good."'

The time was now ripe to dare anew and take the decisive step in the adventure of life. In the spring of 1899 Churchill resigned from the Army. It had always only been a stop-gap because his unsatisfactory school results did not permit anything else, and it did not satisfy his ambitions. No, politics was the goal, the passion of his life. Once again the dubious example of his father played a rôle: to follow his flight to the heights, and if possible even to outdo him—that was the objective. And a practical opportunity appeared soon enough. There was a by-election for the House of Commons in the constituency of Oldham, and the Conservative Party, probably again in memory of the father, offered the son the chance to run. It was, however, a difficult constituency, primarily inhabited by workers, and they knew little about the past fame, or the new fame, of the writer. Churchill fell through. His political career began with a flop.

One may ask whether failure had not been inevitable. Did the former lieutenant of Hussars, coming from far away, know anything at all about the complicated mechanisms of British domestic politics? Indeed, he did. He had read the parliamentary debates as well as the chronicle of current events very carefully, and had studied famous speeches, particularly those of Lord Randolph, and relived them in his mind. He also knew that the ability to speak is of key importance and had prepared himself. He was working at eliminating a slight impediment of speech which handicapped him—not exactly a lisp, but something close. He had particular difficulty in pronouncing 's' correctly. He therefore practised untiringly under the Indian sun, almost as in George Bernard Shaw, and later in the musical *My Fair Lady*, when the simple girl is to be turned into a lady: 'I do not see the Spanish ship because it is not in sight.'

Churchill had never been afraid of hard work, if his ambition, his enthusiasm and his commitment to the matter concerned could be at least half-way combined. This is why he later became a competent professional minister holding many different offices. Perhaps we should add: this zeal for work set him apart from most of the British politicians of the turn of the century, and particularly from the leaders. Most of them were wealthy and distinguished gentlemen, members of an upper class which had ruled since time immemorial. For them politics was the only occupation in keeping with their status, and included a thrill—somewhat like the races at Ascot. It would therefore have been unthinkable to hold Cabinet meetings or sessions in Parliament during Ascot week. In brief, politics was, at the highest level, something for amateurs. But Churchill wanted to be a professional, and he became one — not exactly to the delight of the amateurs.

What should Chuchill do, after he had lost the by-election to the Commons? A way out opened for him with the start of the Boer War in October 1899.

To recapitulate the situation briefly: the Boers were the descendants of the Dutch who had settled in the southern tip of Africa since 1662, intermingled with Huguenots, and partly also German immigrants. To escape the increasing pressure of British rule they moved north in the Great Trek of 1835–38 and founded the republics of Transvaal and the Orange Free State. But when rich gold deposits were discovered in Transvaal in 1886, a mining town developed into the city of Johannesburg, into which hordes of Englishmen streamed. They soon made up half the population, but, in fear of being swamped by foreign influences, the Boers denied them civil rights and the franchise. Tensions grew, and out of them the war.[11]

Churchill decided to go to South Africa as a war correspondent and signed a contract with the *Morning Post*. The fame he had already earned with his reports from Cuba, India and the Nile helped him: 'It was probably the most advantageous contract any war correspondent had signed to date and was to lead to pay for journalists being generally improved.'[12]

On 14 October the war correspondent left Southampton in the same ship which carried General Buller, the commander designate, his staff and other journalists, and there was only one worry among the company: would they reach South Africa before the war was over? After all, what resistance could a handful of armed farmers offer the professional British Army?

The worry was groundless. In the initial months of the war there were only defeats. The ponderously marching and badly led British formations, swarmed about by the mounted and mobile Boers who were familiar both with the use of rifles and with the terrain, lost one encounter after another. Soon they were encircled and besieged in the field camps of Ladysmith, Mafeking and Kimberley. Since the Boers had no heavy artillery with which to pound the camps ready for storming, they settled down to starve them out. Fresh troops for relief had to be brought up as quickly as possible, and new commanders, too, in Field Marshal Lord Roberts and his Chief of Staff Kitchener.

The British public reacted to the reports of disaster from South Africa with confusion and horror. Only one venerable old lady, Queen Victoria, behaved in an exemplary British manner. When her minister James Balfour came to see her in order to discuss the 'black week' of disasters, she interrupted him: 'Please note that in this house no one is despondent. We are not interested in the possibility of a defeat. Such a possibility does not exist.'[13]

But while victories were still not in sight, Churchill provided a welcome distraction. Hardly had he arrived in South Africa than he set off for the Front. He accompanied a British armoured train which the Boers led into an ambush, derailed and then took under heavy fire. The reporter did not restrict himself to observing, but took a hand himself. He managed things so that the locomotive and a part of the train carrying the wounded were able to escape. Immediately thereafter he had to surrender to the Boers, who took him to a camp for officers in Pretoria. 'Armoured Train Trapped — Mr. Churchill Taken — His Sangfroid and Courage', ran the headlines of the *Morning Post* of 15 November. A few days later the story spread that the Boers had shot their prisoner. This was not at all outlandish: he was not, after all, a soldier but an irregular caught in the act.

But he was alive, climbed over the wall of the camp after a few weeks and began an escape which was actually hopeless. He was deep in enemy territory and knew neither the language nor the way, and soon 'wanted' posters were being circulated about him. Almost overcome with fatigue, and tormented by thirst and hunger, he finally knocked on the door of a house — and chanced upon probably the only man far and wide in whom he could confide, a British mining engineer who came from, of all places, Oldham. The man hid him, first in a disused shaft and then in a freight train bound for neutral Portuguese Mozambique. 'Churchill at Liberty Again After Daring Escape!' the sensational report now read.

Churchill had himself reactivated as an officer and took part in the advance which began after the turn of the war. He entered Pretoria, which the Boers were in the process of evacuating, ahead of the Army and liberated the prisoners in the camp in which he himself had been an inmate. Soon after this he returned to England, because, like all the military experts, he believed that with the capture of the enemy capital the war was over. In actual fact it dragged on for two more increasingly bitter years.

At home he was celebrated as a national hero. The only thing to cause offence was that he preached reconciliation and wrote in the *Morning Post*: 'I hope, I expect, I demand that a magnanimous and conciliatory policy be practised.' Of course he also immediately wrote another book, this time not about the war in general but about his personal experiences — *London to Ladysmith via Pretoria*, which appeared in 1900.

The government, which wanted to take advantage of the mood of victory, set general elections for October. For the second time Churchill stood for Oldham, and this time he won with a clear majority. But he only took up his seat in February 1901. Before that he went on a speaking tour of Great Britain and the United States. This was important enough: Churchill needed money. He was living from hand to mouth, and on a grand scale at that. There were no allowances for MPs as yet: these were only introduced in 1911 — at £400, not per month but per year. By speaking and writing Church-ill managed to collect the small fortune of £10,000, which was enough to last him for some time.

At his presentation in New York, his famous writer colleague Mark Twain introduced him with the words: 'Ladies and Gentlemen, I have the honour to present to you Winston Churchill: hero of five wars, author of six books, and future Prime Minister of England.'[14]

An Aside
on Human Passions

Let us leave public events for a while and turn to the private man, the human being. Modern opinion, or possibly only curiosity, has it that we know nothing about a person unless we penetrate into his intimate sphere, into the realm of his passions, and above all uncover the secrets which have to do with his desires, with sex.

In Churchill's memoirs of his youth, *My Early Life – A Roving Commission*, which take us up to the year 1908, the final sentence of the book reads: 'I got married at this time and have lived happily ever since.' But only fairy tales about the enchanted children of kings end that way. All the more are our suspicions aroused. After all, the author was already 34 years of age when he got married. What had gone on before? What in the decades thereafter?

There are few lives which have been so thoroughly studied as that of Winston Churchill. The books dealing with him can hardly be counted, and every stone, so to speak, has been turned in order to see what lies underneath. But hardly anything has been uncovered. Certainly, we meet a Miss Pamela Plowden, the daughter of a colonial official whom the lieutenant of Hussars met in India. The relationship developed in Victorian rectitude all the way to an official engagement, but no further.[1] There are similar reports about a Miss Muriel Wilson and a Miss Ethel Barrymore. The suitor, so it would appear, only knocked timidly without entering.

The first meeting in 1904 with Clementine Hozier, Churchill's later wife, also did not lead to a determined courtship. Clementine has reported:

> Winston just stared. He never uttered one word and was very gauche – he never asked me for a dance, he never asked me to have supper with him. I had of course heard a great deal about him – nothing but ill.

30

A commentary on this runs:

> All his life Churchill was always apt to be gauche when he met women for the first time. He had no small talk. He greatly preferred talking about himself. He could scarcely do this with strangers: hence the embarrassment he often caused.[2]

The second meeting only took place four years later, not without mutual inhibitions. As women are wont to do in such cases, Clementine claimed she had nothing to wear, and Winston declared: 'I am not going. It will be a great bore.' In the end they both overcame their doubts and on 15 August 1908 *The Times* announced what was impending: 'Mr. Churchill. A marriage has been announced between Mr. Churchill MP and Miss Clementine Hozier, daughter of the late Sir Henry Hozier and Lady Blanche Hozier.'

Clementine was again seized by doubts, however, and her younger brother — after the death of the father, the head of the family, so to speak — saved the wedding by explaining to his sister that she had already broken an engagement once before and that he could not tolerate a second incident of this sort, particularly since Churchill was a public figure. And so the couple were married on 12 September.

Winston, in his turn, was obviously only half-present:

> After the wedding ceremony he began to talk politics in the chapel . . . and appeared to have completely forgotten that he was supposed to escort the bride outside.[3]

Who so wishes may talk of a love-match, if this is intended to mean that there were no material advantages involved because the bride had no dowry worth mentioning. But one can hardly speak of stormy passions.

Clementine was a beauty, and an intelligent woman of strong character. When her husband monopolised the conversation at a social gathering, which normally happened, she only listened. But it was she who ruled within her own home, and prevented with determination her husband from developing into a domestic tyrant. Perhaps that was exactly what Churchill needed — not weakness, but a form of strength on which he could rest.[4]

Incidentally, he was a tender and indulgent father, who was apt to spoil his children rather than to treat them with strictness. He probably wanted to make up to them for what he himself had suffered. Diana was born in 1909, Randolph in 1911, Sarah in 1914, Marigold in 1918 and Mary in 1922.

Marigold died at the tender age of 3½, deeply mourned by her father. In the case of the other children, indulgence was urgently required — the older they grew, the more so. Diana got married and divorced, Sarah wanted to become a dancer — something that was really not fitting for a lady — and the heir Randolph, 'handsome as a Greek god and twice as arrogant', broke off his studies. He was never able to cope with the problem of being the son of a famous father. But who is?[5] In all this, the education of the children devoured much money.

If there was ever a crisis in the latter years of Churchill's marriage, then it was due to Clementine, not Winston. In 1934 she went on a cruise to Indonesia lasting several months, to the enchantments of an island world not yet shaken by the fever of modernisation, and the handsome art dealer Terence Philip, several years her junior, became her 'constant companion'. What happened or did not happen must be left to conjecture. All in all, to quote Sebastian Haffner:

> We shall have to be content with the fact that in this adventure-filled life of a man of passion, the great adventure of love and the passion of love do not occur. In the life of Churchill there is no Katharina Orlow who almost knocked Bismarck aside, no Inessa Armand who almost knocked Lenin aside. What did knock him aside — repeatedly — were political passions and military adventures, never erotic ones.[6]

Some biographers, disappointed by their futile turning over of stones, have attempted to define this as a lack of sensuality or even of sexual drive.[7] But that hardly does justice to the facts. Churchill was not a stay-at-home, no thin-lipped, woolly-headed brooder, and least of all an ascetic. He loved life in all its variety and colour. It is hardly a coincidence that he became a painter in his leisure time,[8] and his mastery as a speaker and writer is based on the fact that he did not lose himself in abstractions but instead sought vividness and developed a sense of symphonic qualities, for orchestration, for the music of language.[9] Otherwise, he enjoyed eating and drinking, and often more than was good for him.

He enjoyed it just as much when wealthy friends invited him to spend luxurious vacations by the Mediterranean. He also played cards — and for money, too. Bridge, the English card game *par excellence*, suited him less well, however, and he soon gave it up. What is important here is not self-centredness but partnership. Randolph Churchill was probably quite correct when he wrote:

> It is a curious fact that politicians do not usually make good bridge players. Churchill, Asquith and Birkenhead were all duffers and consistent losers. It may be that politicians, who tend to be wilful men of action, always want to play the hand and overbid. They like one-man shows rather than partnerships.[10]

A lack of sensuality or passion? No, certainly not. One need only consider that there are vastly different kinds of passion, and that among them a ranking inevitably occurs. When one grows and becomes dominant, another one steps back accordingly. The modern spread of sexuality possibly has to do with the fact that the other options are less and less available. The images of the gods have fallen or become unrecognisable; the hunt is no longer a challenge; all that remains of war are its horrors. All the mountains have been climbed, all the deserts crossed and the oceans charted. For Churchill the dominating passion from youth to old age was politics, behind which all the others stepped back. That is why the strange scene in the wedding chapel assumes a symbolic meaning, and he suffered accordingly when he was excluded from political activities.

To venture a comparison: Bismarck's make-up was completely different from Churchill's. In him there was always the tension between two poles — here politics, there the security of country life and the family circle. Nothing ever fulfilled him completely; when he was at one pole, he always longed to move across to the other.[11] For him, therefore, there was the political passion just as much as the private and personal one. And so the passions always fought each other for supremacy, the preponderance of one always threatening the other with wasting away:

> He complains greatly about lack of zest for work, and that politics is 'drying out' everything within him; neither hunting, nor music, nor socialising give him pleasure any more.[12]

With Churchill there were no such complaints, nor any drying out, because with him the ranking order of his passions had been clearly fixed from the beginning. This may possibly help to explain why Churchill alienated so many of his political co-players in Britain: they were simply not, like he was, committed with all of their being.

The Parliamentarian

In 1901, on 14 March, Winston Churchill assumed his seat in the House of Commons and four days later he gave his maiden speech. It was the start of a unique, highly chequered but honourable parliamentary career, which was to last for roughly sixty years with only one short interruption in 1923–24.

The newcomer had, of course, already given political speeches, primarily during election campaigns, but now, in the inner sanctum of British democracy, there was much more at stake. Famous men had been at home here — the elder and the younger Pitt, Charles James Fox and Edmund Burke, Benjamin Disraeli, William Gladstone and Churchill's own father Lord Randolph to name but a few. Churchill thought — or, better yet, felt — in historic terms, and all of these figures were as close to him as if they were sitting there listening to him. What stage fright, what a responsibility and burden on his shoulders!

And, as already indicated, Churchill did not have a natural talent as an orator. He had carefully to prepare everything he wanted to say, calculate its effect and learn it by rote. In his own memoirs of his beginnings in the Commons he writes: 'In those days, and indeed for many years, I was unable to say anything (except a sentence in rejoinder) that I had not written out and committed to memory beforehand.'[1] Nevertheless, during his maiden speech unrest made itself felt on the government benches. The subject was the war in South Africa, which was still going on, and daringly enough Churchill declared: '. . . if I were a Boer, I hope I should be fighting in the field . . . ' The Colonial Secretary Joseph Chamberlain turned to his neighbour and said: 'That's the way to throw away seats.'

But [Churchill elaborated] I could already see the shore at no great distance, and swam on vigorously till I could scamble up the beach, breathless physically, dripping metaphorically, but safe. Everyone was very kind. The usual restoratives were applied, and I sat in a comfortable coma till I was strong enough to go home.[2]

What insufficient preparation could lead to, Churchill was to learn three years later. During a speech on union matters he lost his train of thought, stopped, searched in his pockets for saving notes. No, there was no hope left—he was lost. He was only able to murmer: 'I thank the honourable Members for their attention' before he abruptly sat down. He buried his face in his hands—what a disgrace!

In the course of his long career Churchill gave countless speeches, mediocre and even bad ones occasionally, but as a rule brilliant and sometimes even inspiring ones. He continued to perfect his rhetorical arsenal, so that the Members still came in to hear him even when they disapproved of his position. To give an example: in March 1926 the General Strike broke out. All wheels ground to a halt, no trains ran, no ships were unloaded, no newspapers appeared. The government issued an emergency paper, the *British Gazette*, which was distributed in its millions, and Churchill—at the time Chancellor of the Exchequer and not, as one might have assumed, Home Secretary—struck the sharpest note. He compared the leaders of the Labour Party to bloodthirsty revolutionaries, to Lenin and Trotsky and he demanded the confiscation of union property and the deployment of troops. Even many Conservatives shook their heads about this. When the General Strike finally broke down, a justification in Parliament became necessary:

The speech Churchill gave in the Commons on 8 July was 'inspiring and brilliant'. He declared that he decidedly refused to 'be impartial between the fire department and the fire'. At the close of his speech he addressed himself to the threat of revolution several of the Labour Members had made, and with finger raised and in his most 'dramatic tone of voice' announced to them: 'Should you ever again call a General Strike against us, we will'—and here he paused for a moment while the Opposition tried to shout him down—'unleash a new *British Gazette* against you.' The 'anticlimax was perfect,' as Prime Minister Baldwin wrote to the King, and the stupefaction about the failure of the threat of military intervention everyone had expected to materialize unburdened itself in ringing laughter. According to Chamberlain, Churchill had 'markedly improved his standing' and was not only 'very popular on our side' but, 'because of the wonderful entertainment he offered them', also with the other Members.[3]

Powerful institutions rich in tradition mark the people who serve them, and the British House of Commons shaped Churchill into becoming the great parliamentarian he was. Instinctively we ask ourselves: what would have become of him under different circumstances — in Spain or Italy, in Russia, in Germany — if we consider his passion in the political battle, his will for power, his demagogic abilities, his penchant for military adventure? A revolutionary like the young hero in his novel *Savrola*? Or a counter-revolutionary, a Caudillo, a *Duce*, a dictator, the leader to tyranny? The spirit, the trend of the times between the world wars, ran counter to Liberalism and parliamentary democracy.

In the Germany of the Weimar Republic, Carl Schmitt, a professor of constitutional law, lent his pen to the spirit of the times when he wrote:

> Political thought and political instinct prove themselves . . . theoretically and in practice by their ability to distinguish friend from foe. The high points of great politics are also the moments in which the foe is recognized to be the foe in concrete clarity.[4]

But Liberalism, 'in a dilemma typical of it . . . has tried to turn the foe on the business side into a mere competitor, and on the intellectual side into a mere opponent in debate'.[5] Therefore

> . . . its essence is negotiation, 'wait-and-see' half-measures, in the hope that the definitive conflict, the bloody battle of decision can be turned into a parliamentary debate and by unending discussion be suspended for ever.[6]

As far as Schmitt was concerned, the verdict on parliamentary democracy had now been given — and it had been distinguished from true democracy:

> The stronger the power of the democratic feeling, the surer the recognition that democracy is more than just a system for registering secret ballots. Before a direct democracy, not only in the technical but in the vital sense, the parliament grown out of liberal concepts appears as an artificial machine, whereas dictatorial and Caesaristic methods not only are supported by the acclamation of the people but can be direct expressions of democratic power and substance.[7]

The practical application could later be seen in organised mass acclamation: '*Führer* command; we follow!'

What, then, would have become of Churchill in different circumstances? There are no limits to our imagination. But it was the British House of Commons that shaped him. It made him into a parliamentarian of conviction, and in this form into a counter-player against tyranny. And as a passionate fighter, not only outside but also within Parliament, he was always clearly able to distinguish friend from foe. He would have listened with a complete lack of comprehension to the claim that the parliamentary system was, in its essence, afraid to take decisions and only committed itself to 'wait-and-see' half-measures. He would have rejected Carl Schmitt's apparently brilliant words as being the modernistic nonsense they actually are.

For the almost life-long parliamentarian the issue was not only a useful and practically indispensable institution but also a deep emotional tie, a sort of home. When a bomb devastated the House of Commons during the Second World War Churchill wept—and made provision for having the architecture restored practically unaltered. There were two things of particular importance for him, and he said that these were indispensable.

Firstly, measured against Continental standards, the House of Commons is far too small. When all of the Members actually do assemble, there is a great crush on the sparse benches without lecterns. And still not everyone finds a seat and many have to stand. But this creates the impression of drama— and even during normal sessions the feeling of an intimate get-together. The desolate picture is avoided which, for example, the German *Bundestag* often presents—one or two dozen Members losing themselves in the great semi-circle, while the paper-rustling speaker intones into the void what then disappears into the minutes and is of no further interest to anyone.

On the second attribute it is fitting to give the floor to Mr Parkinson for a typically British speech:

> We are all familiar with the basic difference between English and the French parliamentary institutions; copied respectively by such other assemblies as derive from each. We all realize that this main difference has nothing to do with national temperament, but stems from their seating plans. The British, being brought up on team games, enter their House of Commons in the spirit of those who would rather be doing something else. If they cannot be playing golf or tennis, they can at least pretend that politics is a game with very similar rules. . . . So the British instinct is to form two opposing teams, with referee and linesmen, and let them debate until they exhaust themselves. The House of Commons is so arranged that the individual Member is practically compelled to take one side or the other before he knows what the arguments are, or even . . . before he knows the subject of the dispute. His training from birth has been to play for his side, and this saves him from any undue mental effort. Sliding into his seat toward the end of a speech, he knows exactly how to take up the argument from the point it has reached. If the speaker is on his own side of the House, he will say 'Hear, hear!' If he is on the opposite side, he can safely say 'Shame!' or merely 'Oh!' . . . Nor does it make the slightest difference whether he learned his politics at Harrow or in following the

fortunes of Aston Villa. In either school he will have learned when to cheer and when to groan. But the British system depends entirely on its seating plan. If the benches did not face each other, no one could tell truth from falsehood, wisdom from folly — unless indeed by listening to it all. But to listen to it all would be ridiculous, for half the speeches must of necessity be nonsense.

In France the initial mistake was made of seating the representatives in a semi-circle, all facing the chair. The resulting confusion could be imagined if it were not notorious. . . . Instead of having two sides, one in the right and the other in the wrong — so that the issue is clear from the outset — the French form a multitude of teams facing in all directions. With the field in such confusion, the game cannot even begin. . . .[8]

Let no one claim that these are mere superficialities. Whoever has had anything to do with presentations or lessons knows that almost everything depends on the atmosphere of the room — whether one speaks from a distant lectern into a huge and half empty hall or in intimate security in which the audience presses closely around the speaker. Disaster already announces itself when there are glass fronts which permit eyes and minds to wander far away. It is also nonsense, incidentally, when, in podium discussions in which the issue is debated for and against, the participants sit next to each other like sparrows aligned on a drain instead of facing each other. This provokes the delivery of monologues and not the unfolding of a flowing, occasionally tumultuous exchange of arguments.

And why, in the German *Bundestag*, do the Chancellor and his Ministers sit on a separate government bench facing the Members, instead of joining the coalitions to which they belong? Strictly speaking, this is a relic from the days of the authoritarian state, in which His Majesty the *Kaiser*, and not the *Reichstag*, determined who was to be Chancellor. That was never the case in Britain, even in the days when the franchise was still restricted to a small upper class and the King had a hand in appointing the ministers. Given that, over the centuries, and particularly since the 'Glorious Revolution' of 1688, the House of Commons became the central political institution and Britain made the transition from an oligarchy to a democracy without ruptures, then this also has to do with such a seating plan, which at first glance might appear to be of negligible import.

In Britain the student is already prepared for the rituals that await him when he moves up to become an MP later on. Every university has its debating society, the auditorium for which is modelled on that of the House of Commons. At each meeting a motion is debated. Whoever is in favour of the motion takes his seat on the 'government side', the opponents on the benches of the opposition. Sometimes it is all just fun, for the practice of fencing: 'Moved that this House holds riding on trams to be immoral.' But there are also serious issues. In 1933 in Oxford, the motion was debated and carried by a large majority that 'This House will not fight for King and Country under any circumstances'. At the time this caused great commotion. Even in retrospect from the post-war era, Churchill spoke of an 'ever-shameful' resolution.[9] It is even alleged that Joachim von Ribbentrop, sometime Ambassador in London and then Foreign Minister of the Third Reich, drew his conclusions and supported Hitler in his view that Great Britain would not fight, or at least not seriously.

In the course of arguments within the debating societies it does happen that one changes one's opinion. One then gets up, steps into the centre aisle, bows to the chair (occupied in the House of Commons by the Speaker) and goes over to the other side. One can imagine what a body-blow it is for a speaker who is just in the process of winding garlands of words when someone from his own ranks turns his back on him in such a demonstrative manner. In Parliament this is called 'crossing the floor'. It only occurs rarely, because it involves a change of Party — as a rule, only in the form that in the next General Election one stands for the other Party. In this sense, Churchill crossed the floor twice in the course of his parliamentary career.

A part of the construction of the House of Commons is the first-past-the-post system of elections which favours the concentration on two dominating parties. A pure system of proportional representation, which favours the splintering of parties — as in the Weimar Republic, for example — would hardly be served by opposing rows of benches. Here again we see how the magic of the room and the political system equate one to the other.

During Churchill's early days in Parliament, however, there was substantial disorder. Before the First World War the major issue was the Irish Question. Ireland was still a part of Great Britain and returned elected Members — far more, incidentally, than equated to the population, because the re-drawing of the constituencies had not kept pace with the dramatic drop in population caused by the emigration of millions after the Great Famine of 1845–49. The Irish Nationalists were an obstinate, hardly calculable weight with which to tip the scales, and the other British parties also kept splitting on the question of whether Ireland should or should not be granted Home Rule — and, if so, to what degree. After the First World War the rise of the Labour Party began, while the ancient Liberal Party, the Whigs, fell to pieces. This development did not come about overnight, but in stages. In cases of uncertain majorities, therefore, there were often coalitions and frequent new elections. It was only in the 1930s that the traditional opposition began to stabilise again, but now with the Labour Party taking the place of the Whigs against the Tories.

To return to the beginning: one can only understand Churchill within the context of his shaping by 'the mother of parliaments'. The House of Commons provided him with the atmosphere, the arena he needed and loved, and which he could hardly have found in the German *Reichstag* or the French *Chambre des Deputés*. He was fascinated by the battle, also or especially, in its rhetorical form. To set himself against inimical trends and if possible to win, incidentally often enough against his own party—that was his elixir of life. In his long membership in the British House of Commons he truly became a parliamentarian of note—in fact, one of the greatest history has recorded.

Stages of
a Political Career

In 1906 Churchill published the great two-volume biography of his father Lord Randolph Churchill. *The Times Literary Supplement* accorded it the greatest of praise:

> ... here is a book which is certainly among the two or three most exciting political biographies in the language ... The book is a son's book, of course, written from a particular point of view: and there are, of course, things which might be said against Lord Randolph Churchill but are not said here. That is inevitable; but the worst kind of biographer is not he who has a point of view, but he who has not — and certainly Mr Winston Churchill has not unduly obtruded his. . . .[1]

In actual fact, the author worked with care. He evaluated all the available documents, letters and speeches, interviewed the contemporary witnesses and, in a brilliant portrayal, projected a political canvas of the late nineteenth century. Two years later, after an extended trip through East Africa, there followed *My African Journey*, and in 1909 *Liberalism and the Social Problem*, a political programme. Besides that there was still the reporter.

One asks oneself where Churchill found, or stole, the time to write: he was, after all, an MP, and soon entrusted with state offices. The answer that he had to make money in order to live is correct, but it is not enough. He actually did possess a special, very sensual, not to say erotic, relationship with the language — not only with the spoken but with the written word as well. And so, besides the parliamentarian and the statesman, there was always also the writer, who finally quite deservedly received the Nobel Prize for Literature in 1953.

Actually, a young MP is not supposed to go astray, but to commit himself earnestly in his own field in order to advance his career. He has to take care of his constituency and, if he is as brilliant a speaker as Churchill, to make himself available to the Party at all times. He should not shine through absence from the House, but demonstrate his zeal for work.

And that is exactly what Churchill did, though in a very deliberate manner. Together with other young MPs he formed a circle which did not mince words, nor shy at rudely kicking the grey-haired Party prominents in the shins. Compared to this, the 'young mavericks' of our day hardly deserve their name. In those days they were called 'hooligans', just as if they were football rowdies from a proletarian environment. To Churchill's most important circle of friends there soon belonged Frederick Edwin Smith (1872–1930) – later Lord Birkenhead – an arch-conservative whose ability to formulate was as brilliant as it was witty, and who did not first have to work at becoming an orator. Churchill admired him for this, and they remained lifelong close friends, even after their political paths had led them in opposite directions.[2]

Churchill quickly found a reason to fall out with his Party. His father had preached 'Tory Democracy', a turn by the Conservatives towards the masses, which if it were not to remain pure demagogy would have required a determined step towards developing a social state. There was, however, little or nothing to be heard in that direction. Instead one was fighting for protective tariffs in the interest of the industrialists and the landowners. The poorer classes would then have to bear the burden, because the price of food would rise. In 1904 Churchill took this, in addition to some other questions, as his reason for crossing the floor to the Liberals. Nasty comments, however, could be addressed to the proverbial rat which leaves the sinking ship: Churchill had a nose for the fact that the time in government of the Conservatives was coming to an end and a late flowering by the Liberals was imminent. Pure opportunism then, driven by career ambitions? In any case, many Tories saw Churchill's change of party as being exactly that and never forgave him his 'treason', not even when, twenty years later, he returned to them with the onset of a changing tide.

But there was more to it than that. One could really not do much with the Tories of those days, and certainly not create a Tory Democracy. And not only as the heir, if not to say the avenger, of his father, but from his own volition, the grandson of a duke began to develop 'leftist' tendencies, as so many young people do who have sufficient passions not to be satisfied with the beaten paths.

The rewards were not long in coming. In 1906 Campbell-Bannermann, Liberal Prime Minister since 1905, appointed Churchill as Under-Secretary in the Colonial Office. Here again Churchill demonstrated his instinct. Initially he had been offered the same position in the Exchequer. But that was where Herbert Asquith ruled, the strong and coming man in the Cabinet, who was to inherit the office of Prime Minister from Campbell-Bannermann in 1908. Under him the state secretary could hardly be more than a 'paid echo'. The Colonial Secretary, however, was the Earl of Elgin, who sat in the House of Lords, so that Churchill had the arena of the Commons all to himself. Elgin did not like public speaking anyway and had little political ambition. With an indulgent smile he watched the zeal with which his young subordinate went to work.[3] And this indeed he did. Untiringly he produced memoranda — something he did which quickly became habit and characteristic of later offices as well — often with no regard for departmental boundaries, and therefore frequently calling down aggravation upon his head. As the word went:

> While he was a backbencher, Churchill had spoken as if he were an Under-Secretary, now, as an Under-Secretary, as if a member of the Cabinet; and when he reached the Cabinet he was apt to speak as if he were Prime Minister.[4]

During the time Churchill spent in the Colonial Office the primary issue was the restructuring of the situation in South Africa. To heal the wounds of a bitter war, to reconcile the vanquished with British rule after the peace treaty — that was the great task to which he devoted himself out of conviction. The Boer republics, now British colonies, were given back a large measure of self-administration. In 1907 Louis Botha (1862–1919) was elected Prime Minister of Transvaal, the same man who as a Boer general had led the troops of his country up to the end of the war in 1902. Three years later he advanced to become the first Prime Minister of the newly formed Union of South Africa.

During the peace negotiations something highly unusual occurred. Since the First World War we have become accustomed to the vanquished, who are already ruined, having huge contributions and reparations imposed upon them, which they are supposed to pay. The vanquished Boers, however, were granted a compensation of £3 million — a considerable sum in those days — for, among other things, the rebuilding of the farms which had been burned down during the final phase of the war in order to deprive the partisans of shelter.

In Britain there were, of course, voices raised in outrage, warning against foolishly squandering the fruits of victory. But Churchill defended reconciliation in Parliament and in public with all his persuasiveness. Incidentally, Botha claimed that it had been he who had captured the war correspondent and irregular fighter Churchill during the attack on the British armoured train in 1899 — for the Under-Secretary and later the Cabinet minister all the more reason to reach out his hand to Botha and to support him to the best of his abilities. Later Churchill developed an intimate relationship with Jan Christiaan Smuts (1870–1950), another Boer general turned statesman, and a champion of the British Commonwealth. During the Second World War Smuts was one of the few men whose advice meant anything to Churchill.[5]

In looking back on his experiences during the Boer War and his political occupation with South Africa Churchill wrote:

> Here I must confess that all through my life I have found myself in disagreement alternately with both the historic English parties. I have always urged fighting wars and other contentions with might and main till overwhelming victory, and then offering the hand of friendship to the vanquished. Thus I have always been against the Pacifists during the quarrel, and against the Jingoes at its close. Many years after this South African incident, Lord Birkenhead mentioned to me a Latin quotation which seems to embody this idea extremely well. '*Pacere subjectis et debellare superbos*', which he translated finely 'Spare the conquered and war [*sic*] down the proud.' I seem to have come very near to achieving this thought by my own untutored reflections. The Romans have often forestalled many of my best ideas, and I must concede to them the patent rights in this maxim. Never indeed was it more apt than in South Africa. Wherever we departed from it, we suffered; wherever we followed it, we triumphed.
>
> And not only in South Africa. I thought we ought to have conquered the Irish and then given them Home Rule; that we ought to have starved out the Germans, and then revictualled their country;[6] and that after smashing the General Strike, we should have met the grievances of the miners. I always get into trouble because so few people take this line. I was once asked to devise an inscription for a monument in France. I wrote: 'In war, Resolution. In defeat, Defiance. In victory, Magnanimity. In peace, Goodwill.'[7] The inscription was not accepted. It is all the fault of the human brain being made in two lobes, only one of which does any thinking, so that we are all right-handed or left-handed; whereas if we were properly constructed we should use our right and left hands with equal force and skill according to circumstances. As it is, those who win a war well can rarely make a good peace, and those who could make a good peace would never have won the war . . . [8]

After his probation in the Colonial Office, Churchill was called into the Cabinet in 1908 and took over the Ministry of Economic Affairs. The term requires an explanation. Many of the questions which today are assigned to the Department of Social Security came under the responsibility of the office because there was as yet no Ministry of Social Affairs. Churchill unleashed astonishing activity. He advocated the foundation of job centres and the introduction of unemployment insurance. In actual fact, the foundations of the British welfare state were laid with his energetic support in the years before the First World War. Because these measures cost money, Churchill advocated a progressive income tax and a punitive inheritance tax, according to the motto 'Fleece the rich!' Of course, expenditure for the Army and the Navy was to be reduced as well. 'He is full of the poor; he has just discovered them,' one of his colleagues mocked. For election campaigns the Minister wrote a flamboyant brochure entitled *The Rights of the People*.

The grandson of a duke and the son of a lord as a radical in public service? One can only understand this if one considers three factors. First, the development of a social state was long overdue. The ruling traditional parties had overlooked for far too long the fact that the Industrial Revolution had led to a society in which the upper and middle classes on the one hand and the workers on the other opposed each other more sharply than probably anywhere else. It is hardly a coincidence that Friedrich Engels wrote his famous book *The Situation of the Working Class in England* based on the insights he had gained in Manchester, and supplied Karl Marx with the material he required. Furthermore, the Fabian Society had been founded in 1884. Among its founders were Sidney and Beatrice Webb, its contributing authors including George Bernard Shaw and H. G. Wells. Since 1889 the Fabian Essays were appearing, and these developed a programme of social reform and the intellectual arsenal for the Labour Party.[9] If the Liberals did not want to be swamped by the rising tide, they had to impose their own reform programme.

Secondly, there was David Lloyd George (1863–1945). He was a Welshman who came from humble origins and had been a Liberal MP in the House of Commons since 1890. He owed his rise to his own energy, and above all to his talents as a speaker. He was a demagogue of note. He could, so they said, 'talk a bird out of a tree' – or, more drastically, 'charm the bark off the tree'. He was a colourful figure in other ways as well. There was talk – in those days behind closed doors and not in the newspapers – about his amorous affairs, and later even of corruption: like no other British politician of the twentieth century, he is alleged to have amassed wealth – a fortune – by the sale of offices and titles.

Churchill admired Lloyd George for his talent as a speaker, as he admired F. E. Smith, and the somewhat older man with his already long experience in Parliament became his political mentor. The relationship probably drove the younger man a few steps more deeply into the radical camp than he would have trodden of his own volition. In the Asquith Cabinet, into which Churchill had been called as Minister of Economic Affairs, Lloyd George held the post of Chancellor of the Exchequer, and both worked together so brilliantly that they were soon being called 'the heavenly twins'. For their Conservative opponents, however, they appeared to be more like a pair of hell-hounds. While Churchill was preparing unemployment insurance and developing the job centres, Lloyd George was addressing himself to old age and health insurance. In 1909 he brought in his 'Popular Budget' which was intended to 'fleece the rich', and which led to a dramatic conflict with the House of Lords.[10] The conflict ended with the Lords' right of veto being curtailed in 1911.

In looking back at their joint work, Churchill, with unusual modesty, lauded his mentor and assigned all of the merits to him:

> It was he who gave to orthodox Liberalism the entirely new inflexion of an ardent social policy. All the great schemes of insurance have entered for ever into the life of the British people, originated or flowed from him. He it was who cast our finances intently upon the line of progressive taxation of wealth as an equalizing factor in the social system.[11]

Thirdly, Churchill took over every new office with a zeal for work and an ambition as if it was the most important office on earth, and he wanted to succeed in each. This helped him to acquire quickly the necessary specialised knowledge and to find his way about in unknown terrain. The drawbacks included a narrowing of perspective. When, therefore, the Minister of Economic Affairs responsible for social questions denied that there were any threats from abroad and wished to reduce arms expenditure, only a short time later the First Lord of the Admiralty already saw a war looming and demanded extra battleships. Some observers have deduced a (possibly inbred) character defect from such swings of opinion. But enthusiasm for the new office explains the facts just as well, or even better.[12]

One could say with irony that the only office for which Churchill was suited without any reservations was that of Prime Minister — because it does not restrict the view but establishes a universal responsibility — and it was, of course, already the ambition of the young man to go down in history one day as Prime Minister. 'Facts are better than dreams,' Churchill said when he was actually called to the highest office under dramatic circumstances on 10 May 1940.[13] This statement also tells us something about the dreams of the early years, which then dragged on over the decades to the threshold of old age.

It is appropriate to insert some remarks on Churchill's relationship with Germany and the Germans here—because this relationship, too, was subjected to bouts of 'hot and cold' in the history of the twentieth century. At the time we are dealing with here, sympathy was linked to interest. In 1906 he attended the *Kaiser*'s manoeuvres which took place in Silesia, and was introduced to Wilhelm II. He expressed his thanks by sending the *Kaiser* a copy of his biography of Lord Randolph, and His Majesty reciprocated with the quite thrilling book *Der Kaiser und die Kunst* (The Kaiser and Art).

In his book about great contemporaries, which appeared in 1937, Churchill produced a critical summary of his encounters with the *Kaiser*. He came to a different conclusion from the usual one, and blamed the circumstance more than the man:

> The truth is that no human being should ever have been placed in such a position. An immense responsibility rests upon the German people for their subservience to the barbaric idea of autocracy. This is the gravamen against them in history—that, in spite of all their brains and courage, they worship Power and let themselves be led by the nose. . . .[14]

In 1909 Churchill again visited the martial display, which this time took place in the south-west, but now he also had a look at institutions of the social state, for example employment offices in Frankfurt-am-Main and Strasburg. He noted: 'My heart was filled with admiration of the patient genius which had added these social bulwarks to the many glories of the German race . . .'[15] Bastions of peace! In a speech he gave in August 1908 in Swansea, he said:

> I think it is greatly to be deprecated that persons should try to spread the belief in this country that war between Great Britain and Germany is inevitable. It is all nonsense.'[16]

Somewhat later in the same speech he said:

> . . . far and wide throughout the masses of the British dominions there is no feeling of ill-will towards Germany. I say we honour that strong, patient industrious

German people, who have been for so many centuries a prey to European intrigue and a drudge amongst the nations of the Continent. Now in the fulness of time, after many tribulations, they have by their virtues and valour won themselves a foremost place in the front of civilization. I say we do not envy them their good fortune; we do not envy them their power and their prosperity. We are not jealous of them. We rejoice in everything that brings them good; we wish them well from the bottom of our heart, and we believe most firmly the victories they will win in science and learning against barbarism, against waste, the victories they will gain will be victories in which we shall share, and which, while benefiting them, will also benefit us.[17]

Here we clearly hear the admiration for the social state that Bismarck had founded.

In 1910 Churchill took over the Home Office. There is not much to recount here. His term in office only lasted for a year, and the major topic of the day, prison reform, was not exactly the stuff of headlines. More exciting, and aggravating, was the confrontation with the Suffragettes, who, led by Emmeline Pankhurst, were fighting for women's rights and the franchise, frequently by means of dramatic gestures such as we know today from Greenpeace or the opponents of nuclear power. The only remedy was the truncheons of the police, and a departure from radical positions announced itself in their chief. The Home Secretary is, after all, responsible for law and order.

Then Churchill became First Lord of the Admiralty in 1911, and he devoted himself to this office with a commitment, enthusiam and energy as to no other. David Beatty, whom he made Naval Secretary, noted in May 1912: 'Winston does not speak about anything except the sea and the Navy and the wonderful things he is going to do.'[18]

The new Minister immediately did a dramatic about-face. Prospects of a secured peace and therefore disarmament? No, quite the opposite: the danger threatened from Kiel and Wilhelmshaven. German battle fleet construction was challenging British sea power to a duel. Therefore the First Lord of the Admiralty fought for new, bigger, faster battleships, more heavily armoured and armed than before—and, naturally, as many as possible. The growing fleet in its turn required more sailors, and these had to be better paid if one wished to attract them in sufficient numbers. Therefore the costs rose year on year. In 1913, the last year of peace, the Navy budget reached the—for the times—enormous sum of £46.3 million, compared to £42.8 million in 1911. The comparable figures for Germany were £22.9 and £21.7 million. The race that led to catastrophe was fully on.[19]

On 7 February 1912 Churchill gave a speech in Glasgow, during which he said: 'The British Navy is to us a necessity and, from some points of view, the German Navy is to them more in the nature of a luxury.'[20] German newspapers splashed this across their front pages: the term 'luxury fleet' made the rounds and was rejected with the appropriate outrage. The reaction was probably so sharp because the First Lord of the Admiralty had hit the nail on the head. The Navy actually was of vital importance for the defence of Britain and the Empire, as the historic experience of the victory over the Spanish Armada in 1588 and the struggle against Napoleon had shown.

But what did its Navy mean to Germany? For the protection of the trade routes or the economically unimportant colonies, fast cruisers with a large radius of action were required. All one needed besides that was the friendship of Britain instead of its challenge, as Albert Ballin, the Managing Director of one of the world's largest shipping companies, HAPAG, kept repeating. But what the naval architect Alfred Tirpitz was actually building under the enthusiastic patronage of the *Kaiser* was a battlefleet which was only suitable for a fateful war for naval supremacy one day somewhere between the Heligoland Bight and the Thames Estuary. The battleships which formed the core of the High Seas Fleet were heavily armoured and excellently trained, as the Battle of Jutland was to prove in 1916, but their radius of action, like their speed, remained relatively modest. And how was one supposed to get through the Channel, or around Scotland and Ireland into the Atlantic, far from any supply stations and possibilities of repair? During the war this was never even attempted because it was hopeless.

In looking back at the century, one must not only talk of a luxury fleet but of a fatal fleet, and we can hardly understand any longer why it was built at all. Certainly, in her European central position between France and Russia, Germany was always in danger. In the worst case she had to reckon with a war on two fronts. But for this she had her powerful and tested army. It was all the more compelling to avoid also turning the leading sea power into an enemy. And that is exactly what she did with the building of the battlefleet. Obstinately, she risked the great European war and defeat.

A sober calculation of her interests should have urged Germany to keep the peace with all her might. Only under conditions of peace could her rapid economic growth continue, and she was well prepared for the future. German science and research were in the forefront worldwide, as were her modern chemical and pharmaceutical industries, her optics and her electro-technology. In addition, this rapid progress provided the Germans with jobs and bread. The large numbers of emigrants of the nineteenth century belonged to the past. Why, therefore, the dream, or delusion of 'world power', which she intended to gain in the duel with Great Britain? There was something deeply irrational here, as Michael Stürmer so bitterly wrote:

> Where was the healthy vital instinct which would have exposed the fantasies of omnipotence, of the fleet ideology, to deadly ridicule? Where the sober ability to calculate by industry, which did business all over the world yet still fell victim to heroic nightmares about the final battle? Germany had become the factory of the world. But instead of practising *realpolitik*, the German élites dreamt about world politics, colonial expansion and building a fleet, and if all this was to lead to nothing, then let the factory fall down, like the feasting hall of the King of the Huns which buried the last of the Nibelungen under its ruins — an atavistic nightmare in the world of the design offices.[21]

Let us return to England. The counterpart of Alfred Tirpitz was John Fisher (1841–1920), between 1904 and 1910 the First Sea Lord. He masterminded the jump from battleships to 'dreadnoughts' which were far larger than anything previously known, with far heavier armour and guns.[22] Germany had to follow suit if she did not want to lose the naval race during peacetime, and she also had to enlarge the North Sea–Baltic Canal.

Churchill had always been interested in Fisher, and when war broke out in 1914 he called him back to the Admiralty. Concerning a conversation with Fisher in 1907, he noted:

> We talked all day long and far into the nights. He told me wonderful stories of the Navy and of his plans — all about Dreadnoughts, all about submarines, all about the new education scheme for every branch of the Navy, all about big guns, and splendid Admirals and foolish miserable ones, and Nelson and the Bible, and finally the island of Borkum. I remembered it all. I reflected on it often. I even remembered the island of Borkum when my teacher had ceased to think so much of it. . . .[23]

As First Lord, Churchill had himself advised by Fisher, who in his turn took the stormy young man into his heart when he sensed his enthusiasm for the Navy. 'My beloved Winston . . .' is the way his letters to the First Lord began. But Fisher was a bizarre personality. He was suddenly seized by rage and hatred.[24] He used to say of his enemies, 'their wives should be widows, their children fatherless, their homes a dunghill'.[25] And so it came to pass that one day Churchill was no longer the 'beloved Winston' but had to read: 'First Lord: I can no longer be your colleague.'[26]

Of all the tasks to which the First Lord devoted himself with all his strength, three should be mentioned. He first began with building up an Admiralty staff, against the opposition of the traditionalists. Until then there had been no research institution, no 'think tank' which could compare, even from afar, to the Central General Staff of the Prussian-German Army, and therefore there was just as much a lack of official portrayals of war history as of systematic studies on naval strategy. The only important work on this subject came from an America pen,[27] and Tirpitz immediately had it translated into German in order to use it as an instrument of propaganda for his fleet construction.

Secondly, Churchill advocated something quite new — the development of naval aviation. Because adventure beckoned him, he not only supported the 'daring young men in their flying machines' but joined them. Many hundreds of times he enjoyed a lust for risk with the pilots and lived through their dangers, including a flip-over while landing. In looking back at this period he wrote: 'The air is an extremely dangerous, jealous and exacting mistress. Once under the spell most lovers are faithful to the end, which is not always old age.'[28]

Thirdly, he supported the conversion of ships' engines, or rather their boilers, from coal to oil. This led to several advantages. Ships became faster and gained greater range.[29] They were also able to resupply themselves more easily and more rapidly, even on the high seas, and the job of the heat-washed, furiously shovelling stokers was now performed by pumps. This led to a technical advantage — not least of all over the German Fleet. In wartime the latter would not have access to any secure oil wells and therefore had to stay with domestic coal. In 1914 developments were still in their early stages, but had the war not come, or had it come only some years later, this fact alone would have sent the German High Seas Fleet down the road to defeat.[30]

But peace still reigned and no one anticipated the European catastrophe:

At the end of June [1914] the simultaneous British naval visits to Kronstadt and Kiel took place. For the first time for several years some of the finest ships of the British and German Navies lay at their moorings at Kiel side by side surrounded by liners, yachts and pleasure craft of every kind. Undue curiosity in technical matters was banned by mutual agreement. There were races, there were banquets, there were speeches. There was sunshine, there was the Emperor. Officers and men fraternized and entertained each other afloat and ashore. Together they strolled arm in arm through the hospitable town . . .[31]

The
First World War

Everything is tending towards catastrophe and collapse. I am interested, geared up and happy. Is it not horrible to be built like this? The preparations have a hideous fascination for me. I pray to God to forgive me for such fearful moods of levity.

That is what Churchill wrote to his wife on 28 July 1914.[1] But he did not have to be ashamed of himself. When declarations of war rained down a few days later, and the lights of civilisation went out in Europe, millions upon millions of people were jubilant. The nations sang, like the crowd gathered before the palace in Berlin when mobilisation was announced: 'Now let us all thank God . . .' And no one spoke about catastrophe and collapse but about a great and inspiring awakening. Apparently no one asked himself whether he had an outlandish disposition. A young man nobody knew as yet wrote in retrospect:

For me those hours were like a salvation from the aggravating emotions of youth. Even today I am not ashamed to say that I, overcome by stormy enthusiasm, fell to my knees and thanked heaven from an overflowing heart that it had granted me the joy of being permitted to live in these times.[2]

No, Adolf Hitler did not need to be ashamed either: young men everywhere felt as he did. By the hundreds of thousands, by the millions, they volunteered for war, in Great Britain and France no different from in Germany, and the mothers and girlfriends decorated them with flowers when they reported to the barracks, or wound garlands for the trains when they rode to the Front. The problem was not to find candidates for death, but to organise and arm them because there were so many. The educated, the thinkers and the writers, also hailed the war. In Germany alone it is estimated that in August 1914 about one and a half million poems of awakening and war flowed from the pens—a production record of a unique sort.

In looking back over the orgies of blood and destruction of the twentieth century, all of this may appear ghastly and hardly comprehensible. How was it possible that everyone rushed into disaster so suicidally? One answer must be that the people and the nations did not know war, and certainly not in the form the machine age would bring about. Not even the generals knew what they were letting themselves in for. Nobody had an inkling of soldiers who sat in the mud of the trenches, dirty, lice-ridden and lost, while poison gas choked them or artillery barrages smashed them.

Historical memories were of no help any longer, or led one astray. The horrors of the Napoleonic era lay a century in the past, and more recent horrors took place far away in the Crimea or in South Africa, or amid the barbarity of the Balkans. The wars that took place in cultured Europe only lasted a few weeks, or at worst a few months, like the recent Franco-Prussian War of 1870–71. Everybody would be home by Christmas, wreathed in laurel, and the dead would be revered as heroes.

Churchill was happy because in the Royal Navy he held in his hand one of the most famous instruments of war known to history. It did its duty from the very first day. When the British ultimatum expired on 4 August, British cruisers took up their stations on the blockade line from the Shetlands to Norway, and when dawn broke on 5 August German merchant shipping for all practical purposes came to a standstill, if we disregard the Baltic. No meat and no fat, no grain, no copper and no cotton came into besieged central Europe any longer.

The German battlefleet, however, bobbed at anchor in the Schilling Roads as lacking in purpose as if it did not exist. The few sea battles which took place during the course of the war, and even the Battle of Jutland, had no strategic importance whatsoever, and only confirmed what was clear from the first day of the war. Because of its lack of purpose the High Seas Fleet gradually decayed from within, and in the end became the nucleus of revolution. After a few months the oceans had also been swept clear: on 9 November 1914 the cruiser *Emden*, which had conducted a succesful commerce-raiding war in the Indian Ocean, was shot to pieces, and on 8 December the German Far East Squadron under the command of *Graf* Spee was destroyed off the Falklands.

So far, so good. But by then the war had become set in the trenches, and it could not be foreseen when it would become mobile again and be brought to an end. In weapons technology the defence triumphed under the banner of barbed wire, spade, repeating rifle and machine gun. The days of the cavalry were past, and those of the tank had not yet come. Even day- or week-long barrages were of little help. There were always enough defenders left to mow down the attackers. And because, on the German front, which stretched in north-eastern France from the Swiss border to the Channel coast, it was the French and British who attacked more often between December 1914 and March 1918, they suffered heavier casualties than the Germans.

Few have described the situation as briefly or as clearly – or as darkly – as Winston Churchill:

> There was nothing left on land now but the war of exhaustion – not only of armies but of nations. No more strategy, very little tactics; only the dull wearing down of the weaker combination by exchanging lives; only the multiplying of machinery on both sides to exchange them quicker . . . Good, plain, straightforward frontal attacks by valiant flesh and blood against wire and machine guns, 'killing Germans' while Germans killed Allies twice as often . . . And when at the end, three years later, the throng of uniformed functionaries who in the seclusion of their offices had complacently presided over this awful process, presented Victory to their exhausted nations, it proved only less ruinous to the victor than to the vanquished.[3]

Churchill's restless mind rebelled against such stupidity. There was already much less work for the Head of the Admiralty than had been expected, so much so that he found the opportunity to go to the Front and to interfere unasked – in Antwerp, for example, where he attempted to organise the resistance against the German besiegers, which then quickly collapsed anyway, aggravating British losses. But the blockade at sea for which he was actually responsible went on as a routine without incidents, and could only take effect in the long term anyway, particularly since a far-sighted man such as Walther Rathenau was organising the German war economy. It was only after the 'swede winter' of 1916/17 that hunger began to undermine German morale – though again, only in the long term.

As an aside, the issue here is not the history of the First World War but Churchill's share in it and the portrayal and evaluation of the events, which he himself attempted in his five-volume work *The World Crisis*. Arthur James Balfour, at home in many government offices for decades and Conservative Prime Minister from 1902 to 1905, from whom the Member Churchill defected to cross over to the camp of the Liberals, said with brilliant malice: 'They tell me Winston has written a thick book about himself and called it *The World Crisis.*'[4]

Churchill, however, had never claimed that he wanted to be 'objective'. He said:

> After this volume was far advanced I read for the first time Defoe's *Memoirs of a Cavalier*. In this delightful work the author hangs the chronicle and discussion of great military and political events upon the thread of the personal experiences of an individual. I was immensely encouraged to find that I had been unconsciously following with halting steps the example of so great a master of narrative.[5]

Churchill demonstrates what can be achieved by such a grouping: it is precisely the subjective perspective, the portrayal born completely out of one's own temperament, that makes the history of the First World War such exciting reading and turns it into literature.

There is a basic theme:

> From first to last it is contended that once the main armies were in deadlock in France the true strategy for both sides was to attack the weaker partners in the opposite combination with the utmost speed and ample force.[6]

Of what use were all the attacks on the Western Front?

> In these siege-offensives which occupied the years 1915, 1916 and 1917 the French and British Armies consumed themselves in vain and suffered . . . nearly double the casualties inflicted on the Germans.[7]

And so,

> It is certain, surveying the war as a whole, that the Germans were strengthened relatively by every Allied offensive — British or French — launched against them, until the summer of 1918.[8]

Conversely, the Germans would have been better advised to prepare for the defence in the West in 1914, in order to let the French run up against their positions and bleed themselves to death. This would have avoided the march through Belgium and have at least delayed the declaration of war by Great Britain. In the meantime they should have turned East with overwhelming force, and would then probably have achieved the victory over Russia not in 1917 but two years earlier.[9] The German offensive against Verdun in 1916 was also a costly mistake, as were also, finally, the desperate German attacks in the West from March to June 1918: 'It was their own offensive, not ours, that consummated their ruin. They were worn down not by Joffre, Nivelle and Haig, but by Ludendorff.'[10]

Agreed, but what could the Allies do? Churchill's eye fell on the Dardanelles, the strait leading from the Aegean to the Black Sea. Right at the start of the war the German battlecruiser *Goeben* and the cruiser *Breslau* had run a 'regatta' against the British naval forces in the Mediterranean and won. They reached Turkish waters undamaged and sailed into the Bosporus. This contributed to Turkey's decision to join the war on the side of the Central Powers. At the end of October 1914 Turkish naval forces — in other words, primarily the two German ships — bombarded Russian ports on the Black Sea. In early November Russia, France and Great Britain replied by declaring war on Turkey.

Could naval forces not force the passage of the Dardanelles in a *coup de main*? What would happen if they were suddenly to appear off Constantinople and threaten a devastating bombardment while simultaneous landings by land forces took place? Who would be able to oppose them? The bulk of the Turkish Army was deployed far away in the Caucasus, in Mesopotamia and along the Suez Canal. Germany, too, was far away and could hardly provide any help. It was only in October 1915 that the offensive, under the command of Field Marshal Mackensen, began, leading to the conquest of Serbia and the entry into the war of Bulgaria. Would the Turks, if they were offered an honourable armistice and a generous peace settlement, not be prepared to give in, in order to save their capital from destruction?

The blow against the Dardanelles offered many and tempting prospects. Bulgaria would probably have remained neutral, and Greece would have joined the war on the side of the Allies much earlier. Russia would have been relieved on its Caucasian front, as would Britain from the costly deployment of troops in Mesopotamia and Egypt. One could have provided decisive aid to the Russian ally and strengthened her will to go on fighting. The Tsar was never lacking in men to keep setting up new armies, but was short of equipment, modern weapons and ammunition. This led, almost inevitably, to the fatal failures and huge losses which finally resulted in collapse. But once the Dardanelles were open, the required material could easily be shipped to Odessa and from there to the Front.

It was truly a daring plan, but workable only as long as it was carried out with determination and sufficient strength. A temporary halt in the offensive in France would have provided more than enough troops, and the Grand Fleet stationed in the North Sea could have sent a few battleships at small risk. They would only have been required for a short time anyway, for the decisive break-through. But the British admirals would not take the risk, and the French generals did not want to give up the attacks in France from which they expected victory. A reference work reports on this almost monotonously:

> 16 February to 20 March 1915: winter battle in the Champagne. Break-through attempt by the French is repulsed; 10 to 14 March: break-through attempt by the British at Neuve Chapelle achieves only small gains and is repulsed; 9 May to 23 July: break-through attempts by the *Entente* between Lille and Arras are repulsed after only small loss of ground by the Germans; 22 September to 6 November: Joffre's 'big offensive' fails.

The amphibious operation was approached half-heartedly from the beginning, and almost everything that could fail did fail. There was no determined Supreme Commander, only hesitating and bickering admirals and generals. The bombardment of the Turkish positions and forts protecting the entry into the Bosporus began on 19 February 1915, hesitantly and with insufficient forces. A mine barrier was overlooked and not cleared, and several British and French battleships received hits and sank. The landing operations by the troops on the Gallipoli peninsula began far too late and without effective co-operation from the naval forces. In the meantime the Turks had had enough time to reinforce themselves and to organise a determined defence under the German General Liman von Sanders. The Allied attack ground to a halt with heavy losses, and the end of the Dardanelles operation was not marked by a glorious victory but by a shameful withdrawal.

Churchill commented on this failure with bitterness:

> Coming generations will not understand why the strategy of an island nation, which at the time and during the whole of the war was blessed with the unlimited and unendangered rule of the sea, failed so utterly when it attempted to take advantage of this for her own possibilities of attack.[11]

And, even more bitterly, he added:

> No war is more bloody than the war of attrition, no attack less promising than the one head-on. To these two cruel means of battle the military leaders of France and Great Britain sacrificed the flower of the youth of their nations . . . For later generations it will not only be horrifying, but incomprehensible when they recognise that

such sacrifices were imposed by the holders of military power on a heroic population, which obeyed their orders. Because we are dealing with a history of the torment, the mutilation and the destruction of millions of people, of the slaughter of
the noblest and best of a whole generation.[12]

Churchill remains silent, however, about his own responsibility. He had
devised a brilliant plan, put paid far too little attention to its practical execution. He had not provided clear lines of command, and not even in his own
sphere of influence had he been able to ensure that sufficient ships with
enough combat strength were present. There were also no political drafts of a
peace treaty with Turkey. And Churchill had never hammered home to those
responsible in Great Britain and France what the alternatives were—either to
conduct the operation with determination and strength or to let it be.

In the end, so it would almost appear, personal responsibility fades away
to the notes of a fateful symphony. Vaguely and placatingly he says:

> The greatness of the prize in view, the narrowness by which it was missed, the
> extremes of valiant skill and of incompetence, of effort and inertia, which were
> equally presented, the malevolent fortune which played about the field, are fea-
> tures not easily to be matched in our history.[13]

But the First Lord of the Admiralty did not escape unscathed. Even in
war there are public opinion, a Parliament, the parties and the Press, unlike
in Germany (at least after 1916 under Hindenburg and Ludendorff), where
there was the suffocating omnipotence of the Supreme Army Command.
Consequently the hopes which had accompanied the attack on the Dardanelles turned into disappointment—all the more so since the costly stale-
mate in France was notorious.

Now a guilty person, a scapegoat, had to be found—and who else if not
Churchill? He had advocated the operation like no other, had demanded
it with all of his powers of persuasion and had painted the opportunities
it offered in the most glowing colours. The swing of opinion, therefore, hit
him full blast: suddenly everyone had always known that he only caused
disaster, and the flood of condemnation swept him away. On 18 May 1915
the First Lord of the Admiralty was dismissed and fobbed off with an honorary position of no importance as Chancellor of the Duchy of Lancaster.
But the pressure continued, and Churchill finally evaded it by volunteering
for service at the Front, where he was employed as a battalion commander
in France. 'As in the shades of a November evening, I for the first time led

a platoon of Grenadiers across the sopping fields which gave access to our trenches . . .',[14] then the darkness was truly not only due to the time of day and year: it bore down heavily upon his soul.

Balfour adjuged the guilt fairly justly when he said:

> In the Dardanelles affair the prime movers were a soldier without strategic genius who controlled the army machine [Lord Kitchener], a sailor, also without strategic genius, who should have controlled the naval machine but did not [Lord Fisher], and a brilliant amateur who tried to control both but failed.[15]

Churchill, close to desperation, looked for the guilty in his turn: 'I have been stung by a viper. I am the victim of a political intrigue. I am finished.'[16] He felt like a deep-sea diver who has been brought to the surface too quickly[17] or, to turn the metaphor in the other direction, like a mountain climber who loses his hold and suddenly falls into the void. 'I am so consumed with ambition,' he wrote to his wife from France, and she even feared that he 'would die of sorrow'.[18]

That did not happen, thank God. Churchill was never lacking in personal courage. He proved himself in combat, and after he had thus practised active remorse in the eyes of the public, so to speak, he returned home after six months and in May 1916 again took up his seat in the Commons. A few months later, in December, a change in government occurred. Lloyd George replaced Asquith as Prime Minister — or, rather, he brought him down with the help of the Conservatives and split his own party in the process. He remembered Churchill's fertile mind and untiring industry as well as their former brilliant co-operation and wanted to bring the 'disempowered' man back into the government. He ran into an inexorable 'No' from Bonar Law, however, the leader of the Conservative Party. The renegade, the accursed changer of parties and his crossing the floor, were unforgotten. A short time later, in July 1917, Lloyd George high-handedly called on Churchill anyway, and almost precipitated a Cabinet crisis.

In his memoirs Lloyd George writes:

> Some of them [the Conservatives] were more excited about his appointment than about the War . . . It was interesting to observe in a concentrated form every phase of the distrust and trepidation with which mediocrity views genius at close quarters. Unfortunately, genius always provides its critics with material for censure — it always has and always will. Churchill is certainly no exception to this rule.[19]

Lloyd George takes an even closer look at Churchill's enemies: 'They admitted he was a man of dazzling talents, that he possessed a forceful and fascinating personality. They recognized his courage and that he was an indefatigable worker.' Churchill's opponents apparently often asked themselves what the reason for their mistrust was:

> Here was their explanation. His mind was a powerful machine, but there lay hidden in its material or its make-up some obscure defect which prevented it from always running true ... When the mechanism went wrong, its very power made the action disastrous, not only to himself but to the causes in which he was engaged and the men with whom he was co-operating. That was why the latter were nervous in his partnership. He had in their opinion revealed some tragic flaw in the metal. This was urged by Churchill's critics as a reason for not utilising his great abilities at this juncture. They thought of him not as a contribution to the common stock of activities and ideas in the hour of danger, but as a further danger to be guarded against.
>
> I took a different view of his possibilities. I felt that his resourceful mind and his tireless energy would be invaluable *under supervision*.[20]

The perspicacity of this remark on the relationship or disparity between genius and mediocrity is just as much evident as the proud conclusion: David Lloyd George considered himself to be a genius too, only one without faults, and was convinced he could keep the other genius with the mechanical fault under control. And in fact, in the years together in office until the fall of the Lloyd George government in 1922, he always remained in control and Churchill remained dependent upon him as his servant, because only the firm hand of the Prime Minister kept him in office and protected him from the mistrust, the hostility of the Conservatives.

Churchill was appointed Minister of Munitions. The office encompassed more than the name implied: in practice it was a Ministry for Armament. In the critical situation of 1917 the issue was to mobilise all the forces at home in order to meet the growing demands of the Front. Social problems also came into the equation, of course — the relationship between the employers and the unions, questions of remuneration, overtime and extra shifts. The Minister devoted particular attention to the development of new weapons of attack — the production of tanks. These armoured, fire-spitting monsters would gain increasing if not yet decisive importance in the final phase of the war. In them the military future was announcing itself — the development of the tank armies of the Second World War.

In the meantime two fateful events occurred, one advantageous and the other disastrous for Germany. Lenin, who had been brought to Russia from his exile in Switzerland with German help, set off his October Revolution (according to the Western calendar, in November). This led to Russia's quitting the war. On 15 December 1917 a cease-fire was agreed, and on 3 March 1918 the peace Treaty of Brest-Litovsk was signed. Ludendorff could now bring numerous divisions from the East to the West and prepare for his big offensive.

Before that, on 9 January 1917, unrestricted submarine warfare had been proclaimed on the insistence of Supreme Army Command and the Navy: within a restricted zone drawn widely around Britain, all merchant ships were now to be attacked and sunk without warning. The United States reacted to this by severing diplomatic relations on 3 February and declaring war on 6 April.

The admirals had claimed, and given their word of honour, that the U-boats would bring Britain to her knees 'within six months'. The warnings by Chancellor Bethmann-Hollweg about America's entry into the war were dismissed with the remark that no troop transport would ever reach France. In actual fact, not a single such vessel was ever sunk, and the early successes of the U-boats were not maintained. While merchant ships in the order of a total of six million tonnes were sunk in 1917, the high point was reached in the period April–June. From then on the number of sinkings declined further and further, because the British organised their shipping into convoys which were protected by destroyers. And soon Allied new construction was to exceed losses.

'Our future lies on the waters,' the *Kaiser* had once proclaimed. But this future contained disaster—defeat. The false promises of the admirals can probably only be explained by the condition of their souls, their humiliation and desperation. From the first day of the war it had been the Army which had won all the victories and borne all the burdens, while the expensive battlefleet stayed on the sidelines, useless and without a victory. It had been built in vain. Therefore the submarines were the 'final card'. Miraculously they were supposed to bring about ultimate victory—all or nothing, and they brought nothing.

On 21 March 1918 Ludendorff's great offensive began. Deep penetrations of the Allied front were achieved, and once again victory appeared to be close at hand. But the decisive break-through failed. Further attacks followed, but with gradually diminishing force. The final push failed on 17 July with heavy losses. The following day Marshal Foch, since the crisis in the spring the new Allied Supreme Commander, began his counter-offensive. It was continued without let-up and with shifting focuses until the end of the war—now also with American troops, whose strength increased from week to week, and with rapidly growing armoured forces. Many German soldiers felt that all their efforts had been in vain, and they deserted or surrendered. On 8 August, the 'black day of the German Army', whole divisions broke up.

On 14 August, during a conference at their headquarters in Spa, Hindenburg and Ludendorff declared that a continuation of the war was hopeless, and on 29 September they demanded an armistice. Germany's allies now also began to collapse. On 30 September Bulgaria, on 30 October Turkey and on 3 November Austria-Hungary all signed cease-fire agreements. On 28 October the German Fleet mutinied when the admirals wanted it to put to sea for a final and senseless battle—a sort of Nibelungen finale. On 3 November revolution began in Kiel, on 7 November in Munich and on 9 November in Berlin. On the same day the last Imperial Chancellor, Prince Max von Baden, turned the government over to the chairman of the SPD, Friedrich Ebert. On 10 November *Kaiser* Wilhelm II fled into Dutch exile. On 11 November at 11 a.m. an armistice came into effect on the Western Front as well. A sudden deep silence replaced the thunder of the guns. The great European war was over. It had cost ten million dead.

Churchill experienced the moment of victory in a strangely subdued mood:

> I was conscious of reaction rather than elation. The material purposes on which one's work had been centred, every process of thought on which one had lived, crumbled into nothing. The whole vast business of supply, the growing outputs, the careful hoards, the secret future plans—but yesterday the whole duty of life— all at a stroke vanished like a nightmare dream, leaving a void behind. . . .[21]

The Minister looked out into the street. At the stroke of eleven it suddenly filled with people for a 'pandemonium of triumph'.

In the evening he had a talk with Lloyd George:

> My own mood was divided between anxiety for the future and desire to help the fallen foe. The conversation ran on the great qualities of the German people, on the tremendous fight they had made against three-quarters of the world, on the impossibility of rebuilding Europe except with their aid. At that time we thought they were actually starving, and that under the twin pressures of defeat and famine the Teutonic peoples—already in revolution—might slide into the grisly

gulf that had already devoured Russia. I suggested that we should immediately, pending further news, rush a dozen great ships crammed with provisions into Hamburg.[22]

Towards the end of his great work about the world crisis Churchill writes:

It will certainly not fall to this generation to pronounce the final verdict on the Great War. The German people are worthy of better explanations than the shallow tale that they were undermined by enemy propaganda . . .[23]

Yet in the sphere of force, human records contain no manifestation like the eruption of the German volcano. For four years Germany fought and defied the five continents of the world by land and sea and air. The German Armies upheld her tottering confederates, intervened in every theatre with success, stood everywhere on conquered territory, and inflicted on their enemies more than twice the bloodshed they suffered themselves. To break their strength and science and curb their fury, it was necessary to bring all the greatest nations of mankind into the field against them. Overwhelming populations, unlimited resources, measureless sacrifice, the Sea Blockade, could not prevail for fifty months. Small states were trampled down in the struggle; a mighty empire was battered into unrecognizable fragments; and nearly twenty million men perished or shed their blood before the sword was wrested from that terrible hand. Surely, Germans, for history it is enough![24]

But few Germans have probably ever read this final sentence — or, if they have, they have misunderstood it.[25]

Vladimir Ilyitsh Lenin
and Edmund Burke

In 1703 Tsar Peter the Great founded the fortress of Peter and Paul on the banks of the River Neva, close to its estuary in the Gulf of Finland. With this he threw open Russia's 'window on the Baltic' and the door to the West. The city which grew around the fortress was called St Petersburg. Between 1914 and 1924 it was called Petrograd, and thereafter Leningrad. During the Second World War it was besieged for three years by German troops; about 600,000 inhabitants died under the hail of bombs and shells, but mostly from hunger. In the meantime the subsequent generations of citizens are again living in St Petersburg. When in autumn a mild sun shines through the fog, the city shows itself in all its unique beauty.

It was the door to the West, but also the gateway to many and varied influences. In 1825 the first revolt against Tsarist autocratic rule took place in St Petersburg. In 1905 the revolution which was to lead to the beginnings of popular representation followed. The February Revolution of 1917 which forced the Tsar to abdicate was unleashed in Petrograd. And Vladimir Ilyitsh Lenin also set off the charge of his revolution in Petrograd, according to the traditional Russian calender during the night of 24/25 October, after the Western calender on 6/7 November.

Only a short while later, on 25 November, elections were held for a national constitutional assembly, which the former, now toppled bourgeois government had set. The Bolshevists did not poll even a quarter of the votes. Should they be content with the fact that their revolution would be smothered in Parliament? Lenin had the national assembly dispersed by the bayonets of his soldiers on the very day it first convened, 18 January 1918. He had decided against parliamentary democracy and in favour of the dictatorship of the proletariat, which he himself exercised with the help of a strictly organised party.

Soon civil war raged throughout the country. The 'Red' and the 'White' terror competed with each other. There was no pardon granted. The most prominent victim of the Bolshevists was Tsar Nicholas II. On 17 July 1918 he was shot with his family in Yekaterinburg. But hundreds of thousands suffered the same fate, and many more people were abandoned to death by starvation. An inexorable hunt for 'class enemies' began and did not stop with the end of the civil war. In this the war commanders, the 'national organs' of the Party and, above all, the secret police decided completely arbitrarily who was to be numbered with these class enemies – or was allegedly betraying the just cause to them.

The Stalinist purges were later carried out under similar, perhaps even more sinister auspices, again with hundreds of thousands executed and with millions upon millions who disappeared into the dark world, not to say underworld, of the Gulag Archipelago. The numbers can only be estimated, but if we add up those executed, those who died of hunger and those who became the victims of forced repatriation, hard labour and imprisonment in the camps during the decades of Lenin's and Stalin's rule, and during the reign of Communism in total, then we must speak of eighty, if not of one hundred million – a gigantic Golgotha of horror.[1]

But we are now getting far ahead of ourselves and must return to the beginnings. In far-off London Winston Churchill was watching with dismay what was going on in Russia. Was this not the destruction of civilisation in the Western sense? Were not all human and civil rights being trampled under foot? And must one not fear that the revolution would spill over into vanquished, desperate, starving Germany? Let us turn back a few pages at this point and re-read what Churchill reports about his conversation with Lloyd George in the evening of 11 November 1918. Now there were red flags flying all over Germany, worker and soldier councils were being chosen and nobody could predict with any certainty whether social democracy under Ebert's leadership would succeed in directing the movement on to parliamentary paths and in creating a democratic constitution.

Incidentally, what Churchill feared was what Lenin hoped for. According to Marxist doctrine, the dictatorship of the proletariat could not actually be erected in backward Russia, where there were very many peasants but hardly a working class. Not so in Germany: if, after the initial detonation in

Russia, the revolution were to succeed there as well, the required partner would have been found, and together the achievements of the revolution could be made unassailable. It was only the disappointment of this hope which led to a turning to 'socialism in only one country' and to the Soviet Union being transfigured into the 'fatherland of the worker'.

Churchill again: would not the Bolshevists, as soon as they had won the civil war and stabilised their rule, turn outward as conquerers in order to break out of their isolation? What else did—in 1922—the advance of the Red Army into Poland imply when it was beaten back (though only just) in the 'miracle on the Vistula' with the help of the French General Weygand?

But one should not bet on miracles. It is far better to stamp out a spark before the fire gets out of control and turns into a conflagration. In 1919, after the dissolution of the Ministry of Armaments, Churchill took over the War Ministry, and from then on he preached war. Why not send Allied troops to slay the Bolshevist dragon? This, so he believed, could be accomplished with little effort. Siberia, the Ukraine and southern Russia already belonged to the counter-revolution. One only needed to supply it with weapons, of which there was a surplus in the West since the end of the war, and to support it with one's own forces. Some of these had already landed in the north anyway, in Murmansk amd Archangel. Perhaps one could also gain some supporting forces, possibly even employ some of the German divisions that had just left Russia. 'Mr. Churchill is determined to force a campaign against Bolshevist Russia, which is to be conducted by Allied volunteers, Poles, Finns and anyone else he can get hold of, and to be financed by the Allies,' Philip Kerr, Lloyd George's secretary, noted.[2]

Anyone is free to imagine what course recent history would have taken had Churchill had his way. But no one listened to him. Everyone recalled the failure of his Dardanelles adventure. The statesmen, the soldiers, the nations did not want to hear anything about war any longer: all they longed for was a return to peace and nothing else.

It would, of course, be easy to talk about a belated crusader and to leave it at that. Lloyd George scoffed that his Minister had 'his head full of Bolshevism'[3] and that 'his ducal blood revolted against the mass executions of Grand Dukes'.[4] Even these, however, are also human beings who—in the terms of the American Declaration of Independence—have an inalienable right to life, liberty and the pursuit of happiness.

But British ducal blood and Russian Grand Dukes were really only a side issue. We can only understand Churchill when we recognise how deeply his process of thought was rooted in history, and that all of his convictions had something to do with the experiences of history. One of his examples was Edmund Burke, and we have to elaborate a little in order to make the feelings of affinity between Churchill and Burke, together with their consequences, comprehensible.

Burke, born in Ireland in 1729, was one of the great parliamentarians of the eighteenth century and rose to become one of the spiritual leaders of the Whigs along with Charles James Fox. Time and again he fought for reforms — for the improvement of living conditions in Ireland, for a reform of the administration aimed at curtailing the prevailing corruption, for the abolition of the slave trade, for the abolition of colonial exesses in India, and for the downfall of the allegedly impartial government of King George III. He gave outstanding proof of his courage when he attacked the blindness of British policy in America and defended the rights of the colonies who were threatening to split away. His speech in Parliament on 22 March 1775, *On Moving Resolutions for Conciliation with the Colonies*, belongs among the truly classic speeches known to modern history, comparable to Abraham Lincoln's Gettysburg Address in 1863 and Churchill's 'Blood, Sweat and Tears' speech in 1940. To cite only one passage in which Burke addresses the men responsible for government policy:

> As long as you are wise enough to preserve government by our country as a temple of liberty, as a temple which is dedicated to our common belief, so long will the sons of England, wherever they revere liberty, turn to you. The more numerous they become, the more numerous will your friends be. The more fervently they love liberty, the better will they obey you. Slavery they can have everywhere. That is a weed which flourishes in any soil. Slavery they can have in Spain, and they can have it from Prussia. But as long as you have not yet completely lost all feeling for your true interests and your natural dignity, they can find liberty with no one else but you . . . If you therefore deny the Colonies their just portion of liberty, you will rupture the one and only bond which on which the cohesion of the Empire is based.[5]

Thus Edmund Burke, the protagonist of reform and the advocate of liberty. All the greater was the surprise when he published a fiery manifesto against the French Revolution. His *Reflections on the French Revolution* appeared in 1790, before the revolution had degenerated into terror. In a visionary manner, the author anticipated what was still to come — the slide into terror. In the end, said Burke, there would be a dictatorship by a popular general, whose spirit of command would discipline the soldiers and restore law and order by the rule of the bayonet.[6] The *Reflections* were immediately translated into other languages. They first appeared in German in 1791, and then achieved a lasting success through the brilliant translation by Friedrich Gentz in 1793. Overnight Burke became a figure of European importance in the intellectual debate for or against revolution. His work found many imitators, but also provoked impassioned rejoinders.[7]

Freiherr vom Stein, the leading minister of the Prussian reform movement after the defeat of 1807, said of Burke:

> This great, experienced statesman with a noble character worth revering, defended the cause of legal and religious freedom with forcefulness and captivating eloquence against the meta-political innovators who were devastating France.[8]

In contrast to this, with Thomas Jefferson—the intellectual father of the American Declaration of Independence—his disappointment and outrage comes through:

> The revolution in France astounds us far less than the one in Mr. Burke . . . How terrible it is that this proof of his intellectual depravity now forces us to also have to assume base motives behind his former activities, which we believed had been marked by firmness of character and patriotism.[9]

Churchill takes a third position when he writes in admiration:

> His [Burke's] *Thoughts on the Present Discontents*, his writings and speeches on the conciliation of America, form the main and lasting armoury of Liberal opinion throughout the English-speaking world. His *Letters on a Regicide Peace*, and his *Reflections on the French Revolution*, will continue to furnish Conservatives for all time with the most formidable array of opposing weapons. On the one hand he is revealed as a foremost apostle of Liberty, on the other as the redoubtable champion of Authority. But a charge of political inconsistency applied to this great life appears a mean and petty thing. History easily discerns the reasons and forces which actuated him, and the immense change in the problems he was facing which evoked from the same profound mind and sincere spirit these entirely contrary manifestations. His soul revolted against tyranny, whether it appeared in the aspect of a domineering Monarch and a corrupt Court and Parliamentary system, or whether, mouthing the watch-words of a non-existent liberty, it towered up against him in the dictation of a brutal mob and wicked sect. No one can read the Burke of Liberty and the Burke of Authority without feeling that here was the same man pursuing the same ends, seeking the same ideals of society and Government, and defending them from assaults, now from one extreme, now from the other.[10]

We are of course dealing with mirror-imaging. In the example we recognise the self-portrait. The 'accusation of political inconsistency' had been levelled against Churchill, too, for example when the Minister of Economic Affairs and social reformer wanted to reduce arms expenditure and soon thereafter the First Lord of the Admiralty advocated its increase and painted the picture of impending war on the wall—not to mention crossing the floor. But we are dealing, above all, with the relationship between teacher and pupil.

Churchill learned from Edmund Burke what modern revolutions actually imply. The issues are not primarily reforms, the correction of abuses or the constitution, but an overturn based on principles:

> The current revolution in France appears to me to little resemble the revolutions which occurred in Europe for purely political reasons. It is a revolution of doctrine, of theoretical dogma. Therefore it reminds me far more of upheavals which occur for religious reasons and in which missionary zeal plays a decisive rôle.[11]

And so the struggle inevitably assumes the attributes of a crusade: 'It is a war of religion.'[12] Yet the issues are actually not religious, but have to do with politics and society; an age begins in which traditional religion is fanatically attacked and persecuted by the revolutionary for the very reason that his own ideologies assume quasi-religious overtones and proclaim messages of earthly salvation and redemption. Since 1789, therefore, these are no longer—as in England in 1688 or in America in 1776—acts of resistance against oppression, but something new, formerly unknown: 'Before this took place in France, there was not one single instance of such a total revolution to be found in the history books.'[13]

From the opposite point of view, the 'philosopher of the Prussian state', Georg Wilhelm Friedrich Hegel, applauded the French Revolution:

> The idea, the concept of justice established itself all of a sudden, and this the old structures of injustice was unable to resist. A constitution has therefore now been erected on the concept of justice, and everything is now to be based on this foundation. Since the sun stands in the firmament and the planets circle around it, it has never been observed that man stands himself on his head, that is to say on an idea, and builds reality according to it . . . This was therefore a glorious sunrise. All sentient beings joined in celebrating this age. At this time a noble emotion reigned, an enthusiasm of the spirit permeated the world, as if the true reconciliation between the divine and the worldly had now finally come about.[14]

Certainly, it may well be tempting for philosophers—in modern terms intellectuals—or even be a part of their profession, to practise standing on their heads and to project the world as it should be out of their fantasies. But that is exactly where the evil lies, Burke would answer them. Whoever mixes the divine with worldly matters destroys both. And what justice are we talking about? Whatever deserves this name must be concrete. The law defends a system of human conditions and decides conflicts in order to promote peace instead of unleashing violence. (This becomes far more apparent under Anglo-Saxon case law, incidentally, than it does under Continental codified law.)

The revolution insists on attempting to impose worldly salvation, and by this rejects a fundamental Western conviction which stems from Christianity: by human endeavour alone there is no salvation in this world, and the gates of Paradise remain firmly locked. The revolution, however, rejects the idea of the ever-sinful 'old Adam'. It attempts to create a new man who fits in with its concept of an ideal society. For this it must press the old man into the bed of Procrustes, or, if nothing else is of any help, chop off his head. Forced re-education, violence and persecution are part of the package. Against this Burke remarked sarcastically, long before the revolution: 'Among all the heroes of antiquity, Procrustes will never become my ideal of a law-giver.'[15]

What develops is a fatal circle, an inter-relationship between idealism and violence. Just as the fanaticism of the Inquisition dragged the heretic to the stake and burned him in order to save his soul, the revolutionary zeal persecutes old Adam in order to create a new man and with him a better world. In this sense Dostoyevsky was way ahead of the events in Russia when he told the dark story of the Grand Inquisitor in *The Brothers Karamasov*. And Aldous Huxley said:

> Thinking in terms of first principles entails acting with machine-guns A government with a comprehensive plan for the betterment of society is a government that uses torture. *Per contra*, if you never consider principles and have no plan, but deal with situations as they arise, piecemeal, you can afford to have unarmed policemen, liberty of speech and *habeas corpus*.[16]

Or, to quote Jules Monnerot:

> In order to be able to justify warlike actions, police torture and the re-appearance of slavery in times of peace, one needs nothing less than the promise of paradise. This is the way a direct connection between the certainty of salvation and human atrocity is achieved.[17]

There could have been no better witness for Burke than Maximilien Robespierre who, in a speech in 1794 – in other words four years after the publication of *Reflections on the French Revolution* — held before the National Convention, explained his programme:

> In this country we intend to replace egotism by morality, status by rectitude, habits by principles, the compulsions of tradition by the rule of reason, contempt for bad luck by contempt for vice, impudence by self-respect, vanity by greatness of the soul, avarice by magnanimity, the so-called better society by better men . . . In brief, we want to fulfil the will of nature, to have the destiny of mankind become reality, to redeem the promises of philosophy, to acquit fate of the long reign of crime and tyranny.[18]

The obligation to terror is derived from the fight for virtue, because

> . . . if the motivating force of a popular government in times of peace is virtue, then in times of revolution it is both virtue and terror together: virtue, without which terror would be evil, and terror, without which virtue would remain powerless. Terror is nothing but forceful, inexorable, uncompromising justice. It is therefore a product, a consequence of virtue. It is not a special principle, but a product of the general principle of popular rule, applied to the most urgent matters of the nation.[19]

Churchill did not write any 'reflections on the Russian Revolution', even though he always remained a productive writer. He did not need to write them, because Edmund Burke had already said all there was to say on the subject — and in a manner that could not be surpassed. On top of that, Burke had also preached war, and in his *Letters on a Regicide Peace*[20] castigated the brittle conciliation into which the conservative European powers were prepared to enter with revolutionary France. Churchill's attacks on Lenin, Trotsky and the regime of terror they were creating, however, can hardly be counted and they are unequalled in their sharpness. One of the milder variations is the following sketch which is devoted to Lenin:

> . . . The intellect was capacious and in some phases superb. It was capable of universal comprehension in a degree rarely reached among men. The execution of the elder brother deflected this broad white light through a prism: and the prism was red.[21]
>   . . . His weapon logic; his mood opportunist . . . His purpose to save the world: his method to blow it up. Absolute principles, but readiness to change them. Apt at once to kill or learn: dooms and afterthoughts: ruffianism and philanthropy . . . The quality of Lenin's revenge was impersonal. Confronted with the need of killing any particular person he showed reluctance — even distress. But to blot out a million, to proscribe entire classes, to light the flames of intestine war in every land with the inevitable destruction of the well-being of whole nations — these were sublime abstractions.[22]

71

Churchill's anger was, of course, also directed against the West's fellow-travellers, the intellectuals, artists and writers who were enthusiastic about the distant Soviet paradise of which they knew nothing. An example can again be found in his essay on George Bernard Shaw. Shaw had been invited to the Soviet Union, fêted there effusively and surrounded with all the luxury only a government of violence is able to offer its guests while all about poverty reigns supreme. Shaw's plaudits of the Soviet Union were then appropriately effusive too. Churchill, however, writes:

> Here we have a system whose social achievements crowd five or six persons in a single room; whose wages hardly compare in purchasing power with the British dole [still very low at the time]; where life is unsafe . . . Here we have a state, three millions of whose citizens are languishing in foreign exile, whose intelligentsia have been methodically destroyed; a state nearly half-a-million of whose citizens, reduced to servitude for their political opinions, are rotting and freezing through the Arctic night; toiling to death in forests, mines and quarries, many for no more than indulging in that freedom of thought which has gradually raised man above the beast
>
> Decent, good-hearted British men and women ought not to be so airily detached from realities, that they have no word of honest indignation for such wantonly, callously-inflicted pain.[23]

One underestimates Churchill if all one sees in him is counter-revolutionary zeal or the heir of an ancient upper class whose fear of downfall turns into aggression. Edmund Burke was his mentor and had shown him that the issues were far greater than an overthrow of the power structure such as has occurred a thousand times in history. Tyranny or law, violence and submission or liberty: these were the alternatives. This insight, copied from the historic example and transmitted by a great British parliamentarian, was what enabled Churchill to look deeper than his contemporaries when, in central Europe, that other form of tyranny appeared of which, so far, there has been no mention.

Ireland
and India

One of the results of the French Revolution was the triumphant march of nationalism throughout Europe and the world. When the French Estates assembled in Paris by order of the King, it was initially intended that they should meet and vote separately as the representatives of the nobility, the clergy and the bourgeoisie. It was, therefore, the first revolutionary act when the representatives of the 'Third Estate' proclaimed themselves to be the National Assembly on 17 June 1789, and three days later, together with some defectors, especially from the Second Estate — the clergy — swore not to disband before they had given the country a new constitution. 'Liberty, equality and fraternity' was the rousing slogan, and what it meant in practice was demonstrated in the self-definition as a nation: in future, liberty was no longer a special privilege, but an inalienable right of all Frenchmen, equality described their position as citizens and fraternity was the community of fate of the nation. Strictly speaking, this had not existed before 1789, only the absolute state, embodied by the King. Beside or under him, the Estates, strictly separated according to privilege, led their separate lives following the motto 'Everyone for himself and God for as all!'[1] Now, however, the one and indivisible nation became the new, the secular shrine.

The sons and soldiers of the Revolution carried the ideas of 1789 all over Europe in their haversacks, but with a totally unexpected result. The further their victory marches took them, the more parts of Europe France grabbed for herself or put under her hegemony, the more violently the expectations which had been raised struck back against the conquerors. German nationalism, for example, was thus awakened by France, and turned against France. It reached a high point in the revolt against Napoleon in 1813.

The victorious conservative powers of 1815 knew precisely with what historic dynamite they were dealing and attempted to defuse it by any and all means. In vain. The great political movements and revolutions of the nineteenth century, like those of 1848, were carried by the nationalistic forces, or at least decisively influenced by them. They led to the unification of Germany and Italy. They undermined the venerable, supranational Danube Monarchy of the Habsburgs, and finally destroyed it. They strengthened the longing of the Poles for liberty, which was already inherent in the religious contrast to Protestant Prussia and Orthodox Russia. They shook Turkish hegemony in the Balkans. They reached over to Latin America and supported the revolt of the colonies against Spain and Portugal. Fateful problems announced themselves. What should happen? What was going to happen where peoples were bound together, yet against each other in a mixture?

Great Britain found herself in a strange situation of duality. Essentially she had already been a national state for a long time, and in Parliament she had the political institution at her disposal whose basis in electoral law only needed to be extended to convert it into a representation of the nation in the literal sense. This was then done by the stages of reform of the nineteenth and twentieth centuries. But what about Scotland and Wales? And, above all, what about Ireland, where the Catholic faith created an almost insurmountable barrier to amalgamation? And what about the colonial empire, what about India, its 'crown jewel'? That Benjamin Disraeli had had Queen Victoria crowned Empress of India—much to her delight—was hardly the answer. A modern upper class was gradually developing there which sent its sons to study in Oxford and Cambridge or to London. From there they returned enlightened, in other words full of European ideals, which were to be turned against their originators, as had already happened with French ideas in Germany in the times of Napoleon.[2]

The 'Irish Question' had long been a central issue of British politics. Should the Irish be granted Home Rule for their internal matters or not? And, if so, to what degree? That was the fateful question which occupied the parties, and indeed split them. Normal circumstances were also confused by the Irish Members, who have already been mentioned. To top it all, there was the special problem of Ulster with its Protestant inhabitants, who fought against any attempted solution as relentlessly and violently as they still do today.

William Gladstone, probably the greatest leader the Liberals had in the nineteenth century, brought a Bill on Irish Home Rule into the Commons in 1886 and applied all his skill as an orator to get it passed:

> Ireland [he told the Members] stands at your bar expectant, hopeful, almost suppliant. Her words are words of truth and soberness. She asks a blessed oblivion of the past, and in that oblivion our interest is deeper even than hers. . . . Think, I beseech you — think well, think wisely; think not for the moment, but for the years that are to come, before you reject this Bill.[3]

It was of no help. The Bill was rejected in the House of Lords by the devastating (in every sense) majority of 419 to 41. Gladstone also failed in his second and final attempt in 1893. The Irish Question dragged on unresolved until the First World War and even beyond — until, in the end, what could have led to reconciliation and agreement a quarter of a century earlier was no longer possible. One is involuntarily reminded of the reformer Edmund Burke, who more than a century before Gladstone had said in the Commons:

> I would like to ask the government with great seriousness to consider the wisdom of timely reforms. Timely reforms are like agreements between friends, belated reforms like conditions one imposes on a defeated enemy. Timely reforms take place in an atmosphere of calm, belated ones amid general excitement. Once it has gone that far, a people no longer perceives anything respectable in its government. It falls into the rage of a wild horde which no longer wants to improve anything, but only to tear down.[4]

But who takes such wisdom into consideration? Most people insist on making their mistakes until it is too late — and, most of all, those who shape public opinion and the politicians.

In January 1919 a national assembly convened in Dublin, declared Irish independence and named Eamonn de Valera, who had been sentenced to death because of his participation in the Easter Rising of 1916 and was living in exile, as the first President of the Republic. Great Britain rejected this declaration of independence. A bloody guerrilla war began. Now at last, late in 1920, the House of Commons saw its way clear to enacting a Home Rule law, but split off the six northern Irish counties and granted them their own parliament. This outraged the Irish. In 1921 negotiations were begun which finally led to an agreement.

Churchill took part in the negotiations at the side of Lloyd George, and has described them as dramatically as they probably were. One of the leaders of the Irish delegation was Arthur Griffith, according to Churchill's description a rare example of a taciturn Irishman. To let Churchill speak:

> To Mr. Griffith I said one day:
> 'I would like us to have beaten you beyond all question, and then to have given you freely all that we are giving you now.'
> '*I* understand that,' he answered, 'but would your countrymen?'
> I wonder [Churchill writes, and then turns to one of his favourite topics]. It is extraordinary how rarely in history have victors been capable of turning in a flash to all those absolutely different processes of action, to that utterly different mood, which alone can secure them for ever by generosity what they have gained by force. In the hour of success, policy is blinded by the passion of the struggle. Yet the struggle with the enemy is over. There is only then the struggle with oneself. That is the hardest of all. So the world moves on only very slowly and fitfully with innumerable set-backs, and the superior solutions, when from time to time as the result of great exertions they are open, are nearly always squandered. Two opposite sides of human nature have to be simultaneously engaged. Those who can win the victory cannot make the peace; those who make the peace would never have won the victory. Have we not seen this on the most gigantic scale drawing out before our eyes in Europe? . . .[5]

Churchill was, nevertheless, able to discover some examples of wisdom — Bismarck's conduct after the Prussian triumph over Austria at Königgrätz and the treatment of France at the Congress of Vienna in 1815.

> . . . And we have in our own time South Africa, where decisive victory in arms was swiftly followed by complete concession in policy, with results marvellous to this day.
> Our settlement with the Boers, with my own vivid experiences in it, was my greatest source of comfort and inspiration in this Irish business . . .[6]

But that was not nearly enough. The Irish negotiators were under pressure from the radicals in their own country, who demanded all or nothing: either complete independence or a continuation of the war. Finally Lloyd George handed down an ultimatum, and Churchill again describes the dramatic events:

> The Irishmen gulped down the ultimatum phlegmatically. Mr. Griffith said, speaking in his soft voice and with his modest manner, 'I will give the answer of the Irish Delegation at nine to-night; but, Mr. Prime Minister, I personally will sign this agreement and will recommend it to my countrymen.' 'Do I understand, Mr. Griffith,' said Mr. Lloyd George, 'that though everyone else refuses you will nevertheless agree to sign?' 'Yes, that is so, Mr. Prime Minister,' replied this quiet little man of great heart and of great purpose. Michael Collins [another member of the Irish delegation] rose looking as if he was going to shoot someone, preferably himself. In all my life I have never seen so much passion and suffering in restraint.[7]

In the end history still wrote its inexorable 'Too late!' Arthur Griffith died in 1922, and Michael Collins did not shoot himself — he was shot. De Valera slowly but surely advanced to become the dominating figure. As an uncompromising enemy of Britain he succeeded step by step in making Ireland a completely independent republic and cut all ties with the Commonwealth.[8] Great Britain tacitly accepted this breach of the agreement. De Valera would probably have preferred it if Germany had won the Second World War. In any case, in May 1945 he offered his condolences on Hitler's death to the German ambassador in Dublin.

On New Year's Day in 1921 Lloyd George offered Churchill the Colonial Office, which he accepted and held until the government fell in October 1922. With this Churchill had come full circle, so to speak: his political career had begun in 1906 as Under-Secretary in the Colonial Office.

The Minister's eye soon fell on India, where, shortly beforehand, in 1920, Gandhi had begun to organise civil disobedience and passive resistance against British rule. Of course, there had been stirrings of resistance and dreams of independence before. As early as 1885 the Indian National Congress — which wanted at the very least to achieve greater self-government — had been founded, and of course there had been the Great Mutiny of 1857. But with the appearance of Gandhi the Indian struggle for liberty gained a new quality — and, with passive resistance, an unassailable moral authority. Gandhi also tried to hit the colonial power economically. He called for a boycott of British goods, and his return to the spinning wheel meant far more than a relapse into primitive times. It became a symbol, because, with the development of her modern textile industry, Great Britain had ruined the formerly flourishing crafts in India.

What could be done? Churchill's rule, first to show strength in order then to practise magnanimity, was hardly applicable here. Gandhi was arrested in March 1922 and sentenced to six years in prison because some of his adherents had incited unrest against his will, but little or nothing was achieved thereby. The movement for independence only grew even stronger, because it now had a martyr, who was awarded the epithet 'Mahatma', in India an honorary title for gods or men 'who have a great soul'. Gandhi was released prematurely in December 1924 because of his poor health.

Churchill decided in favour of strength. India, the heart and 'crown jewel' of the British colonial empire, must not be abandoned at any price. To this he committed himself with all his passion, even after (or because) he had lost office. He led a veritable crusade, raved against everybody who tended towards giving in, wrote bitter articles in the newspapers, gave impassioned speeches, and even joined the Indian Empire Society, a refuge for retired colonels and colonial officers who complained in their club rooms that the world was no longer what it was supposed to be.

In an address which he gave to the honourable members of the Society on 11 December 1930, he said:

> Withdrawal of British control [over India] means either Hindu despotism . . . or the return of those cruel internal wars under which the Indian masses suffered for millennia before the British flag was hoisted in Calcutta.[9]

In other words, the white man had to continue to shoulder his burden in order to save the achievements of civilisation and preserve the peace. If that were to fail, it would only be due to 'an obvious lack of will-power and self-confidence which the representatives of Great Britain are displaying'.[10]

By now the quite rapidly changing governments were squirming about and trying to gain time. But it became clearer and clearer that they were headed towards giving in. Churchill lost his campaign. Even Duff Cooper, who stood close to him in many respects, finally noted:

> Strange that he does not understand the game is over. I fear that he will continue to spin intrigues and give speeches in the same way my mother-in-law obstinately continues to paint her face and wears wigs.[11]

Leo Amery commented even more scathingly on the imploring speech given by the Member Churchill in June 1935 against Indian Home Rule: 'Here ends the final chapter from the book of the prophet Jeremiah.'[12] Shortly thereafter the Bill which at least granted India self-government on the provincial level was passed by a majority of 382 to 122.

How must we judge Churchill's position on India? On one point, at least, his evaluation was certainly realistic: once foot had been set on the path of negotiation and giving in, there would be no stopping. Then one would have to go on to the bitter end, to the granting of complete independence, to the loss of the colony. The Indians would only take the first step towards self-government as an encouragement to demand the second. Had not the Irish example already shown where one would inevitably wind up? Many of the Members who voted for the India Bill in 1935 succumbed to an illusion when they believed that they could stop at this intermediary stage. Churchill knew better. In actual fact, twelve years later, in 1947, India was released into independence, not because this was wanted, but because there was now no other solution left. One of the consequences was that the sub-continent was divided between Hindu India and Moslem Pakistan—and that a bitter civil war flared, costing hundreds of thousands of people their lives and millions their homes. Mahatma Gandhi fell victim to the violence as well.

But there are still many questions. Could the historic march to nationalism be stopped at all? Many had attempted this, beginning with the 'carter of Europe' after 1815, Prince Metternich, and all had failed. Bismarck's stroke of genius, on the other hand, consisted in his not blocking the German national movement to the point of self-destruction but making it serve his own conservative purposes. Or how could Churchill ignore the wisdom of his teacher Burke, that timely reforms lead to an agreement between friends whereas belated ones unleash a rage which wants only to tear down? Does not the history of decolonisation provide an example? Taken all in all, Great Britain, with her policy of negotiating and giving in, managed to separate from her colonial possessions in time and with dignity, as opposed to France or Portugal, who let themselves in for costly yet in the end hopeless wars in Vietnam and Algeria, in Angola and in Mozambique.[13]

One may find a first explanation for Churchill's position in the fact that people are formed by the impressions gained in their youth. Perhaps for the rest of his life there was still something left in him of the young lieutenant of Hussars who played polo in Bangalore, read, fell in love and met the adventure he was seeking with the Makaland Field Force. Maybe that is why to him the old, grey colonial officers and servants in the Indian Empire Society did not appear as much out-of-date and dusty as they did to others.

A second explanation, remotely connected to the first, has been offered many times. Churchill, the claim is, was actually a man of the nineteenth century. He grew up in the heyday of the Empire, under the shine of the Imperial crown Disraeli had invented for Queen Victoria. He thought historically in terms of a British global mission to preserve peace and advance civilisation, and he was unable to free himself from this.

If we look back, we find indications of this time and again. As First Lord of the Admiralty, for example, Churchill stated in his Budget speech in 1913 that in three hundred years Great Britain had never misused her sea power but had always only employed it for the common good, for the suppression of slavery, for the charting of the oceans, for the freedom of world trade and for the support of small or young nations who were fighting for independence. 'And because all of this is true, we may rightly claim that, while control of the sea is a vital question for Great Britain, it is also a part of the common treasure of humanity.'

In the German *Taschenbuch der Kriegsflotten* (Handbook of the Battlefleets), 1914 edition, this is quoted and commented upon with scorn:

> Yes, it really is remarkable that none of the other nations has yet become convinced of this, or is grateful for the so ingenuously proffered 'common treasure of mankind'. That's all the thanks you get! And what does the history of the French, Spanish, Dutch and Danish Navies have to say to that?[14]

Scorn is easy to come by. And yet, Churchill's 'old-fashioned' or 'naïve' attitude is worth a second look. Later it was to help him define the British struggle against Hitler as the mission it then actually turned out to be. Furthermore, towards the end of the nineteenth century it was not only in Great Britain but in all of Europe that people believed themselves to be at the centre of the world. World history was European history,[15] and the victory march of nationalism was also a European movement which found its natural conclusion at the borders of the continent. It had nothing to do with Africa or Asia. All the more important, therefore, were colonial possessions, and all the more lasting should they be. They appeared to be one of the foundations of power and wealth—hence the breathlessness and ambition with which late-comers like Belgium, Germany and Italy attempted to secure their fair share.

In Peking there is a temple in which, according to Chinese tradition, the centre of the earth is marked for the Middle Kingdom. Today it is visited by tourists who have their picture taken while standing on it for their collection of curios. But how should we assess the conviction of the Europeans, that they stood at the centre of the world? This conviction, together with the belief in the importance and duration of colonial empires, reached out from the nineteenth into the twentieth century. It was only the age of the world wars which destroyed it. It is easy to be wise in hindsight, but before we condemn a man like Churchill out of hand we should recognise that he was a representative of his age—and that he shared his illusions with our own grandparents and great-grandparents.

Incidentally, one of the illusions was that colonies were of importance for the wealth of the nation, or were even its foundation. The opposite is true. Portugal and Spain, who had conquered vast colonial empires at the beginning of modern times, did not only not become rich by them, but were impoverished and lagged further and further behind the modern development of Europe. The treasures the Spanish silver fleets brought home — swarmed about by royal British pirates — seduced Spain into making herself at home in the comfort of a colonial pensioner instead of developing her own capabilities. At the same time it was also the people with daring and entrepreneurial spirit who left home to make their fortunes in the colonies.

Great Britain owes her rise to become the leading power of the nineteenth century not to her colonies but to the fact that, as the mother country of the Industrial Revolution, she became the factory of the world and sold her products all over the globe. Similarly Germany and the United States, when towards the end of the century they set out to overtake Britain and pass her: not colonial possessions, but only their own power of invention and drive to achieve played the decisive rôle in all this. On the other hand, Great Britain's falling behind, relatively speaking, did have something to do with the Empire: it offered far too many young people seductive positions which prepared them for living the life of a lord instead of becoming hard-working entrepreneurs or managers.

We could continue these briefly sketched considerations on European colonial illusions. In retrospect they may appear to be hardly comprehensible. But they were the illusions of an age. And if Churchill stood head and shoulders above his contemporaries, then he did so also with regard to the magnitude of his errors.[16]

The Return
of the Prodigal Son

In October 1922 David Lloyd George's government fell. For years he had led a coalition in which his own followers had only been a minority. But now the art of the master magician failed him, and while he was to remain a powerfully eloquent Member of the Commons for a long time, almost until the end of the Second World War, he was never again to become a member of the Cabinet, let alone Prime Minister.[1] In a noble gesture in early 1945 – and to spare the old man the efforts of the election campaign looming at the end of the war – Churchill elevated his former fellow-traveller to become Earl Lloyd George of Dwyfor, and thereby transferred him to the House of Lords. But the noble Earl from humble origins died on 26 March 1945. With him Churchill buried his own youth and gave a speech of commemoration honouring him.

He himself lost his seat in the Commons in the elections of 15 November 1922. The Conservatives won, while the Labour Party became the heavyweight opposition and far outdistanced the Liberals. The age-old Conservative–Liberal two party system went awry and a difficult time of transition with often very short-lived governments began. To enable the reader to keep track, there follows a brief sketch of the majorities and governments up to the Second World War.

In November 1922 Andrew Bonar Law formed a Conservative Cabinet, but resigned in May 1923 for reasons of health and was replaced by Stanley Baldwin. The next elections followed in December 1923. This time the Conservatives lost and Ramsay MacDonald became Prime Minister of the first-ever Labour government – but only for a few months. In October 1924 there was another election, and this time with clear-cut results: the Conservatives gained 419 seats, Labour 151 and the Liberals only 40.[2] Baldwin formed his second Cabinet, which was to remain in office until 1929. In May 1929 it was Labour's turn to win again, and MacDonald again took over the government. The world economic crisis which occurred soon afterwards led to the resignation of the government in August 1931. Under MacDonald, a coalition Cabinet was formed, made up of all three parties. In this, however, the Socialists scented some sort of class betrayal, and the majority of the Labour MPs decided to go into opposition. Elections in October 1931 confirmed the coalition and it stayed in office until 1935. Then came the great days of the Conservatives. Baldwin became Prime Minister for the third time. On 28 May 1937, shortly before his 70th birthday, he resigned for reasons of age, this time without any coercion, highly honoured and pleased with himself and the world. His successor was Neville Chamberlain.

And what was happening to Churchill in the meantime? In 1922 an appendectomy prevented his taking an active part in the campaign. In 1923 there was no such excuse. Again he fell through the net, and the only thing left was the bitter admission that even he was no longer able to charm Liberal voters out of the trees in sufficient numbers. Not only for a few weeks or months, but for almost two years his parliamentary career suffered a painful interruption and it became quite clear that it had no future in its former tracks.

It was only typical that he should change sides again, for the second time in his life. When the Chairman of the Conservatives of West Essex, Harry Goschen, asked him in 1924 whether he was willing to stand 'as a representative of the Conservative Party, its leaders and its platform', he seized the opportunity and declared that he saw no difficulties 'as far as the platform was concerned'.[3] He then won against the Liberal candidate with a margin of almost ten thousand votes.

Many of his old/new Party colleagues were, however, more inclined to view this development with cynicism than with joy. They had not forgotten that twenty years ago he had deserted them for the enemy camp, and then had made a career there. The accusation of opportunism was quickly heard, and is still difficult to refute in hindsight.

There are, nevertheless, some arguments to be advanced in defence of the accused, with which to plead mitigating circumstances. In his heart Churchill, like his father, had always been and remained a Tory Democrat. He would probably have returned to his origins far sooner had the magical powers of Lloyd George not prevented it. But this spell was now broken. Furthermore, in the years of the Liberal-Conservative Coalition the fronts had become blurred. Lloyd George himself had moved worlds away from his original, decidedly leftist (not to say radical) point of departure in the pre-war era. But, above all, Churchill in the meantime had stepped forward with arch-conservative zeal, in which he let himself be outdone by no man. One need only recall his crusade against Bolshevism — which expressly included the battle against the local leftists — and his views on India. Opportunism perhaps — but in the end the change of parties was consistent.

The sensation occurred after the election: Baldwin called Churchill into his Cabinet — and as, of all things, Chancellor of the Exchequer. According to traditional ranking, this is the second highest office in the government after that of Prime Minister.

One is unwittingly reminded of the story of the return of the prodigal son, which the Gospel According to St Luke tells in Chapter 15. This son goes off to foreign parts and loses all his wealth and goods. When he finally stands before his father again in rags and tatters and half-starved, his father orders the servants: 'Bring forth the best robe, and put it on him; and put a ring on his hand, and shoes on his feet. And bring hither the fatted calf, and kill it; and let us eat, and be merry.'

This angers the other son, of course, who always stayed at home like a good boy, and in rage he goes and confronts his father: 'Lo, these many years do I serve thee, neither transgressed I at any time thy commandment: and yet thou never gavest me a kid, that I might make merry with my friends: But as soon as this thy son was come, which hath devoured thy living with harlots, thou hast killed for him the fatted calf.'

'Son,' the father replies, 'thou art ever with me, and all that I have is thine. It was meet that we should make merry, and be glad: for this thy brother was dead, and is alive again; and was lost, and is found.'

British politics, however, were not quite so biblically noble as all that. Baldwin, a benign tactician, loved his comfort and wanted peace and quiet. The brilliant parliamentary speaker Churchill was 'a power in the Commons'; he could be useful, but could also create aggravation if he were to become bored on the backbenches. 'If you ignore him,' the Prime Minister was told, 'he will be leading a Tory rump parliament within six months.'[4] It therefore appeared to make sense to keep this dangerous man under control within the Cabinet.

Churchill himself was dumbfounded by Baldwin's offer: 'I would never have guessed that I stood in such high regard with him.' He was also aware that he knew very little about finances and asked himself: 'Will the damn duck be able to swim?' Baldwin was asking himself the very same question: should the shimmering bird turn out to be made of lead and go under – all the better. One could then pull him out of the water with good reason and as a sort of life-saver, and advise him to go rest on dry land for a while. But Churchill had never suffered from inferiority complexes, and the opportunity that was beckoning so unexpectedly was better than nothing. His reply to Baldwin's offer therefore read: 'This equates exactly to my wishes. I still have the robe my father wore as Chancellor. I will be proud to serve you in this honourable office.'[5]

In the end the duck proved that it could swim. Churchill served as Chancellor for five years, longer than in any other office, if we ignore that of Prime Minister during the Second World War. He devoted himself to his new office with all his energy and was wise enough to lean on the expert advice of his officials where his own knowledge was insufficient. However, a feeling of unease, of dependence, always remained. Once the Minister said about his officials: 'I wish they were generals or admirals, because theirs is a language I understand. But these chaps begin to talk Chinese after a while, and then I am lost.'[6] Churchill was never really happy in the Exchequer, in contrast to the Admiralty.

On the other hand, one of the perquisites of the office was that one could interfere in other departments. It is, after all, the Chancellor who must approve – or reject – their budgets. And it is exactly this right of rejection which is one of his traditional advantages: he makes himself popular when he saves money and reduces taxes.

Aggravations were not lacking either. Churchill, for example, got into a deep controversy with the Admiralty which wanted to build new ships he considered to be superfluous and refused to approve. The situation reminds us of the times before the war, of the young Minister of Economics who dreamt of lasting peace and considered the extension of the welfare state to be more important than new, ever more expensive battleships. Soon after this the First Lord of the Admiralty was to paint the devil of war on the wall and could not get enough ships. Now it was a passion for saving again – and the time was not far off when Churchill was to beseech the government to which he then no longer belonged to provide for the arms so urgently required.

Somebody said about him: 'He lives completely in the present, and always assumes the colour of the office he happens to hold.'[7] In a certain sense this is a part of the duty of any office holder — as is professionally caused tunnel vision part of the danger which threatens him. Churchill himself said: 'The only way a man can remain consistent amid changing circumstances is to change with them while preserving the same dominating purpose.'[8] For many if not for most men, however, this dominating objective is only to rise on the career ladder towards wealth and power.

The bitter fight for new battleships and cruisers dragged on for months. At times it looked as if it would end in a government crisis.[9] The First Lord of the Admiralty, William Bridgeman, and the First Sea Lord, Admiral Beatty, threatened to resign. In the end Churchill gave in to some extent, probably because he discovered that the needs of the Royal Navy not only cried to the heavens but also found a vociferous echo in the Conservative Party and the conservative press, but also because he recalled the fate of his father: Lord Randolph had once resigned as Chancellor because he refused to approve the demands of the Navy — and had thereby committed political suicide.

Once a year the British Chancellor of the Exchequer steps into the limelight: on one day in the spring he carries his Budget to Parliament in an old-fashioned briefcase, there to announce the expenditures and the increases or decreases in taxes the government intends to make. This is an important, but basically bone dry matter from which one can hardly strike any sparks. Not so Winston Churchill. In his first Budget speech he unfolded a brilliant fireworks display of rhetoric, which astounded the Members and even provoked the enthusiasm of those belonging to the Government side. Baldwin reported to the King with reluctant admiration that his Minister had risen 'magnificently to the occasion'. In a breathless ride of two hours and forty minutes — rather too long for Baldwin's taste — he had enlivened the dull material with 'witty levity and humour' and had 'soared into emotional flights of rhetoric' on the topic of pensions for mothers and orphans. He had demonstrated that he was 'not only possessed of consummate ability as a parliamentarian, but also all the versatility of an actor'[10] — whatever that may mean by way of praise or censure for an English gentleman. Be that as it may: from this premiere on, the venerable theatre at Westminster was filled to overflowing whenever Churchill gave another presentation of the Budget, because nobody wanted to miss such a performance.

The most important decision to be taken within Churchill's time in office was the stabilisation of the pound in September 1925 by the re-introduction of the gold standard, which had been common throughout Europe before the war. A young and at the time hardly known — but later world famous — economist, John Maynard Keynes,[11] warned against 'Mr. Churchill's consequences': the economy would run into difficulties if there were exaggerated exchange rates — and with it the social structure. And that is what happened. Exports shrank and unemployment and pressure on wages grew. One of the results was the General Strike of 1926, against which the Chancellor took the field as one of the major authors in the *British Gazette*.

But we must take the amateur actor under our protection here. All he did was to carry out what all the experts excepting know-all Keynes were demanding as emphatically as were the government and public opinion. His political position was not damaged. It was even strengthened by the successful conclusion of the conference on the regulation of the inter-Allied war debts in January 1925. This was a condition for the re-introduction of the gold standard. Great Britain's road into the future, so it appeared, led back to the halcyon days before the war.

All in all: Churchill was certainly no great Chancellor of the Exchequer, and even less a lucky one. But he fulfilled the difficult task with which he was confronted with honour, and thereby sealed the return of the prodigal son. The Baldwin government fell in the elections of May 1929 — just in time not to be burdened with the responsibility for the world economic crisis which broke out in October, and with the historic storm this brought about.[12]

A Long Way Through the Desert

The Conservatives were defeated in the General Election of 30 May 1929. The Baldwin Government resigned and Churchill lost his office as Chancellor of the Exchequer. On 3 September 1939 Great Britain declared war on Germany and Churchill was appointed First Lord of the Admiralty. In between lay ten bitter years, years of growing older, of the inexorable march of time.

In 1939 Churchill turned 65, in other words he reached the borderline behind which 'well-deserved retirement' begins for most people — yet which for many still makes them feel as if they were having to lay their heads on the chopping block. During all those years Churchill still held his seat in the Commons, but not any office. The various coalition governments in power from 1931 did not need him. A tired Baldwin no longer wanted to have anything to do with the formentor of unrest, and Chamberlain needed him even less. He gave speeches, and they still shone with brilliant rhetoric, but hardly anybody listened to them. For the man whose whole life was directed towards political effect, this period of waiting was like an endless wandering through the desert under a burning sun or tormented by sandstorms and near to dying of thirst.

One must add, however, that he made it easy for the ruling majorities and governments to leave him in exile. He was their tormenting demon, a constant bone of contention. He protested, scolding like a fishwife about the progress of events. He warned, he threatened, he accused the government almost as if it were committing high treason, because in his opinion it was not doing anything, or at least not enough, to avert the danger which threatened from Germany following Hitler's seizure of power in 1933.

Churchill, so it appeared, no longer had the nose which had once led him with such a sure instinct from the Conservatives to the Liberals and then back to the Conservatives again. That he was moving far, and ever further, from his contemporaries is illustrated by an event that took place in 1936.

King George V died and Edward VIII succeeded to the throne. He was popular, almost a king of the people, who interested himself in social questions, and great hopes were placed in him. All the greater was the subsequent shock in a Britain still encrusted with late Victorian moral concepts when he declared that he intended to marry Mrs Simpson, an American divorcée who had to divorce a second time in order to marry the King. As the Minister responsible for the Crown, Baldwin set the King an ultimatum: either he renounced this marriage or he renounced the throne in favour of his younger brother.

Churchill, however, entered the lists in favour of the King: one should not rush things, but wait and play for time. Months would pass in any case before Mrs Simpson's divorce became final. This was doubtlessly an almost old-fashioned, chivalrous gesture. But to what purpose? A change in British moral concepts? Or—as some newspapers daringly speculated—the formation of a monarchist party which would plunge the country into civil war, like that which occurred during the bloody revolution of the seventeenth century?

With the King there was something far more delicate involved than merely a passing fancy which, one could hope, would actually pass. His inclinations had so far—he was now aged 42—closed him off from any access to the opposite sex. Mrs Simpson, however, and only she, revealed to him the gateway to a life which equated to a far greater degree to late Victorian moral concepts than did loneliness in desperation. For him there was, therefore, no going back but only the renunciation of the throne.

One can say that Churchill acted from a generous heart and Baldwin with the cold steel of national interest. But the Prime Minister saved the monarchy. So when Churchill got up in Parliament to speak for the King, the House of Commons experienced a turmoil such as hardly occurred before or since—and it was the whole House, not only the Opposition: 'Shame, traitor! Stop!' Churchill himself wrote in retrospect:

> There were several moments when I seemed to be entirely alone against a wrathful House of Commons. I am not, when in action, unduly affected by hostile currents of feeling; but it was on more than one occasion almost physically impossible to make myself heard.[1]

And what for? No, no one wanted to have anything to do with this public nuisance any longer, this pig-headed old man whom one could best excuse by his obviously rapidly progressing senility. And when he died one day the newspapers would write in their obituaries that his political career had been a brilliant failure – like that of his father.[2]

And since it really did appear like that at the time, it is appropriate now to talk a little about the private man instead of the politician. At the close of the memoirs of his youth which appeared in 1930 Churchill reported on his marriage and claimed that he had 'always been happy since then'. For his contemporaries who only observed his personal life from afar, or knew about it from hearsay, this may have appeared to be so, and many probably envied him. He was and remained a man of success, if not politically then as an author, and sheltered within his family. With money from a small legacy and the royalties from his five-volume history of the First World War, he bought the country estate of Chartwell in Kent for himself and them, and seen from this perspective *The World Crisis* led directly to an idyll.

Restless as he was, however, he immediately began remodelling, which was to go on endlessly and often spoil the idyll for his wife. Rooms had to be redesigned or added, a heated swimming pool built, bushes and trees planted and walls erected. Above all walls: Churchill learned how to use trowel, mortar, and spirit level – and then insisted in all his newly acquired pride of craftsmanship in joining the bricklayers' union, much to their surprise and anger. They could well recall the Chancellor of the Exchequer who had taken the field against the strikers instead of practising solidarity. And what was one to think about the photograph which showed him at work together with daughter Sarah, a hat on his head, a cigar in his mouth, dressed in suit and vest with tie and collar? No master mason or helper is likely ever to have climbed up on scaffolding in such a get-up.

Chartwell offered a home to the growing children, at least during the holidays when they returned from their appropriately expensive boarding schools, and now their father had time for them. 'During this holiday,' he once told his son Randolph, 'we have spoken together more than my father did with me during all of his life.'[3]

Normal routine included getting up late – though after several hours of reading in bed – and a cosy bath. Where else do the sparks of ideas, softly crackling like the foam, rise more easily upward than in the relaxing warmth of the water? Then to the desk, to formulate sentences out of the ideas. There followed the noonday nap, undressed again in bed instead of half-heartedly on a couch. This made it possible to remain active until late in the evening or at night, and to work with concentration if necessary. Churchill's lifetime achievement could hardly be comprehended without its backdrop of deep and restful sleep.

As a comparison, Bismarck was a notoriously poor sleeper. He therefore constantly complained about exhaustion and from 1871 on spent almost half of his nineteen years as Chancellor not in his office but in the seclusion of Varazin or Friedrichsruh, but without finding recuperation. Of necessity, therefore, he had to leave much undone. But Bismarck and Churchill come together again in their preference for rich eating and good drinking. While the German Chancellor preferred to drink his champagne for breakfast, Churchill liked his with dinner, the social high-point of the day, which was dedicated to conversation and above all to his own flow of words.

Much has been made of Churchill's drinking habits, and much cheap outrage spread, particularly by his enemies. The teetotal and vegetarian Hitler and his Minister of Propaganda Dr Goebbels mocked the 'whisky guzzler on the Thames', who was hardly still sound of mind. No question, sometimes he had 'one too many' — but only rarely. His private secretary of many years, Jock Colville, testifies that the glass of the wartime Prime Minister contained much water and only little whisky.

Far more remarkable is the constant smoking of heavy cigars. If we follow the modern apostles of health, we can hardly comprehend how he managed to live for more than 90 years. In all this Churchill also remained remarkably healthy until his strokes in old age. Feverish colds were not uncommon, and as a schoolboy he barely survived a serious bout of pneumonia. In 1943, too, after the summit meeting at Teheran, an attack of pneumonia (which one can interpret psychosomatically) forced him to take an extended break. But there is little else to report.[4]

There is far more to be said about the accidents. The fall of the boy from a thirty-foot high bridge has already been mentioned. When the lieutenant of Hussars stepped on Indian soil, or rather just before he did that, he grasped a chain fixed to the wall of the quay. The landing boat dropped down into the trough of a wave. Churchill held fast and almost had his arm torn from his shoulder. From then on he remained susceptible.

Let me counsel my younger readers to beware of dislocated shoulders. In this, as in so many other things, it is the first step that counts. Quite an exceptional strain is required to tear the capsule which holds the shoulder joint together; but once the deed is done, a terrible liability remains.'[5]

Churchill was, and remained, handicapped. When playing polo he had to secure his shoulder with a leather belt, and in the Battle of Omdurman he fought with a pistol instead of with a sabre as required by regulations. This, so he stated superstitiously, is probably what saved his life.

In 1931, during a speaking tour of the United States, he suffered a severe traffic accident in New York:

On December 13, when on my way to visit Mr. Bernard Baruch, I got out of my car on the wrong side, and walked across Fifth Avenue without bearing in mind the opposite rule of the road which prevails in America, or the red lights, then unused in Britain. There was a shattering collision. For two months I was a wreck. I gradually regained at Nassau in the Bahamas enough strength to crawl around. In this condition I undertook a tour of forty lectures throughout the United States, living all day on my back in a railway compartment, and addressing in the evening large audiences. On the whole I consider this was the hardest time I have had in my life. I lay pretty low all through this year, but in time my strength returned.[6]

Among the friends who came to visit Churchill at Chartwell was Frederick Lindemann, half-Alsatian and half-American by birth, otherwise Professor of Experimental Philosophy at Oxford:

. . . the 'Prof', as he was called among his friends, became my chief adviser on the scientific aspects of modern war and particularly air defence, and also on questions involving statistics of all kinds. This pleasant and fertile association continued throughout the war.[7]

It must be added that the 'Prof' was, like Hitler (whom he hated all the more), a teetotaller and a vegetarian, and therefore hardly suitable for boozy stag evenings. On the other hand he was 'a snob of gigantic proportions'.[8] With his information about radar development and other questions of electronic detection, he rendered invaluable service to the wartime Prime Minister.[9] A second friend was Desmond Morton, a staff officer in the Army. 'To his Military Cross he added the unique distinction of having been shot through the heart, and living happily ever afterwards with the bullet in him.' It was an advantage that he was a neighbour: his house lay only a mile from Chartwell. He supplied Churchill with military information 'and continued during the war to be one of my most intimate advisers till our final victory was won.'[10] The third man in the trio was Ralph Wigram, 'then the rising star of the Foreign Office . . . He saw as clearly as I did, but with more certain information, the awful peril which was closing in upon us.'[11]

One suspects in this listing that the master of Chartwell did not really need such friends for socialising but had selected them according to their usefulness. And he was not ashamed to admit this in retrospect: it is he who mentions them and no one else. As a man without office, he depended more than ever on the information they brought him. Politics remained his very life-blood, and he had to be prepared at any price if circumstances were to call him back into the arena.

True recuperation, relaxation and distraction were served by a hobby Churchill now began to pursue seriously – painting. This hobby had begun in 1915 as a sort of survival therapy after the painful ejection from the Admiralty. So too now, and again after 1945: the further the distance from political office, the more pressing the need to counter threatening depression with brush and easel. This was also served by separation from the habitual: Churchill preferred to paint under southern lights – on the French Mediterranean, in North Africa or in Italy. Landscapes, including cityscapes, and still lifes were his preferred subjects, but sometimes he even risked portraits.

Of course the artist was no revolutionary, just as little as the politician was: shapes and colours show conventionally what he saw. If his paintings now sell for several hundreds of thousands of pounds each, that is not due to competition with Picasso but to the fame gained elsewhere. But Churchill did surpass mere dilettantism by a long way. A sure sense of composition, for light and shadow, and the brilliance of colours guided him. To name but one example: his seascape of the Adriatic of 1925, with a fishing boat in the foreground and Venice floating between heaven and sea in the background, is one we would like to own.

It was not, therefore, outlandish when the Royal Academy, which has united the more famous British painters since the days of J. M. Turner, made Winston Churchill an honorary member in 1948. Or, to express it in the rather colloquial way of Harry S. Truman (who as President of the United States had seen Churchill go and come back again) after he had wandered through the exhibit his successor in office General Eisenhower had initiated in Kansas City in 1958: 'Damn well done. You can at least tell what he painted, and that is more than you can say about many of these modern painters.'[12]

But besides the hobby there was always serious work. Sometimes weekly, but more generally once a fortnight, he wrote a commentary on political events, including looks back into history and warnings for the future. What he delivered here was first-class journalism. Every topic was presented descriptively and dramatically, brought down to the decisive point, with conclusions drawn without vacillation. These articles were not only read in Great Britain and the United States but reprinted by leading newspapers throughout Europe in a total of sixteen countries—for as long as that was still possible. This job brought the author a lot of money.

And that was bitterly necessary, because 'in actual fact I was living from hand to mouth.'[13] To Clementine Churchill's horror, Chartwell devoured almost as much money as the education of the children, and the grandson of a duke did not intend to accept any reduction in his standard of living. And so the debts grew, slowly but inexorably. By the mid-1930s it looked as if Chartwell would have to be sold—in the economic situation of the times probably well below its long-term value. The Great Depression was still having after-effects. The losses in income it had caused were still a long way from having been made up and emergency sales of property were a daily occurrence. That Churchill had continued with his speaking tour in the United States after his serious accident in 1931, even though he should have spared himself, had to do with the cast-iron necessity to make money.

A comment is called for here. As opposed to what we are used to today, and in particular in Germany, in former times His or Her Majesty's ministers were not sent home with generous pensions when they lost office, but had to look out for themselves. And that was quite deliberate. It was tacitly assumed that the men of power were already wealthy. Pension rights would have changed the career patterns. The statesman for whom it was an honour to do his best for King and Country would have been replaced by the professional politician[14]—a new figure which was alien to the traditional British ruling classes. To prevent that, exceptions to the rule were acknowledged: Lloyd George, for example, who rose from humble circumstances, had, as it were, to feather his nest with anticipatory corruption.

It has often been said of Churchill that he was actually a man of the past, of the nineteenth century, but if we compare him with men like Asquith or Baldwin he proves himself to be far more modern: in essence he was already a professional politician, and remained one even during his time out of office, if necessary in the form of a professional publisher. The strangeness which party leaders and Prime Ministers of the old school always felt in his presence also had something to do with this. In the end, Churchill even became rich, and created a model for the future: the world renown—or, in modern terms, the publicity—he gained during the Second World War guaranteed him continuing, huge world-wide editions of his books.[15] The Nobel Prize for Literature he received in 1953 added further increases in wealth.

But let us return to the bitter years. By the spring of 1938 Churchill's debts had grown higher than ever and he decided—or rather circumstances forced him—to put his beloved Chartwell on the market. In this time of greatest need a helper appeared, the London financial magnate Sir Henry Strakosh, and settled the debts. Sir Henry was a Jew, and, with other British Jews and those who had fled to Britain, he watched with horror the persecutions in Germany. To all of them Churchill, with his untiring warnings about Hitler's tyranny, appeared to be the only saviour from the rising storm flood, and therefore Chartwell—in a *quid pro quo*, so to speak—was being saved from the flood of debts.

It is appropriate to interject a story here, which had occurred earlier. In 1932 Churchill was working on his Marlborough biography and travelled through the Netherlands and Germany in the tracks of his ancestor. He stayed for several days in the Hotel Regina in Munich. There Ernst Hanfstaengl, nicknamed 'Putzi', a restless member of Munich society and admirer of Adolf Hitler, introduced himself. Churchill reports:

> As he seemed to be a lively and takative fellow, speaking excellent English, I asked him to dine. He gave a most interesting account of Hitler's activities and outlook. He spoke as one under the spell. . . . He was a great entertainer, and at that time, as is known, a favourite of the Fuehrer. He said I ought to meet him and that nothing would be easier to arrange.

Churchill emphasises that at this time he had no prejudices against Hitler—be it only out of ignorance:

> I knew little of his doctrine or record and nothing of his character. I admire men who stand up for their country in defeat, even though I am on the other side. He had a perfect right to be a patriotic German if he chose. . . . However, in the course of conversation with Hanfstaengl I happened to say, 'Why is your chief so violent about the Jews? I can quite understand being angry with Jews who have done wrong or are against the country, and I understand resisting them if they try to monopolise power in any walk of life; but what is the sense of being against a man simply because of his birth? How can any man help how he is born?'[16]

That was enough for a negative decision: the meeting between Churchill and the man who stood on the threshold of power in Germany was cancelled. Later Hitler apparently regretted this cancellation and sent two more invitations, but in vain. Churchill felt that the imbalance between the now all-powerful leader of the state and the private individual would preclude any sensible political talk. Lloyd George, who visited Hitler anyway, only made a fool of himself.[17] And so the player for all or nothing and his counter-player never met in person.

During the quiet years at Chartwell between 1929 and 1939 the writing of books stood next to journalism as the primary occupation. It created distraction and a reflection of happiness:

> It was great fun writing a book. One lived with it. It became a companion. It built an impalpable crystal sphere around one of interests and ideas. In a sense one felt like a goldfish in a bowl; but in this case the goldfish made his own bowl.[18]

Of course this also tells us that the author is a lonely man whom an invisible wall separates from his surroundings.

In 1930 the memoirs of his youth appeared. They deal with the adventure of youth, the terrors and enthusiasms of childhood and youth and the discovery of the world, which is as unknown and ready for use for every new generation as if it had just been specially created for it. Young people, above all, should read this book. Of course it talks about circumstances long gone—lightly, yet still with depth, excitingly and with appropriate self-irony. But it resembles a mirror in which we recognise ourselves, and gain courage for the challenges of our own lives and our own times. As for Churchill, what once was always goes under, and, for him, there is always a future worth fighting for.

For the author in Chartwell there followed the encounter with the man who was born in 1650 as John Churchill and who died in 1722 as the Duke of Marlborough. That his biography burst all originally planned bounds and grew to a colossal canvas—a sort of literary Sistine Chapel built and painted by Churchill personally—is understandable. This ancestor, one would like to believe, created the story specifically for his descendant—'a character like out of a Shakespearian drama of kings. Courtier and genius, diplomat and traitor, warlord and statesman.'[19] And, on top of that, one who amassed—almost incidentally, but nevertheless consistently—the gigantic fortune whose shine still fills us with awe today in Blenheim Palace, Churchill's birthplace.

Marlborough was the central figure of the great European War of the Coalition which was waged against the France of Louis XIV under the leadership of Great Britain and Austria, in order to prevent his looming hegemony and the overpowering of his neighbours such as the Netherlands. For Winston Churchill this fact alone turned the story of his ancestor into a schoolbook for the present, except that in the meantime Germany had taken the place of France. The long series of court intrigues, diplomatic manoeuvres, campaigns and battles are also—or almost so—a family affair. Marlborough's brother George was Commander-in-Chief of the Royal Navy, and the other brother, Charles, one of his most important generals. A commander on the other side, James Fitzjames, Duke of Berwick and Marshal of France, was also a Churchill, the natural son of Marlborough's sister Arabella, whom her farsighted brother had directed into the bed of James II, the last of the Stuarts. When, however, this king was pushed off the throne in the 'Glorious Revolution' of 1688 and replaced by William III of Orange, it was again Marlborough who had a very decisive finger in the pie.

A truly fascinating story unfolds before our eyes! And because here an author and his subject were ideally matched, Marlborough is probably Churchill's most important literary achievement. One should read it too, perhaps in more mature youth.

The English original began in 1933 with the first volume and was completed with the fourth in 1938. In the meantime Churchill was already engaged with another work of four volumes, his *History of the English-Speaking Peoples*. It was finished in 1939 for all practical purposes, but publication was postponed by the war and it only appeared, after revision, between 1956 and 1958. Non-Englishmen (and non-historians) in particular may profitably read this work—and with enjoyment too. Churchill pays little attention to the equivocations of the experts; poetry is more important to him. Characteristically he writes at one point, talking about an old legend: 'Grouchy old researchers have destroyed this splendid legend, but it should still have its place in any history book worthy of the name.'[20]

Of course, allusions to the present—the 1930s—are not lacking. For example:

> In bitter and tragic times free men can find comfort in the great lesson of history that tyrants only prevail among submissive peoples. The years one must suffer through may appear to be endless, but in the course of the world they are only seconds of misfortune.[21]

Another example speaks even more clearly:

In a note to the French Ambassador on December 31 [1792] Lord Grenville, the Foreign Secretary, stated the position of His Majesty's Government in words which have ever since been accepted as a classic exposition of English foreign policy: 'England will never consent that France shall arrogate the power of annulling at her pleasure, and under the pretence of a pretended natural right, of which she makes herself the only judge, the political system, established by solemn treaties, and guaranteed by the consent of all the Powers. This Government, adhering to the maxims which it has followed for more than a century, will also never see with indifference that France shall make herself, either directly or indirectly, sovereign of the Low Countries, or general arbiter of the rights and liberties of Europe. If France is really desirous of maintaining friendship and peace with England she must show herself disposed to renounce her views of aggression and aggrandisement, and to confine herself within her own territory, without insulting other Governments, without disturbing their tranquillity, without violating their rights.'[22]

One need only substitute 'Germany' for 'France' in order to see the reality of this for the 1930s. In general, however, the *History of the English-Speaking Peoples* is markedly weaker than *Marlborough* and some other works. Churchill was not a historian, but at the core of his writing of books there always remained a biographer, one who was able to tell exciting tales about people's lives with the highest linguistic artistry—especially evident in his own (self-) portrayals of the First and Second World Wars.

In an attempt at a summary we can say that the years between 1929 and 1939 were fruitful in the sense that they provided much time for reflection, perhaps as a condition for subsequent actions. It is hardly a coincidence that so many old stories tell us of people who went into the desert to gain enlightenment.[23]

But we should not deceive ourselves. For Churchill this was a highly involuntary wandering, and his writing was not only, but certainly also, a means of distraction, not to say anaesthesia. It testifies to the loneliness of the man who saw himself banished into the political desert. Directly underneath the idyll of Chartwell lies despair. There are even reports that Churchill was frequently tormented by nightmares and slept more poorly than during the war years with all their stresses and catastrophes. To watch while the storm of disasters begins to rise, and not to be able to do anything to prevent it—what could be worse than this?

Neville Chamberlain, Adolf Hitler and Winston Churchill

The Chamberlains were a remarkable family – almost akin to a political dynasty. At the beginning there was Joseph Chamberlain (1836–1914). As a successful manufacturer in Birmingham, he acquired solid wealth and was elected Mayor. In 1876 he entered the House of Commons as a Liberal MP. As Minister for Trade from 1880 on he fought for a programme of social reform, just as did one of his successors in office, Winston Churchill, from 1908 onwards. But he was also an Imperialist and rebelled against Gladstone's attempt to pacify Ireland by the Home Rule Bill. Because of this he split the Liberal Party, and led the Unionists who wanted to keep Ireland within Britain proper into the camp of the Conservatives. As Colonial Secretary from 1895 he set out to strengthen the Empire. Kitchener's conquest of the Sudan and the exclusion of France from the Upper Nile, the Boer War and the subjugation of the Boer republics would have been inconceivable without him. It was his dream to ally Great Britain with the two rising powers, Germany and the United States, because this community of three would rule the world – to the latter's benefit, of course.[1]

A fascinating concept, certainly – and we may speculate what course the history of the twentieth century would have taken had it been realised. But reality was quite different. Chamberlain's efforts for an alliance with Germany failed. In the United States the principle developed by George Washington, Thomas Jefferson and James Monroe prevailed, namely that Europe and America should mutually refrain from any interference with each other. Even in Britain things were not all that different, and she only took leave of the 'splendid isolation' which had served her so well in the nineteenth century with great hesitation.

Joseph Chamberlain's last great battle was for the introduction of protective tariffs which were to unite the Empire and seal it off from outside. He lost this battle too. In the 1906 elections the Liberals, who were defending free trade, won one of the greatest victories recorded in British parliamentary history. Shortly thereafter a stroke put an end to the career of this bellicose man who left nobody indifferent.[2]

Austen Chamberlain (1863–1937) was Joseph's eldest son. He served in many offices — as Chancellor of the Exchequer, as Secretary for India, as a member of the War Cabinet under Lloyd George, as Lord Privy Seal and as Leader of the House of Commons. In the end, from 1924 to 1929, he was Foreign Secretary. In 1926, together with Gustav Stresemann and Aristide Briand, he was awarded the Nobel Peace Prize for concluding the Locarno Pact which was to secure lasting peace in Europe.

Neville Chamberlain, Austin's step-brother, was born in 1869. Initially there was little of political passion to be detected in him. As a young man of 21 he took over a plantation in the Bahamas and managed it until 1897. As a manufacturer he then took over his father's legacy. In 1915 he also followed his father into the office of Mayor of Birmingham, and from 1916 to 1917 he ran the conscription office. It was only in 1918 that the now almost fifty-year-old began his career as a Conservative MP. In 1922 he became Postmaster General, in 1923 Minister for Health, then Chancellor of the Exchequer, and from 1924 to 1929 Minister for Welfare. For five years, therefore, the two half-brothers and Churchill were colleagues in the Conservative Cabinet of Stanley Baldwin.

In 1931 Neville Chamberlain again took over the Ministry for Welfare, then, until 1937, the Exchequer. Even though he was not a brilliant speaker, he nevertheless rose inexorably to become the leader of the Conservative Party. When Baldwin vacated the chair of Prime Minister on 28 May 1937, it was by then natural that Chamberlain would be his successor.[3]

The contrast could hardly have been greater. Baldwin was more a corpulent, Chamberlain a bony, gaunt man. His image as the impeccable gentleman with the bushy eyebrows, the moustache, the old-fashioned stand-up collar and the umbrella has become fixed in memory. Baldwin loved comfort, Chamberlain his work. Where Baldwin manoeuvered and postponed his decisions, his successor resolutely grasped the nettle. He understood little of foreign policy. Instead he was the most successful social, economics and finance minister of his times. He would have loved nothing more than to have continued his career as he had begun it, and crowned it with some achievement in domestic policy. But the problem of his time in office was called Adolf Hitler.

This comet from the void, formerly sniggered at and underestimated by friend and foe alike, had been washed up by the world economic crisis in less than three years, from being the preacher of a sect to becoming the leader of by far the strongest party. On 30 January 1933 the democratically elected *Reich* President Paul von Hindenburg appointed him German Chancellor. Over the next eighteen months he removed all the barriers which stood in the way of his unlimited power. The conservatives around Franz von Papen and Alfred Hugenberg, who had intended to tame him, saw themselves pushed to the sidelines. The Enabling Law of 24 March 1933 opened the sluices for the destruction of all political opponents; they were dragged off into concentration camps which were outside the confines of law, or had to flee abroad. The persecution of the Jews began. The parties, except for the NSDAP, were dissolved, and the unions were disbanded and replaced by the *Deutsche Arbeitsfront* (German Labour Front). The unruly storm troop of the movement, the SA, which its Chief of Staff Ernst Röhm wanted to turn into a people's army, was decapitated and sentenced to insignificance in a single night of murder led by the Chancellor in person. In gratitude the *Reichswehr*, which was then renamed *Wehrmacht*, voluntarily swore unconditional obedience to the *Führer*, Adolf Hitler, personally after the death of the *Reich* President on 2 August 1934.[4]

The Third Reich appeared hardly any less menacing to the outside world as well. Germany had already left the League of Nations in 1933. Initially still in secret and cautiously, then openly and ever more massively, she rearmed for war. On 16 March 1935 she officially renounced the arms limitations terms of the Treaty of Versailles and returned to conscription.

The Western Powers stood for all this, and Great Britain went even further. On 18 June 1935 she signed a naval agreement—to vain protests by France—which limited German armament at sea to 35 per cent of British naval strength. With this, diplomatic recognition had been given to the fact that the Treaty of Versailles was no longer valid. The agreement cost Germany nothing, and it would take her years before she reached the agreed upper limit.

Hitler felt encouraged and ventured his next step. On 7 March 1936 German troops marched into the demilitarised Rhineland. At the same time the Locarno Pact, which was supposed to preserve the peace, was renounced. This was probably the last point in time at which the German potentate could have been stopped without having to spill blood. The *Wehrmacht* was still weak and far inferior to the French Army. In actual fact, the troops marching into the Rhineland had orders to withdraw if France replied by a counter-march. Hitler played for very high stakes and won. France, deeply split domestically, left it at a protest on paper. Basically she had long bowed down before the resurgence of German power. How else can we explain that in 1929, when Germany disposed an army of only 100,000, no air force or armoured forces, and the 'spirit of Locarno' was in full bloom, she began the elaborate construction of the Maginot Line for the defence of her eastern frontier?

Nor were developments elsewhere in Europe any reason for hope. In Italy the *Duce*, Benito Mussolini, had established his rule and conquered Abyssinia. The half-hearted attempt to prevent him made him seek the support of Hitler, and the 'Axis' between Berlin and Rome came into being. In Spain a bloody civil war was raging, in which Germany and Italy were supporting the military revolt by General Franco against the Republican government. In the Soviet Union Stalinist terror reigned, and in the summer of 1937 it reached over into the Army, whose leadership was almost totally destroyed. Apart from all other reservations, this meant that one could hardly hope for a powerful ally here. Even in the Far East dark storm clouds were rising. The attempt to reach a naval agreement with Japan failed in 1936, and on 7 July 1937 Imperial troops began their war against China without any formal declaration, after they had already occupied Manchuria some years earlier.

What could Chamberlain do? He was determined to avoid war at almost any price and to preserve the peace, and there were many good reasons for this. First, he was an expert on finance and the economy. He knew British weaknesses far better than Churchill did. The First World War had, to put it mildly, initiated Great Britain's decline from her former position of predominance. The moment for a short and victorious war had been missed, and an extended war was hardly possible without driving the country to the brink of ruin. A dictatorship might be able to afford such a massive rearmament programme as Germany was engaged in, but a democracy never could.[5]

This did not in any way exclude moderate rearmament. In fact, this had already been initiated in 1934. The Navy, and particularly the Royal Air

Force, were being strengthened step by step. But this rearmament had to be kept within bounds and not permitted to get out of hand, so as not to ruin Great Britain in times of peace. Delayed rearmament also had its advantages. For example, fighter aircraft produced in the first half of the 1930s, which Churchill demanded almost hysterically, still looked much like those at the end of the First World War. A machine fit for the future like the Hurricane only took off for its maiden flight on 6 November 1936, and the Spitfire, which decided the Battle of Britain in 1940, came even later, but was therefore more manoeuvrable and better armed than the German Me 109.

Secondly, memories of the Great War still burdened the people and the nations. They now knew war, and they asked: why had it been waged at all? Had not all the effort and sacrifices been senseless anyway? What gains had victory actually brought?

We have already recounted that in 1933, much to Churchill's outrage, students at Oxford debated the motion 'This House will not fight for King and Country under any circumstances' and adopted it by a large majority. And this was no students' joke but the prevailing mood throughout the country, at all levels of society: never again war! Two years later the League of Nations conducted a poll, with a result such as had never been recorded before: 10½ million people came out not in favour of rearmament but of further reductions in arms. In worst cases aggression should be countered by economic sanctions—and only with the approval of the League of Nations at that. The message was unmistakable: whoever defended the peace could expect approval and a following.

In France the fundamentally pacifist mood was even stronger than in Great Britain—and things were not much different even in Germany, despite all the 'fit-for-fighting programmes' and the training of young people for the lives and deaths of heroes. When the Sudeten Crisis escalated in September 1938 Hitler and his Minister of Propaganda Goebbels had troops parade through Berlin—and were horrified at the result: nowhere did people gather on the pavements as spectators, nowhere were there any signs of enthusiasm. All the faces mirrored consternation, even despair, and panic-buying began because the march of the soldiers was read as a sign of impending war. Even generals proved themselves to be defeatists: in August of 1938 Colonel-General Beck, Chief of the General Staff, resigned because he felt it would be irresponsible to begin a war which he believed could not be won.[6]

Thirdly, hesitantly at first but then more emphatically, a change of opinion occurred in Britain: it was finally recognised that the peace diktat of Versailles had been a fateful mistake. The economic and financial demands it contained were ruining the vanquished without benefiting the victors. Initially this may have been apparent only to an expert like John Maynard Keynes, but since the world economic crisis it had been visible to everyone. In his reflections on the First World War Churchill vividly described the dream of the flow of reparations which turned into a nightmare:

> For instance, the Germans could and would readily have set to work to rebuild all the ships their submarines had sunk—but what was to happen to British shipbuilding if they did? They could no doubt make every form of manufactured article; but surely we had not fought the war in order to have all our native industries ruined by state-fostered dumping on a gigantic scale![7]

A possibly even worse effect was caused by the calumny against the Germans which assigned all the blame for the war to them, and thereby justified the burdens which had been placed upon them. Were not Hitler and his successes the fruits of such calumny? People may lose all their worldly goods and accept this, but they turn into killers when their self-esteem is destroyed. This can already be learned from the sinister tale of the original aggression:

> And the Lord had respect unto Abel and his offering. But unto Cain and to his offering he had not respect. And Cain was very wroth, and his countenance fell. . . . and it came to pass, when they were in the field, that Cain rose up against Abel his brother, and slew him.

Churchill tells a story about the shift of opinion in Britain:

> I was asked to address the University Conservative Association in the Oxford Union. I declined to do so, but said I would give them an hour to ask me questions. One of the questions was, 'Do you think Germany was guilty of making the last war?' I said, 'Yes, of course.' A young German Rhodes scholar rose from his place and said, 'After this insult to my country I will not remain here.' He then stalked out amid roars of applause.

Churchill adds: 'I thought him a spirited boy. Two years later it was found out in Germany that he had a Jewish ancestor. This ended his career in Germany.'[8]

From the distance we have happily gained, we can easily recognise the foolishness and untenability of a peace diktat which, instead of bringing about reconciliation, was generated by the fears and hatreds of a long and costly war.[9] On the German side we must guard ourselves all the more against self-righteousness: had Germany won, the future of Europe would have become even more sinister. It is only with a shudder that we read how professors in Berlin and other university cities imagined the fruits of their victory.[10]

We may also regret that the about-turn in public opinion only came to pass after history had already labelled it with her inexorable 'Too late!' But it is still important to explore the details. When doing so, we should keep in mind what Churchill has described so impressively, namely that a completely different attitude is required for waging war than for making peace. Human beings require much time and willpower to move from hatred to reconciliation – if they can succeed in doing this at all.[11] We must both fight or search for peace with our whole soul, but we have only one soul.

The statesmen of 1919 are still being compared to those who assembled for the Congress of Vienna in 1815, and thereby condemned. Yet things were incomparably more difficult for them than for their predecessors. They were living under the conditions of democracy, which include the inertia and tidal swings of public opinion. The statesmen of 1815 did not have to listen to the voices of their people when, after a quarter of a century of bloody warfare, they welcomed back vanquished France. And Bismarck, when he imposed a conciliatory peace with Austria after the Prussian victory at Königgrätz in 1866, only had to fight against the intoxication of victory that permeated his King and the generals – and this was difficult enough.

Seen with the required sobriety, the problem of today is even doubly difficult: once the shift from hatred to reconciliation has been achieved, it becomes almost impossible to recognise new dangers and to arm oneself against them. Should one return to the hostility one has just escaped? No, nobody wants to decipher the words of fire on the curtain to the future, and the prophet who reads them out loud enough is despised and cast out.

And this was exactly the situation in Britain during the 1930s – and the situation in which Winston Churchill found himself. He describes to us what was happening to him using the example of a debate in the Commons in 1935 on the subject of air armament:

> Although the House listened to me with close attention, I felt a sensation of despair. To be entirely convinced and vindicated in a matter of life and death to one's country, and not to be able to make Parliament and the nation heed the warning, or bow to the proof by taking action, was an experience most painful.[12]

After a long detour we return to Prime Minister Neville Chamberlain, in the hope of now being better able to understand his thoughts and actions. Hitler might put him off; he was certainly not a gentleman, and to British ears it sounded rather bizarre when he kept emphasising that he was pursuing his objectives 'fanatically'. And one certainly did not have to approve of his methods. But he was, after all the *Führer* of Germany, who apparently enjoyed increasing support among the population. His achievements in domestic policy could not be overlooked. Unemployment, which had stood at 29.9 per cent in 1932, the year of crisis, went down to 4.1 per cent by 1937. In 1938 it dropped again to 1.7 per cent. By way of comparison, in Great Britain unemployment lay at 'only' 22.1 per cent in 1932, but in 1938 it was still 12.9 per cent. In the United States things were even worse: unemployment declined slowly from a peak of 35.3 per cent in 1933, only to jump up again in 1938 to 26.4 per cent. In the meantime, in 1936, a proud Third Reich welcomed the youth of the world to the brilliantly organised Olympic Games in Berlin.

Hitler, so it appeared, wanted to restore Germany's dignity and welfare, and to secure it by the military power the *Reich* in the centre of Europe needed. And he kept repeating that he, as a soldier who had been in the front lines for four years, knew the horrors or war far better than any diplomat or civilian politician, and that he therefore wanted peace, only provided one permitted him to achieve his objectives. Should he not be taken at his word?

Incidentally, he always spoke about Great Britain and her Empire with respect, as of a potential ally. On the other hand, he always behaved — 'fanatically' again — like an anti-Bolshevist, and the *Lebensraum* about which he had written in his book *Mein Kampf*, and which had to be conquered, lay in the East. If that were to come true, and the great tyrannical regimes in Europe were to be at odds, or even go to war against each other — then all the better.

And there was one more factor, possibly the deciding one: when Germany requested an armistice in the autumn of 1918, she appealed to the 'Fourteen Points' put by American President Woodrow Wilson, in which the right of self-determination of the peoples played a major rôle. The victors of 1919 had sworn themselves to this right, but refused it to the vanquished. German Austria was not permitted to join the *Reich*, and millions of Germans lived under foreign rule, especially in Czechoslovakia and Poland. How could one object when Hitler claimed this right of self-determination? Was this a reason to declare war on him?

On the morning of 12 March 1938 German troops marched into Austria. Hitler followed in the afternoon, welcomed by the ringing of bells, inundated with flowers, surged around by jubilation. Via the town of his birth, Braunau on the River Inn, he drove to Linz, where in the evening he signed the 'Law on the reunification of Austria with the German Reich'. Next day he made his entry into Vienna, and during the mass rally on the Heldenplatz the enthusiasm rose to a storm when he stood to attention before his so often evoked 'destiny', or world history (which amounted to the same thing), to declare: 'As *Führer* and Chancellor of the German nation and *Reich* I now report to history the entry of my homeland into the German *Reich*.'[13] 'German' *Reich* was now redesignated 'Greater German' *Reich* and the completion of the 'reunification' was confirmed by a plebiscite in which the 'Yes' votes came to 99 per cent and in places even higher. And it was hardly necessary to intervene or manipulate. The enthusiasm for the 'man of destiny' had reached its apogee.

What did it matter when, immediately after the occupation of Austria, an uninhibited persecution of the opponents of the regime and of the Jews began?[14] Europe may have held its breath, but it remained silent. From Mussolini – who during the National Socialist *putsch* attempt in 1934, to which Federal Chancellor Dollfuss fell victim, had moved Italian troops to the border – his Axis partner learned on the telephone via the German envoy, the Prince of Hessia: 'The *Duce* has received the whole affair in a very friendly manner. He sends you his heartiest regards.' To which Hitler replied: 'Then please tell Mussolini that I shall never forget this . . . Never, never, never, come what may.'[15] What was to be heard from Paris and London, however, Italian Foreign Minister Count Ciano described with malicious accuracy as 'outraged acquiescence'.[16]

The annexation of Austria also helped the over-stretched armaments industry because in the *Ostmark*, as it was now called, there were still plants working under capacity and a reserve army of unemployed. Furthermore, the gold and foreign currency reserves of the Reichsbank, which had sunk to 76 million, could be replenished with 1.4 billion Reichsmarks. But, above all, a new strategic situation had come about, which Hitler's military adviser Jodl, later Colonel-General, described:

> Whereas formerly Czechoslovakian territory had jutted into Germany as a threat, Czechoslovakia in her turn now had the screws put on her. Her own strategic situation had now become so unfavourable that she would have to suc-

cumb to a determined attack long before effective help could be expected from the West.[17]

Incidentally, Czechoslovakia had protected her frontiers with the 'Old Reich' in the north and west by building strong border fortifications, but to the south, against Austria, she was almost completely unprotected.

Hitler wasted no time. Only two weeks after the annexation of Austria he received the leader of the Sudeten German Party, Konrad Henlein, and compelled him to make demands of the government in Prague that could not be fulfilled. A problem actually did exist: within the border areas of Czechoslovakia there lived three and a half million Germans who felt themselves encouraged by the unexpected events and were now demonstrating under the slogan 'Home to the Reich!' In the ensuing weeks and months the mood continued to heat up, incidents were staged and thousands fled over the border to Germany.

Henlein also went to England. In Chamberlain and his Foreign Secretary Lord Halifax he found a certain degree of sympathy. They spoke, so it was said, about Czechoslovakia as 'a combination of bits and pieces, thrown together by the Treaty of Versailles, for whose protection no one wanted to die'.[18] In the meantime Hitler was discussing 'Case Green', the plan for a military campaign of destruction, with the Commander-in-Chief of the *Wehrmacht*, General Keitel. Then, on 20 May, the government in Prague announced the mobilisation of its armed forces. The surprised Western Powers approved of this measure and pointed to their treaty obligations, as did the Soviet Union.

The confused to-ing and fro-ing which followed can safely be skipped here. Hitler, who initially flinched, still showed himself to be determined. In a directive concerning 'Case Green' on 30 May he said: 'It is my unalterable decision to destroy Czechoslovakia within a foreseeable time by means of military action.'[19] And, in contrast to all his public declarations for peace, he said to his adjutant Wiedemann a short time later: 'Every generation has to have taken part in a war . . . War is the best means of education for the youth of Germany.'[20] When the crisis dramatically came to a head in September, he gave a speech in the Sports Palace in Berlin in which he threatened Czech President Benesch:

He now holds the decision in his hands! War or peace! He will . . . now finally grant the Germans their freedom, or we will go and get this freedom ourselves.

With an eye on Britain, on the other hand, the speech also contained some enticements and promises:

> And we now face the final problem which has to be solved and will be solved! It is the last territorial demand I have to make in Europe, but it is the demand which I will not give up, and which I, God willing, will fulfil.[21]

At the close of the speech there was thundering applause and chants of '*Führer* command; we follow!'

The course of the September crisis has been recorded in the history books. Neville Chamberlain did everything in his power to preserve the peace and went all the way to the limits of self-denial. On 15 September he travelled to Germany and was received by Hitler on the Obersalzberg. The meeting did not lead to any result. Chamberlain therefore literally forced a second meeting upon an unwilling Hitler. It took place in Bad Godesberg. But Hitler remained obdurate and rejected all the suggested solutions: 'I am sorry, Mr. Chamberlain, that I can now no longer entertain such matters. After the events of the past few days' — the Czech government had again ordered mobilisation — 'this solution will no longer work.'[22] In the end, all that was left to the Prime Minister was to resign himself: 'I must say with great disappointment and deep regret, *Herr Reichskanzler*, that you have not given me even the smallest support in my efforts to preserve the peace.'[23]

Through the mediation of Mussolini, the conference in Munich finally came about on 29 September 1938, in which the Italian dictator, Hitler, Chamberlain and the French Minister President Edouard Daladier took part. An agreement was reached late at night: Czechoslovakia had to cede all territories with German majorities unconditionally, and in exchange her new, decidedly more restricted frontiers were guaranteed. The government in Prague was not even consulted; it had to submit to the inevitable. From now on it was defenceless, because all of its so carefully built up border fortifications had been lost. Nor, of course, were the men of the German resistance asked; they had hoped for a military *putsch* in case of war. As one of the leaders of the resistance, Carl Goerdeler, said bitterly: 'Chamberlain has saved Hitler.'[24]

The British Prime Minister was fêted as the saviour of peace, much to Hitler's rage, by the people in Munich as his car drove by. And grateful acclaim rose about him on his return to London when he waved a piece of paper and in four words which became famous proclaimed 'Peace for our time'. The saviour was also applauded in the House of Commons. Only a very few did not join in, among them Alfred Duff Cooper, who demonstratively resigned as First Lord of the Admiralty.[25]

Churchill gave a great and gloomy speech in which he said:

All is over. Silent, mournful, abandoned, broken, Czechoslovakia recedes into the darkness. She has suffered in every respect by her associations with France, under whose guidance and policy she has been actuated for so long . . . I say that the Czechoslovakian nation can no longer remain independent. I believe that within a span of time which may last a few years or only months, it will fall under Nazi rule.

Churchill ended his speech with the words:

I do not grudge our loyal, brave people, who were ready to do their duty no matter what the cost, who never flinched under the strain of last week, the natural, spontaneous outburst of joy and relief when they learned that the hard ordeal would no longer be required of them at the moment; but they should know the truth. They should know that there has been gross neglect and deficiency in our defences; they should know that we have sustained a defeat without a war, the consequences of which will travel far with us along our road; they should know that we have passed an awful milestone in our history, when the whole equilibrium of Europe has been deranged, and that the terrible words have for the time being been pronounced against the Western democracies: 'Thou art weighed in the balance and found wanting.' And do not suppose that this is the end. This is only the beginning of the reckoning. This is only the first sip, the first foretaste of a bitter cup which will be proffered to us year by year unless, by a supreme recovery of moral health and martial vigour, we arise again and take our stand for freedom as in the olden time.[27]

The rest of the story is quickly told. Hitler was not at all grateful to Chamberlain for his having saved the peace. On the contrary, it appeared to him as if the British Prime Minister and the French President had stolen his war from him, which he had wanted and could have won. As late as February 1945, in the bunker under the crumbling *Reich* Chancellery in Berlin, he harked back in anger:

The war should have been waged in 1938. That was the last opportunity to localise the war. But they accepted everything. Like weaklings they gave in to all of my demands. Under such circumstances it really was difficult to suddenly start a war. In Munich we missed a unique opportunity to win the inevitable war easily and quickly.[28]

On 9 November 1938 a barbaric program against the Jews took place. All over the *Reich* the Houses of God, the synagogues, went up in flames, as a fiery token of the insanity which sought to expunge an imagined crime by committing a real one. The date had been selected for its symbolic value. On 9 November 1918 an era came to an end. The *Kaiser's* Empire fell with the proclamation of the Republic. This was soon to become the 'November crime'. Hitler had always, and very personally, referred to this fateful date and emphasised that it had selected him to become the future *Führer*. He had already deliberately scheduled his Munich Beer Hall *Putsch* for 9 November. Later, after his seizure of power, the annual march on the *Feldherrnhalle* was celebrated in sombre pomp as a secular hallmark of death and resurrection. And did he not keep repeating 'fanatically' that a 9 November 1918 would 'never be repeated again in German history'?

That day in 1938 proved that success was not making the regime become more reasonable, but radicalising it further. Only one day later, on 10 November, Hitler gave a secret speech to representatives of the Press in which he put this radicalisation into words:

> For decades circumstances have forced me to speak about almost nothing except peace. Only under the constant emphasis of the German will for peace and intent for peace was it possible for me to gain its liberty for the German nation step by step, and to give it the armaments which were always required for the next step. It is self-evident that such a peace propaganda over decades also has its questionable side, because it can easily lead to the idea becoming fixed in the minds of many people that the present régime is identical with the decision and the will to keep the peace under any circumstance.

A change would have to come about here. It was important

> . . . that the German people be psychologically readjusted and to gradually make it clear to them that there are things which, if they cannot be put through by peaceful means, must be put through by means of violence.[29]

Churchill's prophecy came true all too soon. On 12 March 1939 Hitler decided to destroy Czechoslovakia. On 13 March Slovakian leaders reported to Berlin. With German support they declared the independence of their country on 14 March. On 15 March Czech President Hacha was forced by blatant threats to sign a treaty on the establishment of the '*Reich* Protectorate of Bohemia and Moravia'. On the same day German troops marched into Prague. From then on the German '*Reich* Protector' gave the orders in the country.

With this a line of demarcation had been crossed. Until then Hitler had based his claims on the right of self-determination of the people. Now he was trampling this right under foot. In Britain a drastic swing of opinion set in. In a speech in his home city of Birmingham Chamberlain announced the end of appeasement. On 31 March there followed an Anglo-French guarantee for Poland, and on 26 May Great Britain introduced conscription for the first time during peace. But Hitler could no longer be stopped. He got his war. With the conclusion of the German-Soviet treaty of non-aggression on 23 August, whose secret clauses gave up large parts of eastern Europe to the Soviet Union, he gained an accomplice. And so, on the morning of 1 September 1939, the German armies marched into Poland. Two days later Great Britain and France declared war on Germany.

What is left on the balance sheet? What with regard to Neville Chamberlain? When he—now terminally ill—resigned his office in October 1940, Churchill spoke of the 'respect and admiration for the courage and sense of honour which had determined all of his actions'.[30] Those born later should not demur from this verdict. The man with the umbrella is not a ridiculous but a tragic figure. Unwaveringly, with all his heart, he fought for the preservation of peace. That the war he had prevented in 1938 came about after all was truly not his fault.

The fault lay basically in only one person—his counter-player Hitler. The story of Hitler's rise to the pinnacle of power is the story of his underestimation and misinterpretation—and this is based on his cheating. The Germans trusted him, and the world saw him as a patriot and statesman who wanted to do the best for his country, albeit with ill grace and by rough methods. Had he been this, at least comparable to a Bismarck or a Gustav Stresemann, a Heinrich Brüning or a Konrad Adenauer, the peace policy would have stood a chance and today we would be honouring Chamberlain as a model.

But Chamberlain erred, he let himself be deceived, as were all his age with him. Hitler was not a patriot. The Germans, with all their diligence, abilities and willingness to obey, only served him as a means to an end, to gain power, absolute, unrestricted power, power over life and death. This adoration of power found its vocal expression in his delusions about the master race of heroes, which no longer had anything national about it anyway, only the singular objective to destroy the 'sub-humans' and subjugate the inferiors. And in case the nation was to fail in the task of obtaining this absolute power for its ordained leader, it was condemned. 'I will not shed a single tear of regret for the German nation,' Hitler declared in November 1941.[31] His conclusion in the final phase in 1945 was:

If the war should be lost, the nation will also be lost. There is no need to make any allowances for the foundations which the German people need for their basic survival. On the contrary, it would be better to destroy these things ourselves. The nation has shown itself to be the weaker, and the future belongs exclusively to the stronger eastern nation. What will be left after the battle will only be the inferior ones anyway, because the good ones will have fallen.[32]

And the statesman? Sebastian Haffner said of him:

He did not want to be the first servant of the state, but the *Führer*, an absolute ruler, and he recognised quite rightly that absolute rule is not possible in a healthy state, but only in a controlled chaos . . . The German *Reich* had to stop being a state in order to become a complete instrument of conquest. In this sense there can be no greater contrast than that between Hitler and Bismarck, who became a politician of peace once he had achieved the achievable.[33]

Chamberlain was a politician of peace from the beginning, and not made for war. When he then had to wage it, life appeared to him to be nothing except 'one long nightmare'.[34] Or, as he said with self-critical insight: 'I hate and deplore this war. I am not made to be a Minister of War.'[35] It was almost symbolic that he was replaced as Prime Minister on 10 May 1940, the day the war between Germany and the Western Powers began in earnest, and his illness and his death on 9 November 1940 may possibly also be interpreted in this light. In any case, it is only too readily understandable that Hitler remained an enigma for him.

In the end we are left with questions of comparison. What was the difference between Churchill and Chamberlain? Why was the former able to look more clearly and more deeply than the Prime Minister? How did he see through Hitler? What made him continue without compromise on his long way through the desert, when public opinion declared him to be an incorrigible complainer, know-all and prophet of doom? His contrariness almost reminds us of the whipped boy withdrawn within himself that he had once been. What pointed beyond this into the future? Any attempt at an answer must be given at many levels.

One could begin by speaking about opportunism, which is human—all too human. If one has to become an outsider, one would at least like to enjoy the advantages to the full which this uncomfortable position still offers. One recognises the superficiality, sometimes absurdity, of existing trends almost automatically, and enjoys the rôle of the merciless critic who is hoping for a shift in the tide and insists on having been right. As far as Churchill is concerned, he had been an outcast since 1929, and not only since the Nazis' seizure of power in 1933. The tendency to play down and give in had already outraged him in British domestic politics, and, faced by the German menace, this outrage only had to be reformulated and newly reasoned.

Churchill had erred with regard to India, but not with regard to Hitler. The prophetic power with which he recognised the rising storm, and the desperation with which he implored the government, Parliament and his compatriots to arm themselves against it, cannot be explained away so cheaply. Therefore a second and important interpretation follows from the fact that he, as opposed to Chamberlain, was a born warrior. It was not the tenaciously and conciliatorily negotiated balance of interests which awakened his energies and passions, but the battle for all or nothing. One is almost tempted to speak with Thomas Mann about 'Brother Hitler'. In this man from the void Churchill instinctively recognised the lust for violence that was worth opposing.

Thirdly, Churchill was deeply rooted in history. For him it was the basic foundation of truth, and the condition for being able to recognise oneself. When, therefore, all of his books — compressed into biographies — talk about historic experiences, they also serve self-experience and show autobiographical traits. In this sense it is no coincidence that in the uncertainties of the 1930s Churchill turned to the history of the English-speaking peoples. The recording of the past was designed to lead into the future.

It is a part of the teachings of history that Britain's task has always been to prevent any dominating or overwhelming power from arising on the Continent, in order to secure by her own liberty the diversity and liberty of Europe. In the confrontation with Spain, this was also a reason why British sea power was developed. And for this, the ancestor Marlborough had fought against France and Great Britain had remained at war for almost a quarter of a century against the armies of the French Revolution and Napoleon. The First World War had been fought for this. And if now, mightier than ever, a power was growing in the heart of Europe which wanted to dominate and subjugate, then Britain would once again have to shoulder her historic burden and fight, cost what it may.

Fourthly and finally, guided by history and Edmund Burke, Churchill was aware of the destructive power of modern doctrines of salvation, which promise paradise on earth only to create hell. This knowledge had armed him against Lenin, his teachings and Bolshevist practice. He recognised the destruction of justice and liberty as an inevitable result of ideological fanaticism. The racial delusions and the sort of natural philosophy which Hitler had put together for himself as a *Weltanschauung* might be light years away from Marxism and Leninism, but it was not difficult to recognise within it the same drive towards destruction, persecution and annihilation.[36] Had Churchill read Heinrich Heine, he could have quoted:

> Far more terrible than anything else would be for natural philosophers to actively interfere in the German revolution and identify themselves with the work of destruction . . . Do not smile about the dreamer who expects the same revolution in the material world that took place in the world of the intellect. The idea precedes the act, like lightning the thunder. The German thunder, however, is still German and is not very flexible, and comes rolling along rather slowly. But come it will, and when you hear a clap one day such as there has never been a clap before in the history of the world, then know: the German thunder has finally reached its goal. At this sound, the eagles will fall dead from the sky and the lions in the most distant desert of Africa will pull in their tails and creep away into their royal caves. A piece will be enacted in Germany, compared to which the French Revolution will appear to have been only a harmless idyll.[37]

All in all, it was not Neville Chamberlain who was prepared to step upon the stage as Hitler's counter-player, but Winston Churchill.

'Winston
is Back'

In London the Second World War began with an air raid warning. But even more impatiently than for the sirens to sound the all clear, Churchill was waiting for the call of the Prime Minister. Thank God he did not have long to wait. To Churchill's delight, he was offered the Admiralty and returned with satisfaction to his old offices, in which he had been at home once before from 1911 to 1915. 'Winston is Back', the Admiralty signalled the Fleet.

And now to work! After the long years of enforced abstinence there just could not be enough of it. Churchill recalls how, as a man of retirement age, he was able to cope—with the help of the noonday nap:

> Nature had not intended mankind to work from eight in the morning until midnight without that refreshment of blessed oblivion which, even if it only lasts twenty minutes, is sufficient to renew all the vital forces. I regretted having to send myself to bed like a child every afternoon, but I was rewarded by being able to work through the night until two or even later—sometimes much later—in the morning, and begin a new day between eight and nine o'clock. This routine I observed throughout the war, and I commend it to others if and when they find it necessary for a long spell to get the last scrap out of the human structure. The First Sea Lord, Admiral Pound, as soon as he had realised my technique, adopted it himself, except that he did not actually go to bed, but dozed off in his arm-chair. He even carried the policy so far as often to go to sleep during the Cabinet meetings. One word about the Navy was however sufficient to awaken him to the fullest activity. . . .[1]

It should be added, however, that many of the junior officers complained about Churchill's schedule. On the one hand they were forced to take a break with which they could do little—most of them did not have a bed nearby like their chief—and on the other they had to remain capable of working late into the night. One can stand this for a few days but hardly for weeks or months, let alone years.

As quickly as possible Churchill went to visit Scapa Flow, the naval base in the Orkneys. From there he sailed across in the flagship *Nelson* to Loch Ewe in Scotland, where the major part of the fleet lay at anchor. *Nelson* was one of the newly constructed battleships the Navy had been able to wrest with difficulty in the 1920s from Chancellor of the Exchequer Churchill. The longer the visit lasted, however, the more the First Lord was overcome by strangely discordant recollections of his former time in office:

> Most of the captains and admirals of those days were dead or had long passed into retirement. The responsible senior officers who were now presented to me as I visited the various ships had been young lieutenants or even midshipmen in those far-off days. . . . The perfect discipline, style, and bearing, the ceremonial routine—all were unchanged. But an entirely different generation filled the uniforms and the posts. Only the ships had most of them been laid down in my tenure. None of them was new. It was a strange experience, like suddenly resuming a previous incarnation. It seemed that I was all that survived in the same position I had held so long ago.
>
> . . . [After the visit] I motored from Loch Ewe to Inverness, where our train awaited us. We had a picnic lunch on the way by a stream, sparkling in hot sunshine. I felt oddly oppressed with my memories.
>
> > For God's sake let us sit upon the ground
> > And tell sad stories of the death of kings.
>
> No one had ever been over the same terrible course twice with such an interval between . . . If we were in fact going over the same cycle a second time, should I have once again to endure the pangs of dismissal? . . .
>
> > I feel like one
> > Who treads alone
> > Some banquet hall deserted,
> > Whose lights are fled
> > Whose garlands dead,
> > And all but he departed.[2]

It says much for Churchill that he does not hide his strange feelings, and we understand how welcome work was—the more the better. A letter he received also helped him:

President Roosevelt to Mr. Churchill   11.IX.39
It is because you and I occupied similar positions in the [First] World War that I want you to know how glad I am that you are back again in the Admiralty. Your

problems are, I realise, complicated by new factors, but the essential is not very different. What I want you and the Prime Minister to know is that I shall at all times welcome it if you will keep in touch personally with anything you want me to know about. You can always send sealed letters through your pouch or my pouch.

I am glad you did the Marlborough volumes before this thing started—and I much enjoyed reading them.[3]

This opening set off an avalanche. During the course of the war Churchill sent 950 messages and letters to Roosevelt and received about 800 replies.[4] In these he always signed with the words 'Naval Person', and after he had become Prime Minister with 'Former Naval Person'. In his memoirs he writes:

My relations with the President gradually became so close that the chief business between our two countries was virtually conducted by these personal interchanges between him and me. . . . Thus a very high degree of concert was obtained, and the savings in time and the reduction in the number of people informed were both invaluable. . . . I felt I was in contact with a very great man, who was also a warm-hearted friend and the foremost champion of the high causes which we served.[5]

That it was precisely this close relationship which could also lead to frictions will be shown later.

'But the essential is not very different.' Just as in August 1914, the British Fleet took up its blockade stations and, as then, German maritime trade quickly came to an end with high losses. Because Hitler had wrapped his plans in deep secrecy, there had been no warning. Many freighters and passenger liners were at sea somewhere on the oceans. They were brought to bay or scuttled themselves when British cruisers found them. Others sought refuge in neutral ports, which later often became hostile, as for example, in America. That the pearl among the passenger liners, the *Bremen*, succeeded in escaping from New York to her home port via Murmansk remained an exception.

In many respects the task of the Royal Navy in 1939 was easier than in 1914. The powerful German Imperial battlefleet no longer existed. The huge battleships *Bismarck* and *Tirpitz* were still under construction. *Scharnhorst* and *Gneisenau* were inferior in gunpower even to the British battleships which were twenty years older.[6] And all there were in addition were the pocket-battleships *Deutschland*, *Admiral Scheer* and *Admiral Graf Spee*. There was no naval aviation at all: Hermann Göring's jealousy as Commander-in-Chief of the *Luftwaffe* had destroyed it. While the aircraft carrier *Graf Zep-*

pelin was built, she was never put into commission, even though she would be needed desperately.

The situation only changed—but then dramatically—after the German Navy took possession of the Norwegian fjords and of French ports on the Atlantic like Brest and St-Nazaire. This applied particularly to the submarine war. But in the autumn of 1939 the initial successes by the U-boats declined rapidly.[7] The Royal Navy did lose the aircraft carrier *Courageous* on 17 September, and on 14 October Commander Günther Prien penetrated into Scapa Flow and sank the battleship *Royal Oak*. These events caused enthusiasm in Germany and consternation in Britain, and it took a long time before Scapa Flow could again be used as an anchorage after new security measures had been installed. British prestige was half-way restored when two months later a cruiser squadron in the South Atlantic brought *Admiral Graf Spee* to bay, damaged her and forced her to run into port in Montevideo. *Spee* then scuttled herself.[8]

In the meantime Hitler's armies had overrun Poland in only a few weeks with their first *'Blitzkrieg'* campaign, while Soviet troops occupied eastern Poland. The French Army did not budge an inch, even though it was initially only faced by a few divisions of reserves. What followed was a six-months *'Sitzkrieg'* or, in to a phrase coined by Chamberlain, a 'Twilight War',[9] during which almost nothing happened. 'Nothing to report in the West,' the *Wehrmacht* repeated with almost monotonous regularity, and sometimes it even restricted itself to these three words: 'Nothing to report.'[10]

One could almost say that the war was suffocating in boredom. All the greater, therefore, was the excitement when in its shadow the Soviet Union made territorial demands on Finland and, when these were rejected, declared war on her little neighbour on 30 November 1939. All over the world, even in Germany, hearts beat for the Finnish David in his fight with the Russian Goliath. Sympathy even increased when David stood fast against all expectations and dealt the armoured giant heavy wounds. Germany's hands were tied. Hitler was preparing the attack in the West, and the secret clauses of the German-Soviet non-aggression pact of 23 August had placed Finland within the Russian sphere of influence. Great Britain and France, however, were almost forced into an absurd additional war against the Soviet Union by public opinion, and only the fact that Finland's resistance finally did tire and compel the country to give in to the Russian demands in the peace treaty of Moscow on 12 March 1940 prevented this.

119

What was left was Norway. How else except via northern Norway could Western aid have reached Finland at all? And how was it to be secured, if not by control of all of Norway? Even after the end of the Finnish-Russian 'Winter War' a tempting target still remained: Narvik. From there the Swedish iron ore her steel industry needed so urgently was shipped to Germany. Cutting this line of supply would have dealt a heavy blow to the armaments industry. And so the Scandinavian adventure was decided. On 8 April 1940 the mining of Norwegian coastal waters began and an Allied expeditionary force set off on its trip into the unknown.

What was in the offing had, of course, not escaped Hitler's notice. Operation *'Weserübung'* was prepared in deep secrecy, and during the night of 9 April landing operations began in all the important ports, while troops also marched into Denmark. The Norwegians, although taken completely by surprise, resisted with all their might. On a rocky island in the Oslo Fjord, for example, lay the fortress of Oskarsborg, which boasted three ancient Krupp guns built in 1892. They bore the nice old biblical names of 'Aaron', 'Moses' and 'Joshua'. The even more ancient commander, Colonel Eriksen, who was close to retirement, detected the shadow of a big warship and fired a single salvo—quite without authority. He hit the heavy cruiser *Blücher* and started a fire. Visible far and wide as a flaming torch, *Blücher* was finally sunk by two torpedoes from a coastal battery. This accidental success delayed the occupation of Oslo and gave the King and the government time to flee inland and organise resistance. Elsewhere, too, things did not all go according to plan. The cruisers *Karlsruhe* and *Königsberg* were lost off Kristiansand and Bergen. At Narvik British naval forces destroyed a whole flotilla of destroyers. Nevertheless, the element of surprise and the initiative lay with the Germans from the start. And, as Churchill bitterly recorded, they showed more fighting spirit, were better equipped and were more energetically led than the Allies. Where their commanders declared a road to be impassable, the Germans were soon to be seen marching along, obviously without any difficulties. Even in Narvik, where they actually were at a disadvantage, 'a motley troop of barely six thousand men held an Allied force of twenty thousand at bay for six weeks—and stood fast until the Allies withdrew.'[11] After only four weeks it became clear that the Germans would be the winners in the Norwegian campaign.

On 7, 8 and 9 May 1940 there was an excited debate in the House of Commons. At first glance it could have made Churchill's oppressive vision of history repeating itself come true and driven him from office, just as the failure of the Dardanelles operation had in 1915. He was, after all, the responsible Minister who had emphatically supported the operation against Norway. But the revolt hit Chamberlain. Very foolishly and prematurely he had declared on 4 April that Hitler has 'missed the bus' — and when things turned out differently this brought all the anger, and worse still the scorn, down on his own head. Everyone sensed that he was only taking part half-heartedly and that a man was now required who would wage the war with real determination. Everyone recalled Churchill's untiring warnings about the approaching danger.

One of the great parliamentarians, Leo Amery, dealt his 'old friend and fellow-traveller' Chamberlain a fatal blow when he said to him what Cromwell had once said to the Long Parliament: 'For the little good you have done, you have been sitting here too long. Away with you, I say, we want no more to do with you. For God's sake, go!'[12] When Churchill took part of the blame upon himself and loyally defended the Prime Minister, Lloyd George called out to him that he should not 'let himself be turned into an air raid shelter' and keep the bomb splinters away from others, and then violently attacked Chamberlain. Following this, Duff Cooper gave a devastating speech. Harold Nicolson drew a sort of summary on 7 May:

> There is more than just worry, there is a sort of fear, but this fear is leading to determination, not to hysteria or cowardice. I have rarely admired the spiritual climate in the Commons as much as today.[13]

Chamberlain initially attempted to save himself by replacing a few ministers and forming a coalition government with Labour. But the Labour leaders refused his overtures and it became obvious that he would have to resign.

The next morning, 10 May 1940, the storm flood of alarming reports began: German troops had crossed the Dutch and Belgian borders. Chamberlain wavered yet again: in view of new developments it might be his duty to remain in office. But he let himself be dissuaded. And no one can tell us what happened next as well as Churchill himself:

> At eleven o'clock I was again summoned to Downing Street by the Prime Minister. There once more I found Lord Halifax. We took our seats at the table opposite Mr. Chamberlain. He told us that he was satisfied that it was beyond his power to form a National Government. The response he had received from the Labour leaders left him in no doubt of this. The question therefore was whom he should advise the King to send for after his own resignation had been accepted. His demeanour

was cool, unruffled, and seemingly quite detached from the personal aspect of the affair. He looked at us both across the table.

I have had many important interviews in my public life, and this was certainly the most important. Usually I talk a great deal, but on this occasion I was silent.... a very long pause ensued.... Then at length Halifax spoke. He said that he felt that his position as a Peer, out of the House of Commons, would make it very difficult for him to discharge the duties of Prime Minister in a war like this. He would be held responsible for everything, but would not have the power to guide the assembly upon whose confidence the life of every Government depended. He spoke for some minutes in this sense, and by the time he had finished it was clear that the duty would fall upon me me — had in fact fallen upon me....[14]

The rest of the day was filled to the brim. First came the audience with the King and his invitation to form a government. Even in this dramatic situation there were still the gambits of British humour. His Majesty began the conversation with the statement: 'I suppose you don't know why I have sent for you.' Churchill replied that no, he had not the slightest idea. Then came the numerous telephone calls and meetings required to finalise the invitation — a busy coming and going. Churchill summarises:

Thus, then, on the night of the 10th of May, at the outset of this mighty battle, I acquired the chief power in the State ...

During these last crowded days of the political crisis my pulse had not quickened at any moment. I took it all as it came. But I cannot conceal from the reader of this truthful account that as I went to bed at about 3 a.m. I was conscious of a profound sense of relief. At last I had the authority to give directions over the whole scene. I felt as if I were walking with destiny, and that all my past life had been but a preparation for this hour and for this trial. Ten years in the political wilderness had freed me from ordinary party antagonisms. My warnings over the last six years had been so numerous, so detailed, and were now so terribly vindicated, that no one could gainsay me. I could not be reproached either for making the war or with want of preparation for it. I thought I knew a great deal about it all, and I was sure I should not fail Therefore, although impatient for the morning, I slept soundly and had no need for cheering dreams. Facts are better than dreams.[15]

Yes, they probably are — when these dreams come true. In his memoirs Churchill also writes:

In my long political experience I had held most of the great offices of State, but I readily admit that the post which had now fallen to me was the one I liked the best. Power, for the sake of lording it over fellow-creatures or adding to personal pomp, is rightly judged base. But power in a national crisis, when a man believes he knows what orders should be given, is a blessing. In any sphere of action there can be no comparison between the positions of number one and numbers two, three, or four.[16]

It would be difficult to find two other texts that tell us so much about Churchill as the two we have just cited.

On 13 May the new Prime Minister stood up before the House of Commons to make his policy statement. It is probably the shortest one on record,[17] and certainly the most famous. It went down in history as the 'Blood, Sweat and Tears' speech. In actual fact he speaks about blood, toil, tears and sweat. This sounds impressive, but the change around and shortening makes it even more powerful.[18] At the close of the speech he said:

> I would say to the House, as I said to those who have joined this Government: 'I have nothing to offer but blood, toil, tears and sweat.' We have before us an ordeal of the most grievous kind. We have before us many, many months of struggle and suffering.
>
> You ask, What is our policy? I will say: 'It is to wage war, by sea, land, and air, with all our might and with all the strength that God can give us: to wage war against a monstrous tyranny, never surpassed in the dark, lamentable catalogue of human crime. That is our policy. You ask, What is our aim? I can answer in one word: Victory—victory at all costs, victory in spite of terror; victory, however long and hard the road may be; for without victory there is no survival. Let that be realised: no survival for the British Empire; no survival for all that the British Empire has stood for; no survival for the urge and impulse of the ages, that mankind will move forward towards its goals. But I take up my task with buoyancy and hope. I feel sure that our cause will not be suffered to fail among men. At this time I feel entitled to claim the aid of all, and I say, 'Come, then, let us go forward together with our united strength.'[19]

The House of Commons accepted this declaration of policy by unanimous vote.

The Player
and His Counter-Player

The stage is set, the great play can begin, and the audience is already impatient for the curtain to rise. As in Shakespeare's *Macbeth*, the drama will begin with a murderous triumph, which then still turns into defeat and ruin. Or, from the counter-perspective, the first act deals with catastrophe, the last with victory. But before the two leading figures appear, it may prove useful to learn more about the player and his counter-player.

We begin with the statement: the counter-player needs the player. Churchill would not have become Churchill without Hitler, at least not a historic figure of importance. It is hardly a coincidence that in the context of his appointment as crisis Prime Minister on 10 May 1940 he speaks about his feeling that his whole life had only been a preparation for this moment and test of fate. If Hitler had been content with what he had achieved in 1938 by the Munich Agreement, as he had so solemnly promised, we would remember Chamberlain and not Churchill as the great British statesman who had saved us. But Hitler, too, would not have been Hitler if he had done so. Or to speculate with a greater degree of probability: had Georg Elser's bomb torn Hitler to pieces in the *Bürgerbräukeller* in Munich on 8 November 1939, then, according to everything we can predict, negotiations with the objective of reaching a compromise peace would most probably have begun between his successor Hermann Göring and Chamberlain.[1]

Hitler was one thing before everything else—a gambler; only he played for incomparably higher stakes than the normal visitor to a casino, for all or nothing, life or death, absolute power or oblivion. He had not acquired a decent education, and was not suited for any middle-class profession. He was actually a professional gambler out of passion—not to say a gambling

124

addict through and through. And because he was, he could not stop and had to increase the stakes after each success. His whole career demonstrates this, from its obscure beginnings to the bizarre finale.

First we meet the demagogue who develops the sado-masochistic game of domination and submission to perfection. In his book *Mein Kampf* he writes:

> The psyche of the masses is not receptive to half measures and weakness. Like the female, whose spiritual feeling is less determined by reasons of abstract thought than by those of an undefinable, emotional force, and who would therefore rather submit to a strong man than dominate a weakling, the masses too love the ruler more than the supplicant, and feel themselves more satisfied inside by a doctrine which does not tolerate any other next to itself than by the granting of liberal freedoms, which they normally do not know what to do with anyway, wherefore they easily feel themselves abandoned. They consciously perceive the impertinence of their mental terrorisation as little as the revolting mistreatment of their human liberties, because they have not the slightest inkling of the inner madness. And so they only perceive the ruthless power and the brutality of its determined expression, to which they always submit in the end.[2]

Leadership and obedience as an erotic power relationship? That is not absurd; it is the reality of an inter-relationship between master and servant, in which the servant, as a condition for his commitment and self-sacrifice, does not demand restraint or tolerance from the master but instead the display of absolute power. What we dismiss from a safe distance with a shaking of the head when we see films of Hitler's appearances and speeches, and can hardly comprehend any longer, is exactly this erotic relationship of power between the leader and his followers, and nothing else.

In *Mein Kampf* the conditions for the staging of this power are precisely described, including the details and formalities. Even the time of day turns out to be important. Hitler describes the failure of a morning event:

> I believe I did not speak any worse than usual, yet the effect appeared to be nil. I left the rally totally dissatisfied but richer by a new experience . . . In the morning, and even during the day, the human will appears to still resist with utmost energy any attempt to impose a foreign will or a foreign opinion upon it. In the evening, however, it succumbs more easily to the dominating power of a stronger will. Because, in truth, each such rally resembles a wrestling match between two opposing forces. The outstanding rhetoric art of a dominating apostle type will succeed all the more readily in gaining those people for the new purpose who have already experienced a natural weakening of their power to resist than those who are still in full possession of a vigorous mentality and will.[3]

Increasing the stakes, Hitler, after he had become the leader of by far the greatest mass movement in 1932, rejected the offer of the Vice-Chancellorship in a conservative government, which would have imposed restrictions on him. After he had become Chancellor, things still did not satisfy him, and he deliberately set about trampling down all the constitutional limitations to his power. When he had 'torn off the fetters of Versailles' and achieved military equality for Germany, this was again not enough. Rearmament was stepped up even further, to achieve superiority. The gaining of the Sudetenland was followed by the march into Prague, Prague by the war against Poland, the victory over France by the war of extermination against the Soviet Union. After failure had begun to loom in December of 1941, war was even declared on the United States. When it became clear that the war had been lost, there was only one way left in which the stakes could still be increased—by the intention to annihilate. In essence this was the extermination of the Jews, which by 1942 had gone far beyond any historically known examples and given the Holocaust its unbounded and unique dimension. In the end Germany, too, was to be annihilated. As his mouthpiece Goebbels screamed: 'But when we step down, then will the globe shake!'[4] All that was lacking was the atomic bomb, to be set off at the final moment in the ruins of the *Reich* Chancellery in conquered Berlin.

The future remains obscure to the gambler. He does not know whether the ball will fall on red or black. This is what gives him his kick—and his torment. That is why he needs the feeling of being predestined for success. And therefore not man in general, but the adventurer and gambler, needs, to quote Ernst Jünger,

> . . . the belief we require deep inside—namely that we are sworn to the world to be in agreement with it. When the ball rolls for us, the card falls, we savour a refined enjoyment, the enjoyment of a most secret material intelligence. Luck is in truth nothing but the elementary form of intelligence—in luck material things, the world at large, think for us.'[5]

But for the passionate gambler luck already slips through his fingers with success. Therefore he must constantly bet again and increase the stakes.

For Hitler the key term was 'destiny'. Is there possibly an indication here of a subliminal connection with Churchill? Why does the Englishman say that, during the night of 10 May 1940, 'I felt as if I were walking with Destiny'? We have already looked for an explanation why it was Churchill and not Chamberlain who recognised what was approaching in the guise of Hitler, and we have given reasons. Maybe we must now add the final and deepest: only a counter-player can recognise the player.

This is probably from where stem Churchill's unshakeable will to play the game for the highest stakes, cost what may, and his confidence that he would win. He has often and bitterly been criticised for having rejected any sort of compromise peace.[6] Yet Hitler was simply not a statesman, but a gambler through and through, and one cannot reach an understanding with someone like that: one can only fight him to the bitter or glorious end. In this, too, Churchill saw more clearly and more deeply than most of his contemporaries or the latter-day know-alls.

If we leave the gambler aside, all we can see at first glance is the incomparable. There the man from the void with his dark insecurities and bad manners, here the grandson of a duke who was a natural member of the establishment, of the upper ten thousand. There the demagogue with the simplistic choice of words who did not tolerate any objections, here the linguistic master craftsman who wielded his blade in duels. But there are still similarities. Both Hitler and Churchill had an unhappy childhood, in which they sealed themselves off in defiance. Neither gained the major part of their knowledge within the normal system of education. Both were, each in his own and then again quite different ways, adventurers and outsiders. Both talked a lot and with perseverance, frequently to the point of exhaustion, even the desperation of their audiences. Both were basically driven by only one passion, the political one, to the neglect of all the others. And did Churchill's policy statement as Prime Minister not also announce the game of games for all or nothing, for life or death? Did this not contain the fulfilment of his life?

It should be noted that the rôles for the great play are distributed as contrasts and remain so. Hitler is always the gambler who hates everything that goes to make up European tradition, someone who tramples down traditional structures and their convictions and rights, in order to create room for violence and destruction within the chaos. Churchill recognises and hates this destruction. He is rooted in history. He wants to preserve what stems from it. He defends liberty and justice. And that is exactly the reason why the player has the first move, and why the counter-player only gains his historic ranking through him.

His
Finest Hour

Now at last the slowly-gathered, long-pent-up fury of the storm broke upon us. Four or five millions of men met each other in the first shock of the most merciless of all the wars of which record has been kept. Within a week the front in France, behind which we had been accustomed to dwell throughout the hard years of the former war and the opening phase of this, was to be irretrievably broken. Within three weeks the long-famed French Army was to collapse in rout and ruin, and our only British Army to be hurled into the sea with all its equipment lost. Within six weeks we were to find ourselves alone, almost disarmed, with triumphant Germany and Italy at our throats, with the whole of Europe open to Hitler's power, and Japan glowering on the other side of the globe. It was amid these facts and looming prospects that I entered upon my duties as Prime Minister and Minister of Defence . . .

These are the words with which Winston Churchill begins the second volume of his history of the Second World War. It bears the title 'Their Finest Hour'. What is meant are the British, the sailors and soldiers, particularly the young fighter pilots who won the Battle of Britain, but also the people in London and other cities, who defied the hail of bombs. What is meant is a nation which did not panic when everything appeared to be lost, but stood fast and did its duty. But it was above all his – Churchill's – finest and greatest hour especially because it began with disaster, with catastrophe. Where else do we learn anything about historical greatness if not in the clash with a disaster no one else proves able to cope with? And Churchill knew that, of course. When the old man was asked long after the war if he would like to relive one of his by then more than 70 years, he replied without hesitation: '1940 any time, any time.'[1]

Some key data on the course of the catastrophe. When the German armies jumped off to the attack on the morning of 10 May 1940, first into the

128

Netherlands and Belgium, the French and British divisions responded and advanced to meet them. They left their prepared positions on the Franco-Belgian border, on which they had been working for months, and involved themselves in a war for which they were not ready. The French Army in particular, from generals all the way down to common soldiers, had committed itself to standing fast, and gave up when it was attacked while on the move.[2] Furthermore, France's generals had sworn that at the hinge of the movement the Ardennes offered natural protection, because they were impassable to armoured divisions and other motorised forces. So there were only a few French divisions there, and that is exactly where the German 'hook' was applied, which in only a few days led to the Somme and down the river to the Channel coast. The Allied forces in north-eastern France were encircled and ground down in a gigantic pocket, forced to surrender or driven towards the sea to their destruction.

After the mopping-up of the pocket and a short rest, the German armies again went on to the offensive on 5 June and overran all of France. Five days later Italy entered the war, assured of cheap spoils. France signed an armistice on 22 June and quit the conflict. Marshal Pétain, the famous victor of Verdun in the First World War, formed a government which set itself up in Vichy to administer the unoccupied territories in the centre and the south of the country—closely tied to the directives of the victors, of course. German casualties during the six-week campaign amounted to 27,074 killed, 111,034 wounded and 18,384 missing,[3] as compared to 1.9 million enemy captured—who were very welcome because they could replace German personnel drafted into the Army, especially on the farms. A huge mass of weapons was also captured, and the French armaments industry worked for Germany from then on.

Churchill did what he could, and that was little enough. He flew to France several times to persuade the government to hold out. But during his first visit on 16 May he came upon signs of hopelessness and disintegration. When he asked the French Commander-in-Chief where the strategic reserve was, the reply was a shrug of the shoulders and a single word *'aucune'*—'there is none'.

Churchill described his reaction:

> *'Aucune.'* I was dumbfounded. What were we to think of the great French Army and its highest chiefs? It had never occurred to me that any commanders having to defend five hundred miles of engaged front would have left themselves

unprovided with a mass of manoeuvre. No one can defend with certainty so wide a front; but when the enemy has committed himself to a major thrust which breaks the line one can always have, one *must* always have, a mass of divisions which marches up in vehement counter-attack at the moment when the first fury of the offensive has spent its force.

What was the Maginot Line for? It should have economised troops . . . enabling large forces to be held in reserve . . .[4]

In the silence which followed the fatal *'aucune'* Churchill looked out of the window. There were already fires burning into which files were being thrown so that they would not fall into the hands of the enemy when he marched into Paris.

Churchill, of course, also sent urgent messages to the American President, for example on 18 May:

I do not need to tell you about the gravity of what has happened. We are determined to persevere to the very end, whatever the result of the great battle raging in France may be. We must expect in any case to be attacked here on the Dutch model before very long, and we hope to give a good account of ourselves. But if American assistance is to play any part it must be available soon.[5]

But there was hardly anything Roosevelt could do, tied as he was to the Constitution and confronted with a Senate and a House of Representatives who both rejected by a clear majority any intervention in the European war.

Amid all the disaster there was one unexpected ray of hope — the drama at Dunkirk which unfolded between 26 May and 4 June. At first it looked as if nothing could stop the German armoured forces who were advancing past Boulogne and Calais from the west. If they took Dunkirk by *coup de main*, like so many other towns before it, there was no saving the British Army which was still fighting far inland. But the attack was delayed, and the reason for this is still controversial. Some talk about a deliberate intervention by Hitler, who was worried about the battleworthiness of his armoured forces for the further attack on France. Others point to commanders like General von Rundstedt. What also doubtless played a rôle was Göring's promise that, with his *Luftwaffe*, he would prevent any evacuation by sea.

However it may have been, a miracle came to pass. Hundreds of ships rushed to the rescue, not only warships but private yachts, tugs, cutters, motor boats. Afterwards 861 vessels of all types were counted, sailing back and forth between the French and English coasts. Two hundred and forty-three of them were sunk, of which 226 were British. But a total of 338,226 soldiers were rescued from death or capture between 27 May and 4 June, including almost 100,000 off the beaches instead of from the port of Dunkirk.[6] The major part of the British Army was saved — with the loss, however, of almost all its equipment if we disregard rifles and at best a few machine guns.

On 4 June Churchill gave a speech to the House of Commons in which he said:

> When I requested one week ago to reserve this afternoon for a statement, I feared it would be my bitter duty to report to you on the greatest military catastrophe in our long history. I believed — and not merely a few people with judgement agreed with me — that at best 20,000 or 30,000 men could be saved . . . The enemy attacked from all sides with the greatest strength and determination, and threw his numerically far superior air force into the fray . . . We must, of course, be very careful not to assign to this deliverance the attributes of a victory. Wars are not won by evacuations.

And yet there was the achievement that the major part of the Army had been rescued. The equipment which had been lost could be replaced, though hardly the experienced officers and soldiers who were required to create the army of the future.

At the close of his speech Churchill addressed himself to the now looming invasion:

> I am convinced: if everyone does his duty, if we overlook nothing, and to the best of our abilities continue with our preparations which have already begun, we will succeed yet once again in defending our island home, in surviving the storm of war and outlasting the afflictions of tyranny, if necessary for years and if necessary alone. His Majesty's Government is determined to do this — everyone who belongs to it. And that is the will of Parliament and of the nation . . .
> . . . we shall not flag or fail. We shall go on to the end. We shall fight in France, we shall fight in the seas and oceans, we shall fight with growing confidence and growing strength in the air; we shall defend our Island, whatever the cost may be. We shall fight on the beaches, we shall fight on the landing-grounds, we shall fight in the fields and in the streets, we shall fight in the hills; we shall never surrender; and even if, which I do not for a moment believe, this Island or a large part of it were subjugated and starving, then our Empire beyond the seas, armed and guarded by the British Fleet, would carry on the struggle, until, in God's good time, the New World, with all its power and might, steps forth to the rescue and the liberation of the Old.[7]

It is reported that many of the Members had tears in their eyes when they stood up after the speech to demonstrate by their applause that the Prime

Minister had spoken for them all and for the nation. And truly, in those days and weeks of disaster, there was nothing Churchill could do that was more important than, by his words, arm the people with the hope and confidence they needed to survive the trials and tribulations which had only just begun.

Churchill flew to France on two further occasions, first to Briare on the River Loire, then in a wide swing to Tours, and preached holding out – or, in the worst case, continuing the battle from the colonies. The French replied, quite understandably, with desperate pleas, with demands: all available British troops, and especially the RAF, should be thrown into the battle with full commitment. But besides encouraging words, they received little in the way of help. It had long become evident that the fates of France and Great Britain were separating, and that the issue for the British was to prepare themselves for the Battle of Britain.

Included among the encouraging words was the more romantic than realistic idea that France and Great Britain form a Union with mutual citizenship and a joint constitution.[8] In France this suggestion awakened mistrust rather than enthusiasm: it was believed that Britain intended to seize this opportunity to annex the French colonies. In retrospect Churchill himself only says: 'Of all this Parliament was informed in due course. But the issue by then had ceased to count.'[9]

Incidentally, there were still several British divisions which had been pushed west by the disintegration of the French front or destroyed, or had reached ports like Cherbourg, Brest and St-Nazaire. The *Luftwaffe* did what it could to prevent their evacuation, and there were some catstrophes. In St-Nazaire on 17 June, for example, the fully loaded *Lancastria* was hit by bombs and turned into a flaming inferno. More than 3,000 men perished in the fire. Churchill forbade any reports on the incident: 'The newspapers have got quite enough disaster for to-day at least.' Nevertheless, 136,000 British and 20,000 Polish soldiers reached the island of salvation.[10]

On 18 June Churchill gave a speech in the Commons which was later also broadcast on the radio. At the close he said:

> What General Weygand called the Battle of France is over. I expect that the Battle of Britain is about to begin. Upon this battle depends the survival of Christian civilisation. Upon it depends our own British life, and the long continuity of our institutions and our Empire. The whole fury and might of the enemy must very soon be turned on us. Hitler knows that he will have to break us in this Island or

lose the war. If we can stand up to him, all Europe may be free and the life of the world may move forward into broad, sunlit uplands. But if we fail, then the whole world, including the United States . . . will sink into the abyss of a new Dark Age, made more sinister, and perhaps more protracted, by the lights of perverted science. Let us therefore brace ourselves to our duties, and so bear ourselves that, if the British Empire and its Commonwealth last for a thousand years, men will still say: 'This was their finest hour.'[11]

This 'finest hour' began with a dark deed. It was of decisive importance for the coming battle not to let the French Fleet fall into German hands. During his penultimate visit to France, Churchill had obtained the promise of Admiral Darlan, Commander-in-Chief of the French Navy, that this would never happen. But could he depend on it? Darlan was a dubious character and he held a key position in the pro-German government of Marshal Pétain.[12] When the French government asked the British to be released from its treaty obligations so as to be able to conclude an armistice, the reply was that they would 'agree under the condition, but only under the condition, that the French Fleet sail to British ports before negotiations begin' and thus be taken out of German reach. But nothing of the sort took place. There were several ships in British ports on the day of the armistice, which were then seized in early June, but the major part of the French Fleet was at anchor at Toulon in southern France, at Oran and at the adjoining naval base of Mers-el-Kebir in Algeria. That was also where the modern, fast and powerful battleships *Strasbourg* and *Dunkerque* were located. It would be unfortunate if these vessels, together with *Gneisenau* and *Scharnhorst*—reinforced in 1941 by *Bismarck* and *Tirpitz*— were to form a battle group for attacks on British traffic in the Atlantic!

The War Cabinet in London decided to send the task force stationed in Gibraltar to Oran and confront the French commander with the alternatives either to follow the British with his ships or to let them be destroyed. It was, Churchill writes, 'a hateful decision, the most unnatural and painful in which I have ever been concerned'. But it was taken, and communicated to Vice-Admiral Somerville, the man in command: 'You are charged with one of the most disagreeable and difficult tasks that a British Admiral has ever been faced with, but we have complete confidence in you and rely on you to carry it out relentlessly.'[13]

On the morning of 3 July 1940 the British task force appeared off Oran. The negotiations dragged on and ended with a French 'No' to the British demands. At 5.54 p.m. the battlecruiser *Hood* and the battleships *Valiant* and *Resolution* opened fire; the elderly *Bretagne* exploded, *Provence* was beached and *Dunkerque* ran aground. *Strasbourg*, though pursued by torpedo planes, escaped to Toulon. Altogether 1,720 French seamen lost their lives.

It was a truly grim business. It cannot even be compared to the Japanese attack on Pearl Harbor. The Empire of the Rising Sun and the United States had long faced each other in hostility. Here we are dealing with an ally with whom one had fought shoulder to shoulder in the First World War, and in the Second as recently as only days beforehand. But in Britain the 'deed of Oran' was applauded and on the other side of the Atlantic it was taken as a sign of British determination to continue the fight to the end. That the French government broke off diplomatic relations with Great Britain can readily be understood.

Before we continue to discuss further events of the war, we must turn to the battle Churchill had to fight on the home front. It was not at all the fact, as it appears in retrospect or in the results of votes in Parliament after one of his great speeches, that he was unassailable. In the early weeks after he assumed office, it was the man of peace, Neville Chamberlain, who was demonstratively applauded by the Conservative majority when he appeared in the House of Commons. Churchill, by comparison, received only meagre applause, and then mostly from the Labour MPs.[14] The reservations reached deeply into the ranks of the government. 'Rab' Butler, the Secretary of State in the Foreign Office, expressed a widely held opinion when he told Churchill's personal secretary Jock Colville that the new Prime Minister was 'a catastrophe . . . We have foolishly entrusted ourselves to a half-American who seeks advice and support from incapable, garrulous people of the same sort.'[15] When the reports from France became dramatically worse, 'the higher social classes were seized by panic'.[16]

A crisis occurred on 26 May when the French Prime Minister Paul Reynaud came to London and suggested asking the Italian dictator Mussolini to mediate, as he had already done in Munich in 1938, with the object of reaching a cease-fire and beginning peace negotiations. A serious dispute developed within the British Cabinet, beginning between Churchill and Foreign Secretary Lord Halifax, whom Chamberlain had favoured as his successor. Halifax declared that one should explore all possibilities, in order to avoid a catastrophe which would break not only over France but over Britain as well. When Churchill did not want to make a peace offer but only to listen to one — and only if Hitler promised to renounce all of his conquests — His Lordship exploded:

I thought Winston was talking the most frightful rubbish . . . and after I had listened to him for a while, I told him plainly what I thought about it, and added that our ways would have to separate if that was truly what he thought. And that is what it came to.[17]

A breach would have made the disunity apparent — with disastrous effects — and only with difficulty was one prevented. Later, after success proved Churchill to have been right, his opponents tended to go into hiding and to play down their own importance. But there can hardly be any doubt about the fact that he was walking very close to the brink and that his great hour could soon have come to an end. He would have been the wrong man for negotiations, whereas Lord Halifax would have been the right one. And what Philipp Bell writes is certainly true:

Had the War Cabinet acceded to the French suggestions and asked Mussolini to mediate, a withdrawal of this step would no longer have been possible. If even the mere possibility of negotiations had been opened, it could not have simply been closed again. And how could the government then still have led the nation to resistance against German superiority?[18]

It is impossible to overestimate the importance of this final sentence. To use a metaphor: instead of standing firm against the flood, the government would have breached the dyke itself. The will to resist at any price would have been irretrievably broken. And this applies to every point in time, no matter if negotiations had been taken up during the battle for France or at any point thereafter. Whoever claims that negotiations should at least have been begun in order to explore what they could lead to, and that in the worst case a return to unconditional resistance could have been made, succumbs to the sort of cleverness which already contains its own hidden error.

In the end death also helped Churchill. Chamberlain, who would have been indispensable for bringing the Conservatives to a restructured government and its new policy aimed at negotiations, died on 9 November 1940. Shortly thereafter the British Ambassador in Washington, Lord Lothian, also died and Churchill appointed Lord Halifax to succeed him. The position appeared to be honourable and important. But in reality the uncomfortable critic and dangerous rival saw himself banished into exile: all the important decisions were taken as a result of direct contact between the American President and the British Prime Minister.

And how did things look in the opposing camp? Germany celebrated a memorable victory. Church bells rang for days on end, and Hitler made his entry into Berlin as the conquering hero. On the evening of 19 July he entered the *Reichstag* and gave a long speech. It lasted for two hours and seventeen minutes. He described the campaign in the West in detail, the bravery of the German soldiers, the superiority of their weapons and their leadership—in other words his own.[19] Generals were promoted to Field Marshals in droves, and Hermann Göring, who was one already as Commander-in-Chief of the *Luftwaffe*, was permitted to decorate himself with the hitherto unknown title of *Reichsmarschall*. It was only towards the end that the political part came, a vilification, a threat and an avowal of peace all wrapped in one. First, the vilification directed against Churchill personally:

> I feel an inner revulsion for that sort of unscrupulous parliamentary destroyer of nations and states . . . My intention was not to wage wars, but to erect a new social state of the highest level of culture. Every year of this war robs me from this work. And the reasons for this robbery are ridiculous ciphers . . . Mr. Churchill has just declared once again that he wants war.

Furthermore, he had been the first to have non-military targets bombed:

> Until now I have hardly had any reply made to that. But this does not mean that that is or will remain the only reply.
>
> It is clear to me that, from our coming reply, unspeakable pain and suffering will break over the people. Not over Mr. Churchill, of course, because by then he will certainly be sitting in Canada . . . And this time Mr. Churchill should make an exception and believe me when, as a prophet, I say the following: a great empire will be destroyed thereby. An empire it was never my intention to destroy, or even to damage. But it is clear to me that the continuation of this struggle will only end with the complete destruction of one of the protagonists. Mr. Churchill may believe that this will be Germany. I know that it will be Great Britain.
>
> In this hour I feel it to be my duty before my own conscience to appeal once more to reason in Great Britain as well. I consider myself in a position to make this appeal, since I am not a vanquished foe begging for favours, but the victor, speaking in the name of reason. I can see no reason why this war need go on . . . Possibly Mr. Churchill will brush aside this statement of mine by saying it is merely born of fear and doubt of final victory. In that case I shall at least have relieved my conscience with regard to the things to come.[20]

If we analyse this text, three things become clear. First, the vilification proves that Hitler is taking Churchill seriously. The player has recognised his counter-player and knows that he is blocking his path. Both are fighting their duel for all or nothing.[21] Secondly, the accusation of being a destroyer of nations and states serves to mask his own intentions. Whoever opposes Hitler's will for greatness, unrestricted rule and unlimited power deserves destruction. And, by this, barbaric actions, not only in the 'eradication' of British cities, are justified in advance. Thirdly, the appeal to 'reason' is intended to put the opponent out in the cold, and he hopes that instead of 'ciphers' men will seize the reins who are prepared to negotiate, if not to submit. But nothing concrete is demanded or offered. The conditions for a negotiated peace remained totally obscure, but it becomes all too clearly visible that German hegemony over Europe is going to be one of them. With this, however, Churchill's position was reinforced, not weakened.

One final remark: of course Hitler did not feel himself to be prevented from erecting a social state of the highest level of culture, but from beginning the one war which was really important to him—the campaign in the East which was to bring *Lebensraum* and destroy the Soviet Union. This factor tempts us to speculate: what would have happened if Britain had given in? The German armaments industry could then have concentrated on building tanks instead of having to deliver submarines. The *Luftwaffe* would not have taken the field weakened and dispersed but with fully concentrated strength. Many additional divisions would have been available, which instead were needed in Norway, in France, in the Balkans and in Africa, including air defence divisions from the *Reich*, incidentally, whose 8.8cm guns had shown themselves to have a penetrating effect against enemy tanks. And finally, instead of at the end of June, the campaign could have been launched four to six summer weeks earlier. Would the collapse of the Soviet Union possibly have been achieved by all this? We do not know, but there is much favourable evidence, including Hitler's rage against his obdurate opponent Winston Churchill.

Let us return to the events of the war. On 22 May an Emergency Bill was voted in Britain which obliged women as well as men to serve, if not in the armed forces, then in the armaments industry. This Bill was rushed through the Commons and the Lords in a single afternoon and signed the same evening by the King. With it a degree of mobilisation was achieved which was far higher than in Germany. Germany basically only followed suit in 1942 or 1943 when the energetic Albert Speer was appointed Minister of Armaments with comprehensive powers.

But mobilisation required time. The equipment the Army had lost in France could be replaced only gradually, and with American help. The greatest short-falls were in tanks and anti-tank guns. In August 1940 there were only eight infantry divisions deployed in southern England for the repulse of a German invasion. By September there were thirteen, plus two armoured divisions. In addition there were several hundred thousand, mostly sparsely equipped men for local defence in the Home Guard. In a battle on the Continent this force would have been overwhelmed in a twinkling.

But the *Wehrmacht* had to cross the Channel, and therein lay the problem. A surprise attack as in Norway was out of the question, and there were soon more than 800 ships, ranging from destroyers to armed patrol boats, available for defence. While aircraft could hit at this swarm of hornets, they could hardly drive it away or destroy it. Events during the British evacuation from Dunkirk had already shown up the limited effectiveness of the *Luftwaffe*. The German Navy, on the other hand, was far inferior to its opponent, and weakened further by the losses in Norway. Even if the establishment of a beach-head on the coast of England were to succeed in the first rush of attack, the supply of troops, tanks, guns, vehicles, ammunition and fuel would have to be provided for over an extensive period of time.

The German Navy had already prepared plans for invasion some time earlier, and with the conquest of the Netherlands, Belgium and northern France the preconditions appeared to have been fulfilled. On 21 May, and then again on 20 June, Admiral Raeder, Commander-in-Chief of the Navy, discussed these plans with Hitler. Operation 'Sealion' began to take shape. On 2 July the first directives were issued, and on 16 July Hitler decided to have all the necessary preparations made. These were to be completed in August, and when this proved impossible, by mid-September.[22] There were, however, no specialised landing craft such as the Allies used later. Therefore all half-way serviceable ships were confiscated in Germany and in the occupied countries and brought to the Channel ports. Whether they actually would have fulfilled their purpose remains a moot question because the invasion never took place. Many vessels — ferries for example — appeared to be quite exotic.

Controversy broke out between the German Navy and the Army. The Army wanted a widely spread landing operation; the Navy claimed that it could, at best, only guarantee a narrow corridor between Calais and Dover. As planning progressed, so too did the unease grow. In a fit of rage the Chief of the General Staff, Colonel-General Halder, declared that if he were to agree to what the Navy was proposing, he might just as well put his troops 'through the meat-grinder straight away'.

On the other shore, it says in Churchill's memoirs:

. . . our many anxieties and self-questionings led to a steady increase in the confidence with which . . . we had viewed the invasion project. On the other hand, the more the German High Command and the Fuehrer looked at the venture the less they liked it. We could not of course know each other's moods and valuations; but with every week from the middle of July to the middle of September the unknown identity of views upon the problem between the German and British Admiralties, between the German Supreme Command and the British Chiefs of Staff, and also between the Fuehrer and the author of this book, became more definitely pronounced. . . .[23]

There was one point which was never in dispute between the German admirals and generals: the precondition for invasion was complete mastery of the air, and that was not their department. The responsibility lay with *Reichsmarschall* Hermann Göring, who set to work full of optimism. Numerically his *Luftwaffe* was far superior to the RAF — in fighters, for example, by a ratio of 2 to 1 — and until now he had always won. And so with an initial attack on 10 July the memorable Battle of Britain began, which reached its high point in August and September of 1940 and gradually fell off in October. After a phase of feeling each other out, the *Luftwaffe* attempted to destroy the enemy's air bases by unrelenting attacks and thereby actually did force the British into a critical situation. But on 7 September Göring gave the order to attack London from then on, and thereby made, in Churchill's words, a 'foolish mistake'.

The British had two advantages. In their Spitfire they had the best fighter aircraft of the day. The story is told that one day Göring asked the assembled commanders of his fighter squadrons what they would like to have from him. One of them answered: 'Spitfires!' — whereupon the insulted *Reichsmarschall* left the scene without saying goodbye. Secondly, many of the pilots and crews of aircraft shot down were still able to save themselves by parachute or by emergency landing. Because they were fighting over home territory their pilots were not lost to the British, whereas the Germans went into captivity. On the British side the losses in men were therefore lower than the losses in machines, and the decisive factor was the availability of experienced pilots.

Understandably enough, both sides overestimated their successes. Fighter pilots want to distinguish themselves and often report 'kills' even when the results are doubtful. The way human beings are made, fame has a magical attraction for us. This has been true through all the ages and is even more true for young people. That is why the Victoria Cross, established in 1856, was just as much sought after on the one side as the *Ritterkreuz*, which had replaced the *Pour le Mérite* in 1939, was on the other.[24] It is unsurprising, therefore, that between 10 July and the end of October the British counted 2,698 German machines shot down even though in fact the number was only 1,733. Against this stood a loss of 915 fighter aircraft.[25] But these losses could be replaced. The production of fighter aircraft increased by a factor of three between January and July 1940, and during the whole of the Battle of Britain the number of combat-ready machines remained almost constant: on 10 July there were 656, on 25 September 665.[26]

Meanwhile time was running out for Operation 'Sealion'. It would have to be launched no later than in September. In October either autumn storms or fog threatened and the nights quickly became longer. Yet it was only by day and with good visibility that the *Luftwaffe* could — provided it no longer had an opponent of its own — make even a show of protecting the invasion fleet. When, therefore, all of its efforts did not bring about victory, the plan of attack was first postponed until the coming spring, then to a time after victory over Russia, finally to disappear and never be seen again.

In a sacrificial battle, a few hundred young men had saved Great Britain. In the House of Commons Winston Churchill coined one of his memorable phrases: 'Never in the field of human conflict was so much owed by so many to so few.'[27]

Alone

When Churchill became Prime Minister on 10 May 1940 he also invented the office of Minister of Defence for himself. With this he took over not only the political but also the military leadership of the war. He achieved omnipotence, became a sort of 'Generalissimo' who could appoint and dismiss subordinate generals at will as, for example, in North Africa from Wavell through Auchinleck to Montgomery. *Alone* is the title of the second book in *Their Finest Hour*. What is meant, of course, is that for one bitter and glorious year, from 22 June 1940 to 22 June 1941, Great Britain stood alone in her battle against German superiority which reigned over Europe from the North Cape to Sicily and from Brest on the Bug river to Brest on the Atlantic coast. But the title can also be interpreted in another way: Churchill, and he alone and unrivalled, embodied British perseverance and the waging of war at any price.

The situation suggests a further comparison with Hitler. He too was the omnipotent political and military leader who embodied Germany triumphant. In the winter crisis of the Russian campaign he even assumed command of the Army on 19 December 1941, and in the course of the war he put tighter and tighter reins on his generals and replaced them at ever shorter intervals.[1]

But with this the possibility of comparison has already been exceeded and the contrasts become visible. Churchill had to convince his colleagues in the War Cabinet and the Members in the House of Commons. Despite all the friction, differences of opinion and sometimes even serious controversies — all of which occurred, of course — basic unanimity was preserved. To use a metaphor: Churchill was always the captain of a team, and not 'The *Führer*' to whom everyone had sworn unconditional obedience. Hitler, on the other hand, did decide and give orders directly and by himself. Cabinet meetings of the *Reich* Ministers under his direction were long things of the past. He directed the Party through Martin Bormann, propaganda through Joseph Goebbels, the armaments industry through Albert Speer, the SS state of terror and extermination through Heinrich Himmler, and all this in parallel to the normal systems of law and administration which also still existed. Haffner was quite correct when he spoke of a 'tamed chaos' which was controlled solely by the will of the *Führer* and which made him all-powerful.[2]

Churchill still read books;[3] Hitler did not. The latter's education process had long since ossified in what he had already acquired by reading. Churchill liked to travel, all the more so the longer the war lasted, and he describes the sometimes dramatic circumstances with visible relish. Adventure attracted him magically, just as if he were still the young lieutenant of Hussars in India or the Sudan. On D-Day, the day of the invasion on 6 June 1944, he would have preferred to land in France in person with the first wave of troops, and only an urgent admonition by the King held him back from actually doing so.[4] But four days later he was on the spot.[5]

Hitler withdrew into himself more and more. After the start of the Russian campaign he spent most of his time in the 'Wolf's Lair' in East Prussia, his dark vault of bunkers and barracks under a roof of leaves which hardly permitted a ray of sunlight to shine through. The only exceptions were his stays on the Obersalzberg. Churchill sought the public; Hitler avoided it and hardly gave speeches any more. He was indifferent to the sufferings of the people. Churchill, on the other hand, tells a story which is typical for him. After an air raid he visited a housing area south of the Thames where poorer people lived and where a particularly heavy bomb had destroyed several houses. He was immediately surrounded by more than a thousand people who waved to him and applauded him as if he were their saviour, touched him, wanted to shake his hand. Churchill's reaction:

> I was completely undermined, and wept. [General] Ismay, who was with me, records that he heard an old woman say: 'You see, he really cares. He's crying.' They were tears not of sorrow but of wonder and admiration. 'But see, look here,' they said, and drew me to the centre of the ruins.[6]

No scene has been recorded about Hitler which could be even remotely compared to this. He never visited a German city devastated by bombs, never talked to any people there.

Churchill as well as Hitler liked to talk, and both talked a lot. But Churchill spoke with friends and opponents of standing, Hitler preferably with
adjutants and secretaries, like the jovial boss who is holding forth in the factory canteen. Churchill lived with his family and had friends. Sometimes
he even tried to convert political associations into friendships, as for example in his relationship with President Roosevelt. Hitler had no friends; he
only saw Eva Braun—in every respect unimportant—during his visits to the
Obersalzberg. The only emotional tie which may have touched him and was
with him day by day was that to his Alsatian bitch Blondi.[7]

Enough! We return to Britain's lonely battle against Germany. Hitler and
Göring reacted to their failure in the Battle of Britain with increasingly more
enraged night attacks on London and other British cities, which were continued until the *Luftwaffe* was required in the Balkans in the spring of 1941 and
subsequently in Russia. The expectation, however, that such attacks could seriously damage the British armaments industry or break the will to resist of the
people turned out to be a mistake, as was subsequently to be the case with
the British air offensive against Germany, which we will discuss later. Anti-
aircraft artillery and British night fighters extracted a slowly increasing toll,
and Churchill describes the partially successful attempts to lead German
squadrons astray by interfering with their radio directional finding systems.[8]
But the attacks could not really be repulsed.

Of more practical importance was the battle at sea. If the enemy were to
succeed in cutting off supplies to Great Britain, the island empire would
be lost. However, attacks by German surface vessels—such as the battleships *Gneisenau* and *Scharnhorst*, the pocket-battleship *Admiral Scheer* and
the heavy cruiser *Admiral Hipper*—brought little success. The adventure of
the *Bismarck*, the most powerful battleship in the world at the time, ended in
May 1941, after the destruction of the battlecruiser *Hood*, in a catastrophe of
her own making. Later her sister-ship *Tirpitz* was sunk in a Norwegian fjord
by British bombs, and *Scharnhorst* in the Arctic Sea by British naval forces.
The aircraft carrier *Graf Zeppelin*, which could have become so important,
was built but never put into service. There was no longer a naval aviation
element anyway because Göring's jealousy, or vanity, had not permitted
any.[9]

But in the battle with the U-boats the issue really was life or death, and the
Battle of the Atlantic was more fateful for Great Britain than any other. 'The
only thing that ever really frightened me during the war was the U-boat

peril,' Churchill admitted in retrospect.[10] With the Norwegian fjords and the French Atlantic ports, the German submarines now had strategic points of departure of which the Imperial Navy in the First World War had not even been able to dream. All the more, therefore, did it make sense to build as many as possible, and in excess of one thousand were launched in the course of the conflict.[11]

The Royal Navy staked everything on the convoy system which had been successful in the First World War. Twenty, thirty or even fifty merchant ships sailed together, closely grouped into several columns. This was almost an adventure in itself. In rough seas and poor visibility, particularly at night with position lights extinguished, seamanship of the highest quality was required. Everything else depended on destroyers or other escorts protecting the convoys in sufficient numbers. But in the summer of 1940 it was the destroyers which were lacking. The strongest flotillas were required in the Channel to prevent the expected invasion, others in the Mediterranean after Italy had entered the war. Churchill therefore sent urgent calls for help to Roosevelt and requested older American ships which had been taken out of service. On 31 July 1940, for example, he wrote:

> Destroyers are frightfully vulnerable to air bombing, and yet they must be held in the air-bombing area to prevent seaborne invasion. We could not sustain the present rate of casualties for long, and if we cannot get a substantial reinforcement the whole fate of the war may be decided by this minor and easily-remediable factor.
>
> This is a frank account of our present situation, and I am confident, now that you know exactly how we stand, that you will leave nothing undone to ensure that fifty or sixty of your older destroyers are sent to me at once. I can fit them quickly with Asdics and use them against U-boats on the Western Approaches, and so keep the more modern and better-gunned craft for the Narrow Seas against invasion. Mr. President, with great respect I must tell you that in the long history of the world this is a thing to do *now*. Large construction is coming to me in 1941, but the crisis will be reached long before 1941. I know you will do all in your power, but I feel entitled and bound to put the gravity and urgency of the position before you.[12]

The deal was closed on 3 September 1940. The United States delivered the so urgently needed 50 destroyers and in exchange was granted ninety-nine-year leases on British naval bases in the Western Atlantic and the Caribbean. This exchange has frequently and bitterly been criticised in retrospect. On the one hand the number of combat-ready U-boats was still small in 1940; the Battle of the Atlantic only reached its apogee between 1941 and 1943.

On the other hand the American destroyers, almost fit for scrap, had to be thoroughly overhauled; by the end of 1940 most of them were still not ready for action. And for this the British naval bases had been given away for a long time. Was it worth it, or had Churchill not behaved 'hysterically'?

There are, however, also some counter-questions to be raised. Who could really know in the summer of 1940 what would happen in the next few weeks and months? Was it not therefore the duty of the British Prime Minister to do everything conceivable to save his country from catastrophe? Was not the deal also an important signal—for friend and foe alike—of the determination of the United States to support Britain? And do naval bases in the Caribbean—now truly seen with informed hindsight—actually still have the value that was once attributed to them?

In any case, the Battle of the Atlantic remained a battle of fate for Great Britain. More than half of the Allied merchant ships sunk during the Second World War were British. Of the 630 U-boats that did not return from combat patrol, 500 were destroyed by British naval and air forces.[13] Churchill was quite right when he wrote:

> The Battle of the Atlantic was the dominating factor all through the war. Never for one moment could we forget that everything happening elsewhere, on land, at sea, or in the air, depended ultimately on its outcome, and amid all other cares we viewed its changing fortunes day by day with hope or apprehension. The tale of hard and unremitting toil, often under conditions of acute discomfort and frustration and always in the presence of unseen danger, is lighted by incident and drama. But for the individual sailor or airman in the U-boat war there were few moments of exhilarating action to break the monotony of an endless succession of anxious, uneventful days. Vigilance could never be relaxed. Dire crisis might at any moment flash upon the scene with brilliant fortune or glare with mortal tragedy. Many gallant actions and incredible feats of endurance are recorded, but the deeds of those who perished will never be known. Our merchant seamen displayed their highest qualities, and the brotherhood of the sea was never more strikingly shown than in their determination to defeat the U-boat.[14]

From the other side we must add that the crews of the German submarines were pushed to the limits of their abilities and capacity for suffering, and that they suffered higher casualties than any other branch of the services.[15]

Some further comments on the course of the Battle of the Atlantic follow. In 1939 German submarines sank merchant ships of the order of 412,000 tonnes. In 1940 the number rose to 2,125,000 tonnes and remained at almost the same level in 1941. In 1942 it jumped to 6,250,000 tonnes. This was due in particular to successes in the Western Atlantic and the Caribbean, where the United States had — astonishingly enough — made no preparations for her defence. But the turn came in 1943: the sum of sinkings went down to 2,580,000 tonnes. At the same time Allied new construction reached 14,600,000 tonnes, primarily due to American series production. In 1944 sinkings then dropped to 770,000, and in 1945 to 260,000 tonnes.

This turn, which only made the massive intervention by the United States in the European war possible, was, of course, due to the constantly increasing deployment of ships and aircraft, and also to technical advances. The U-boats were basically still operating with the techniques of the First World War. On the surface they were powered by diesel engines and when submerged by electric motors whose batteries only permitted low speeds or quickly ran dry. Therefore attacks were generally carried out on the surface and at night. Only then did the boats dive down into the saving depths to avoid the enemy destroyers. This possibility disappeared with the development of radar. The U-boats could be detected before they reached their attack positions, and the hunters became the hunted and were additionally threatened by asdic detection. On top of that, the British succeeded in breaking the German radio codes and thereby learned where the U-boats were. Hunter groups could then be directed against them and the convoys re-routed to safer waters.[16]

The U-boat peril would have become unforeseeably greater if Spain had joined the Axis Powers. The approaches to Brest or St-Nazaire could still be watched and attacked by air from Britain, but not the Spanish bases far out in the Atlantic. Furthermore, Gibraltar would probably have been stormed and British entry into the Mediterranean sealed off. In Germany models of the Rock were already being made in order to prepare the attack.

In the Spanish Civil War, which began in 1936 and ended in 1939 shortly before the Second World War, Germany and Italy had supported General Franco and helped him to victory. Was it therefore not time, after the German triumph over France, to demand payment of the debt of gratitude? Hitler met with Franco on 23 October 1940 in Hendaye on the Franco-Spanish border. But this meeting was ill-starred. The *Caudillo* first angered the *Führer* by arriving late. He then swamped Hitler with words of admiration, but also with very concrete demands. Spain needed modern weapons in addition to regular deliveries of grain and fuel. In addition to Gibraltar, his spoils would have to include large areas of French colonial possessions.

And so forth. A hard bout of haggling began, about which Hitler later said to Mussolini that he would rather have three or four teeth pulled than to go through it again.

Further German urging did not lead to any better results. Franco behaved more cleverly than the Italian *Duce*. He kept on inventing excuses and further needs which would have to be satisfied before Spain joined the war. The operation against Gibraltar, planned for 10 January 1941, had to be cancelled in the end. Later, after the start of the campaign against Russia, Franco sent his 'Blue Division' to the Eastern Front in a grandiose gesture—and silently withdrew it again when the turn of the war became visible. By means such as these the dictator managed to survive until his natural demise in 1975.

Churchill was watching events in tense worry. He urged the American President to send Spain the grain Hitler was unable to deliver.[17] In retrospect he wrote:

> This great danger [Spain's joining the war] had in fact passed away. . . . It is fashionable at the present time to dwell on the vices of General Franco, and I am therefore glad to place on record this testimony to the duplicity and ingratitude of his dealings with Hitler and Mussolini.[18]

Must we therefore certify the rectitude of the Italian dictator by way of contrast? From initially despising Hitler he developed into his admirer, and then got on to the descending path which in the end led to his being shot by partisans on 28 April 1945 as the despised puppet of his Axis partner. He had entered the war with complete confidence of victory shortly before the French surrender in order to seize the chance which, as his son-in-law and Foreign Minister Count Ciano wrote, 'comes only once in five thousand years' and share in the spoils. Churchill's sarcastic comment was: 'Such chances, though rare, are not necessarily good.'[19]

The Italians' ability to fight turned out to be unexpectedly poor. On paper Mussolini disposed a strong army and a mighty fleet. But even the attack on long-defeated France turned into a disgrace. Occupation of the British island fortress of Malta, which was initially hardly capable of defence, was criminally neglected. British ships and planes operating from Malta were later able to attack the convoys supplying the forces in Libya. While the army stationed there did advance towards Egypt, it was soon brought to a standstill by numerically inferior British forces. The same happened in East Africa. The occupation of British Somaliland was followed by a British counter-attack.

The Italians were pushed back step by step and finally forced to surrender. On 5 May 1941 the hereditary ruler of Abyssinia, Emperor Haile Selassie I, again entered his capital of Addis Ababa, from which he had been driven five years earlier. The attempt to conquer Greece from Albania turned into an even greater disgrace. Not only did the Greek Army stand fast, it went over to the attack and advanced into Albania.

For a Britain fighting alone, the war with Italy was, of course, a heavy burden. While troops for the repulse of a German invasion had to be built up and equipped as quickly as possible at home, further troops and weapons had simultaneously to be shipped on the long route around Africa for the defence of Egypt. The Royal Navy not only had to defend its home island against invasion and protect the Atlantic convoys, but also to fight in the Mediterranean, divided in two as a western fleet in Gibraltar and an eastern fleet in Alexandria, while the Italian Navy occupied the superior central position.

Nevertheless, the British seized the initiative and made Churchill 'purr like six cats'.[20] On 11 November torpedo planes from the aircraft carrier *Illustrious* attacked the Italian Fleet at Taranto and damaged three battleships so heavily that they were out of action for many months.[21] On 9 February 1941 the task force from Gibraltar bombarded Genoa. In a battle off Cape Matapan in Greece on 28 March three Italian cruisers and two destroyers were sunk, while a battleship escaped with heavy damage. On 15 and 16 April British destroyers operating out of Malta put paid to a convoy off the Tunisian coast. Five days later British battleships and cruisers bombarded the port of Tunis.

Before that, on 9 December 1940, the army of General Wavell, composed of a colourful mixture of British, Australian, New Zealand and Indian units, had begun its offensive from Egypt which within two months was to lead more than 500km straight across Cyrenaica to El Agheila on the Great Sirte. The Italian army in North Africa was mostly destroyed and 130,000 prisoners were counted for a loss of 500 killed on the British side. Only difficulties of supply and the fact that troops had to be withdrawn in order to be able to employ them in Crete and on the Greek mainland brought the advance to a halt.

What was left for Hitler except coming to the aid of his hard-pressed accomplice? The deployment of the German *Afrika Korps* began in February 1941 under the command of a general who was as yet hardly known —

Erwin Rommel, who was quickly to become famous as the 'Desert Fox'. In order to hold down Malta and thus secure supplies to North Africa, a *Luft-flotte* (air fleet) was transferred to Sicily. And on 6 April 1941 the campaign in the Balkans began, crowned by the capture of Crete at the end of May. A period of British reversals began. But we are getting ahead of ourselves and must stop and look back. Churchill draws a proud summary for the fateful year of 1940:

> We were alive. We had beaten the German Air Force. There had been no invasion of the Island. The Army at home was now very powerful. London had stood triumphant through all her ordeals. . . .
>
> With a gasp of astonishment and relief the smaller neutrals and the subjugated states saw that the stars still shone in the sky. Hope, and within it passion, burned anew in the hearts of hundreds of millions of men. The good cause would triumph. Right would not be trampled down. The flag of Freedom, which in this fateful hour was the Union Jack, would still fly in all the winds that blew.[22]

And, if this were true, there was no one who deserved more gratitude than Winston Churchill, the indomitable opponent of tyranny.

A Hell
of a Mess

The British habit of first losing battles and then going on to win the wars continued in 1941. On 31 March General Rommel went over to the attack with the still relatively weak forces of his *Afrika Korps*. He forced the British into a costly withdrawal all the way to the Egyptian border. Only the fortress of Tobruk still proved to be invulnerable for the time being.

The chequered war in North Africa, which lasted until the German-Italian surrender in Tunis in May 1943, became uniquely popular with friend and foe alike, and has remained so, because while it was fought with utmost severity, it was also fought with an almost old-fashioned chivalry. A contributing factor to this was certainly that the battles mainly took place in desert areas in which no civilian population was involved. But probably even more important was Erwin Rommel's personality. Churchill paid his respects to his opponent:

> Throughout the African campaign Rommel proved himself a master in handling mobile formations, especially in regrouping rapidly after an operation and following up success. . . . At first the German High Command, having let him loose, were astonished by his successes, and were inclined to hold him back. His ardour and daring inflicted grievous disasters upon us, but he deserves the salute which I made him — and not without some reproaches from the public — in the House of Commons in January 1942, when I said of him, 'We have a very daring and skilful opponent against us, and, may I say across the havoc of war, a great general.' He also deserves our respect because, although a loyal soldier, he came to hate Hitler and all his works, and took part in the conspiracy of [20 July] 1944 to rescue Germany by displacing the maniac and tyrant. For this he paid the forfeit of his life. In the sombre wars of modern democracy chivalry finds no place. Dull butcheries on a gigantic scale and mass effects overwhelm all detached sentiment. Still, I do not regret or retract the tribute I paid to Rommel, unfashionable though it was judged.[1]

The loss of Crete hit British self-confidence even harder than the reversals in North Africa. When on 20 May 1941 German paratroopers, followed by mountain troops, began their landing operations, there had been six months to prepare a defence. Yet much had been neglected, one of the many reasons being a constantly changing high command.[2] Although the attackers suffered heavy casualties, including 2,071 killed and 1,788 missing, they prevailed against the initially numerically superior British and New Zealand forces. In the end all that was left once again was the evacuation of the vanquished, which also demanded heavy sacrifice by the Navy. A total of 12,245 men were captured. Churchill consoles his readers with a rather strange viewpoint:

> Goering gained only a Pyrrhic[3] victory in Crete; for the forces he expended there might easily have given him Cyprus, Iraq, Syria, and even perhaps Persia. . . . He was foolish to cast away such almost measureless opportunities and irreplaceable forces in a mortal struggle . . . with the warriors of the British Empire.[4]

What remains unsaid is how, without a navy and without air forces which by now were urgently required elsewhere, he was to reach Cyprus and even deeper into Asia. Maybe in the suspicion that he is talking nonsense, the author adds a quote from the record of an interrogation of a prisoner to his considerations on the battle for Crete:

> As regards the spirit and morale of the British troops, it is worth mentioning that in spite of the many setbacks to the conduct of the war there remains, generally, absolute confidence in Churchill.'[5]

The lack of naval and air forces, incidentally, led to the conquest of Crete losing all strategic importance. In the end the German occupation forces resembled, according to Churchill's quite accurate statement, 'prisoners who for the time being are guarding themselves'.

But in reality another aspect was far more important: the battles in the Mediterranean theatre tied down forces and cost time. Hitler had to postpone the start of his campaign against the Soviet Union from the originally planned 15 May to 22 June 1941. This war of conquest in the East had always been his goal, and the signing of the treaty of non-aggression in August 1939 only a calculated interim move. The gain in *Lebensraum* and raw materials were to lift his *Reich* to the level of an invulnerable world power. Britain's obdurate resistance played at least an indirect rôle in the decision to attack: if, as planned, a new and triumphant *Blitzkrieg* were to bring victory in 1941, the island kingdom would be faced with the alternatives either to submit to German hegemony after all or to continue fighting without any prospect of winning.

June 22 was a Sunday, flooded by the light of the summer sun. Yet it still marked the beginning of a darkening, a turning point in the Second World War. Right from the start the campaign in Russia was fought with a brutality such as had not been seen in recent European history. And it had little or nothing in common with the campaigns in France or North Africa. Law no longer applied, neither for soldiers nor for civilians. In the end the terrible revenge of the victors was to fall on the vanquished.

Churchill, the dyed-in-the-wool anti-Communist, was put in a strange situation by the German attack in the East. Until 21 June 1941 Stalin had been Hitler's accomplice, to whose unleashing of the war in September 1939 he had contributed decisively. He had brought home his share in the eastern European spoils and literally to the last minute continued to support Germany by deliveries of grain and raw materials. The Communist parties in the West had also discontinued their anti-Fascist struggle since 1939 — as Churchill grimly remarks in his look back at 1940: 'The smear of Communists who obeyed their Moscow orders gibbered about capitalist-imperialist war.'[6] But now, since dawn on 22 June, the accomplice of the enemy had turned, if not into Stalin the party comrade, then at least into a comrade in arms.

The allegedly omniscient father of the working class had let himself be completely surprised by the German attack despite all the warnings which had reached him, even from Britain. The Soviet leaders, Churchill writes,

> . . . had shown a total indifference to fate of the Western Powers, although this meant the destruction of that 'Second Front' for which they were soon to clamour. . . . War is mainly a catalogue of blunders . . . But so far as strategy, policy, foresight, competence are arbiters Stalin and his commissars showed themselves at this moment the most completely outwitted bunglers of the Second World War.[7]

In the evening of 21 June Jock Colville asked Churchill whether a partnership with Moscow would not get him, the arch-enemy of Communism, into a 'hell of a mess'. The reply was:

> Not at all. I have only one purpose, the destruction of Hitler, and my life is much simplified thereby. If Hitler invaded Hell I would make at least a favourable reference to the Devil in the House of Commons.[8]

The following evening Churchill gave a speech on the radio in which he said:

> No one has been a more consistent opponent of Communism than I have for the last twenty-five years. I will unsay no word that I have spoken about it. But all this fades away before the spectacle which is now unfolding. The past, with its crimes, its follies, and its tragedies, flashes away . . .
>
> I have to declare the decision of His Majesty's Government—and I am sure it is a decision in which the great Dominions will in due course concur—for we must speak out now at once, without a day's delay. I have to make the declaration, but can you doubt what our policy will be? We have but one aim and one single, irrevocable purpose. We are resolved to destroy Hitler and every vestige of the Nazi régime. From this nothing will turn us—nothing. We will never parley, we will never negotiate with Hitler or any of his gang.[9] We shall fight him by land, we shall fight him by sea, we shall fight him in the air, until, with God's help, we have rid the earth of his shadow and liberated its peoples from his yoke. Any man or state who fights on against Nazidom will have our aid. Any man or state who marches with Hitler is our foe. . . . That is our policy and that is our declaration. It folllows therefore that we shall give whatever help we can to Russia and the Russian people. . . .[10]

On 12 July 1941 Great Britain and the Soviet Union concluded a treaty of alliance in the battle against the common enemy. But what practical importance would this have? Everybody reckoned with a rapid collapse of the Soviet Union—not only Hitler and the German General Staff but the Western military experts too. Everyone recalled the Russian-Finnish 'Winter War' which lay only one and a half years in the past and in which the Red Army had played a pitiful rôle. And did not the initial successes of the *Wehrmacht*, its rapid advance, the gigantic pocket battles, the hordes of prisoners all speak a similar and clear language?

Yet two things were obvious. The Soviet Union now bore the brunt of the battle, not only by unheard of casualties in its fighting forces, but also by the sufferings of the civilian population.[11] And the longer the war lasted, the more its steadfastness impressed the people, the nations of the West. By this it regained the moral credit which its leaders had formerly coldbloodedly or foolishly gambled away. The past, with its foolishness, crimes and tragedies, actually did appear to be flying away as if it had never been.

Secondly, it was in the British interest to provide every conceivable aid so as to prevent a collapse. But for the time being there were only few possibilities. Rommel's attack in Africa was barely being contained. The Battle of the Atlantic was still a long way from being won and was tying down a major part of production capacity. Except on the long route via Persia, shipments to the Soviet Union could only be made by convoys to Murmansk, in a constant battle against U-boats and *Luftwaffe* forces operating from northern Norway. The convoy battles in the Arctic Ocean were among the hardest and most sacrificial the Royal Navy had to fight in the Second World War. At times no further ships could be sent because losses had become unbearable.[12]

And what about the 'Second Front' which not only the Soviets but also their adherents in the West were calling for ever more urgently? In anticipation of what was to become a long story, Churchill described the problems involved here in his considerations on the war in 1941:

> The Russians never understood in the smallest degree the nature of the amphibious operation necessary to disembark and maintain a great army upon a well-defended hostile coast. Even the Americans were at this time largely unaware of the difficulties. Not only sea but air superiority at the invasion point was indispensable. Moreover, there was a third vital factor. A vast armada of specially constructed landing-craft, above all tank landing-craft in numerous varieties, was the foundation of any successful heavily opposed landing. For the creation of this armada, as has been and will be seen, I had long done my best. It could not be ready even on a minor scale before the summer of 1943, and its power, as is now widely recognised, could not be developed on a sufficient scale till 1944. At the period we have now reached, in the autumn of 1941, we had no mastery of the enemy air over Europe, except in the Pas de Calais, where the strongest German fortifications existed. The landing-craft were only a-building. We had not even got an army in Britain as large, as well trained, as well equipped as the one we should have to meet on French soil. Yet Niagaras of folly and misstatement still pour out on this question of the Second Front. There was certainly no hope of convincing the Soviet Government at this or any other time. Stalin even suggested to me on one occasion later on that if the British were afraid he would be willing to send round three or four Russian Army Corps to do the job. It was not in my power, through lack of shipping and other physical facts, to take him at his word.[13]

In this text one senses, however, how far Churchill feels himself to have been put on the defensive by his war comradeship with Stalin and still to be surrounded by mistrust long afterwards. It was unfortunately not true that the past simply flew away. People felt that the fervent anti-Communist was quite capable of betraying his ally, or even assumed he had. Was it not in his nature—or in the British interest as he defined it—to sit back with arms folded, so to speak, while Hitler and Stalin were fighting each other for life or death, when Germany and Russia bled to death against each other?

Such a question is a grave injustice. Churchill's whole passion was committed, as he states, to the destruction of Nazi tyranny. He was therefore not spared the counter-accusation that he had let himself far too deeply and almost blindly into the comradeship with Stalin and had thereby forgotten and betrayed Poland.[14]

That is not true either, as we shall see. What does become visible, however, are the pressures on Churchill. He had got into a 'hell of a mess' unwittingly, out of which mere compliments to Satan could no longer extricate him. Hitler's attack on Russia did create a welcome relief for Britain, and, if the Soviet Union stood firm, unexpected prospects of victory. But at the same time the situation was no longer as simple and unequivocal as during the bitter but glorious year of standing alone. It had become complicated and contradictory: whatever the responsible British statesman did or left undone in the alliance with Stalin, it could be used against him, or actually be wrong. For the time being, however, the urgent question was: how could the war be waged effectively at all, and how could the hard-pressed ally be relieved as long as the Second Front still had to wait? The next chapter deals with the answer.

The
Barbaric War

It is part of human nature that man asks to be given commandments and then even obeys them as a rule. All things noble have to do with this: the appeal to conscience, the acceptance of responsibility, the fulfilment of duty, resistance against injustice, protection of the weak and oppressed, telling the truth even when it hurts.

'Thou shalt not kill' is one of the basic commandments. Living together only becomes possible when it is at least half-way observed. But the differentiation has always been made between 'in' and 'out', between friend and foe, between one's own group, tribe or nation and 'the others'. The lines of demarcation become visible by the fact that, where they extend, wars become possible that not only repeal the injunction against killing but turn it into its opposite. Down through all the ages and in all cultures, man has differentiated between the murderer, who is outlawed, and the warrior or soldier, who is revered as a hero when he takes foreign life and gives his own in exchange.

Pacifism would like to abrogate the difference and during the 1930s it reached a high point as a readily understandable reaction to the senselessly suicidal First World War. And then it ran into fundamental problems, of course. How should Hitler's tyranny be dealt with? One of its more sinister hallmarks was the breach of the taboo. The 'SS State' developed to become the core of the Third *Reich*. In it the proof of absolute power lay in the commandment 'Thou shalt not kill' being repealed with regard to the weak, the helpless, those 'unworthy of life' according to a simple *Führer* directive.[1] In retrospect no doubts can be admitted any longer: had we listened in time to those who, like Winston Churchill, admonished us to stand firm, and if

156

necessary to go to war against tyranny, we would have been spared having to gird our loins, now and forever, when looking back into the abyss.

And to scotch any lurking misunderstandings: in the age of 'globalisation', which affects far more than only economic relationships, the objectives of pacifism are no longer a luxury of peaceful people in times of peace but a necessity. Only if we succeed in transferring the injunction against killing from the part to the whole, from the individual nation to global society, will mankind have gained an even half-way secure chance of survival. We must only guard against the danger which still — or especially — threatens the most noble intentions, namely that they lead us into blindness, into misapprehending the differences.

This is also true historically. Wars are not all the same. There are marked differences in European history. The seventeenth century was a time of barbaric conflicts. One need but recall the Thirty Years' War which crippled Germany. Accidentally or even deliberately, sometimes incited by religious fervour, peasants and burghers, women and children were affected just as much as the armies.[2] Sometimes not military victory but the destruction of villages and towns, of whole regions, became the objective — as in the ravishing of the Palatinate by the French in 1689.

Things were different in the eighteenth and nineteenth centuries. A remarkable differentiation between the political-military sector and civilian society was achieved and for the most part observed. Ideally the population was not supposed to notice that their rulers were waging a war. Frederick the Great, Napoleon and Bismarck all unleashed wars under the flimsiest of pretexts, and highly questionable wars of aggression and conquest at that. But the Silesians remained Silesians whether as subjects of Maria Theresa or Frederick, and the Rhinelanders remained Rhinelanders even if they were first declared to be French and then to be Prussian. During the Seven Years' War the East Prussian Estates zealously paid tribute to the occupying power, in other words the Russian Tsarina, much to Frederick the Great's annoyance, but otherwise without any scruples, because they knew that after that they no longer had to fear for their livelihoods. What a contrast to the events in 1945!

The civilisation of war was a great cultural achievement of the European modern era, but was then destroyed in the twentieth century. In the First World War it was still preserved to a substantial degree. As horrifying as the slaughter at the Fronts was, it took place between armies and spared the

civilian population. Yet there were already danger signs: when Allied propaganda invented horror pictures of German atrocities in Belgium, it opened
the sluices to a hatred which excited the peoples and took effect. From this
followed the inability after the war to conclude a wise peace aimed at reconciliation, instead of at the return and increase of evil.

In the Second World War there is a distinct fissure. Hitler crossed the line
with Operation 'Barbarossa', the opening of the campaign against the Soviet
Union. From the beginning he was not aiming at a military victory but at
the conquest of *Lebensraum* and thus, to achieve this goal, the enslavement
or destruction of the 'inferior' races, to which—besides the Jews—the Slavs
also belonged. The persecutors and exterminators followed on the heels of
the soldiers. Meanwhile there is a controversy about how far the *Wehrmacht*
let itself become involved in the crime.[3] But the roots go far deeper. Whoever treats at all with the barbarities of persecution and destruction can no
longer prevent their spilling over into the conduct of war. In this sense we
must talk about the guilt of the generals in the year of peace 1934, when the
Reichswehr stood by and watched during the orgy of murder in the 'Röhm
Putsch'. Gordon A. Craig was quite correct when he wrote at the end of his
book about the Prussian-German Army:

> Until the very end the commanders of the German armies continued to display
> the technical virtuosity and physical courage that had always been a characteris-
> tic of the Prussian officers' corps since its resurrection after Jena and Auerstedt.
> But what most of them did not display during these final years of desperation
> was what they had already not displayed when Hitler stood on the threshold of
> the Chancellorship in 1933, what they had not displayed when he let his killer
> gangs loose against the people in June 1934, what they had not displayed when
> Schleicher was murdered and Fritsch demoted, namely a trace of that moral cour-
> age, that intellectual independence, that deep patriotism, which distinguished
> such great soldiers of the past as Scharnhorst, Boyen and Gneisenau. Without these
> attributes their other capabilities were worthless, and they themselves powerless
> to avert the catastrophe which to such a large degree was the result of their own
> lack of political responsibility.[4]

If we were to arm ourselves with the political cynicism of a Talleyrand,
it would be appropriate to repeat what he is alleged to have said to Napoleon after the abduction and execution of the Duke d'Enghien: 'Sire, that
was worse than a crime, that was a mistake.' In the Russian campaign, the
barbaric way the war was waged prevented its being won. When two and
a half million prisoners of war were left to starve to death, it was only natu-

ral that resistance by the Red Army stiffened to the extreme. When extermination squads followed on the heels of the armies, it became inevitable that partisans soon reigned where initially the German soldiers had been welcomed with flowers or with salt and bread, the traditional symbols of hospitality, in the hope of liberation from Stalinism. Liberators find allies; exterminators themselves become entangled in death and extermination. Seen in this sense, even cynicism resolves itself: crimes and mistakes no longer form an either/or, but an interlinked system.

After this rather involved prologue, we now approach Winston Churchill. In his history of the First World War he had impressively described the decline of the art of war, its fall into monotonous slaughter. And like a *leitmotiv* through his portrayal of the Second World War as well, and on through the sum of his speeches and articles, runs his complaint about the degeneration of war, which can be traced back just as much to the amalgamation of state and society in the age of democracy or of totalitarian regimes as to the advances in the technologies of destruction. In the end, and faced with nuclear weapons, the old man became a prophet of peace, and this must be valued all the more highly when we consider that with this the born warrior, the descendant of the Duke of Marlborough, said goodbye to the dream and the adventure of his life. He had recognised that the great achievement of the European modern era, the civilisation of war, could no longer be saved.

But the question must be asked whether Churchill himself did not make a fatal contribution to this relapse into barbarity. He was politically responsible for unleashing the war of bombing and destruction against German cities, which hardly hit military objectives or arms factories but instead the civilian population all the more, and deliberately so.[5]

Of course there are excuses — first the appeal to the crimes of the enemy. On Hitler's request Göring's *Luftwaffe* had attacked British cities between the autumn of 1940 and the spring of 1941 and sown destruction to the best of its ability. It was only the insufficiency of the means which set limitations. Göring would have liked very much to 'eradicate' the cities in the way Hitler had announced with such hatred. Hitler, in his turn, pointed to earlier British attacks on Berlin and other German cities.

But these appeals are of little worth and we must reject them. Hitler wanted to force Great Britain to surrender, and he was prepared to employ any means. Churchill wanted to vanquish Germany, and the bombing war served this purpose. In any case, no crime can be justified by pointing to another crime. Whoever attempts this is only promoting crime.

It is therefore more fruitful to explore the motives which unleashed barbarity. In first place we find the illusions. Hitler and Göring probably actually did believe they could bomb Britain into surrender if this could not be achieved in any other way. That this was an illusion has been described by no one as impressively as by Churchill himself.[6] The far more likely result was the awakening of defiance: Do your worst! It is therefore all the more difficult to understand that Churchill and his military advisers fell prey to the same illusion. Why did their own experience not warn them? And should they not have to take into consideration what they were constantly emphasising elsewhere, namely that once he had established his tyranny, the Germans hardly had a choice except to submit to their *Führer*?

The technical problems were much more difficult. Far too often it is the means which determine the action, and the technical possibilities that are available are applied. The four-engine Lancaster bomber, which had been developed for the bombing war, was capable of carrying heavy bomb loads over long distances, and it was far superior to the standard German bomber, the He 111. But in daylight raids losses would have been unbearable. It was only the American Flying Fortresses which brought about a new situation, and they too only achieved real success after they were accompanied by fighter aircraft of comparable range. In night attacks, however, cities or city districts could be hit, but individual arms factories could not be pin-pointed. Furthermore, the greatetst effects were not achieved by explosive bombs but by incendiaries, especially when individual fires joined together to form devastating firestorms. This was possible within the concentrated build-up of inner cities or housing areas, but hardly in spread-out industrial sites or suburbs, in which every garden acted like an isolating protective wall.

The firestorm capable of devastating large areas was generated for the first time in the attacks on Hamburg from 24 July to 3 August 1943. A later example is the attack on Dresden on 13 and 14 February 1945. In both cases the number of victims is estimated to have been at least 50,000 dead. The destruction of the Saxon 'Florence on the Elbe River' is also quite macabre for the reason that it took place at a time when the war had long been decided. But it belongs to the bitter experiences, and not only in the Second World War, that once barbarism has been unleashed it can no longer be contained. In the final days of the war the historic city centres of Würzburg,

Hildesheim, Paderborn and Münster were destroyed, and finally, on 12 and 13 April 1945, Potsdam. In 400,000 sorties during the course of the war, the RAF dropped one million tonnes of bombs, two-thirds of which fell on Germany. The number of German civilians killed in air attacks is estimated rather conservatively at 500,000.

In retrospect Churchill writes:

> In judging the contribution to victory of strategic air-power [i.e. Bomber Command] it should be remembered that this was the first war in which it was fully used. We had to learn from hard-won experience. . . . We certainly underestimated the strong latent reserve in Germany's industry and the great resources she had gained from Occupied Europe. Thanks to well-organised relief measures, strict police action, and innate discipline and courage, the German people endured more than we had thought possible. But although the results of the early years fell short of our aims we forced on the enemy an elaborate, ever-growing but finally insufficient air defence system which absorbed a large proportion of their total war effort. . . .[7]

That, however, is a pathetic result, and one simply cannot help but ask the counter-question: how much of the British war effort was consumed by the build-up and maintenance of Bomber Command? Was it less? Would increased production of tanks, destroyers or landing craft not have achieved far more?

Regarded soberly, we must speak about a total failure. A huge armaments effort was made for nothing, and the young bomber pilots and crews who were shot down sacrificed themselves senselessly. The German arms industry — hardly affected — increased production month by month, year by year, until the summer of 1944, and the claim by Air Marshal Arthur Harris that the bombing war would bring Germany to her knees turned out to be just as untenable as the claim by the German admirals in the First World War that unrestricted submarine warfare would bring victory. Crimes and mistakes, tied together once more. In the end an astonishing effort — when seen purely technically — only led to death by burning of human beings and the destruction of irreplaceable historic buildings.

Such a result again demands raising the question of the motive. At the beginning of the war Prime Minister Chamberlain had declared in the Commons:

> No matter how far others may go, for purposes of terror His Majesty's Government will never take recourse to a deliberate attack against women and children or other civilian persons.[8]

There was, therefore, a clear awareness of barbaric war—and the line of demarcation around it.

Why, then, did Churchill and his War Cabinet decide in favour of exactly this barbaric war against the civilian population? Why did they support it with all possible means, and doggedly cling to it until 1945? A possible answer must be: for reasons of helplessness, if not desperation. Foreseeably, and taken by itself, the British Army was never a match for the German Army. The Navy protected the country and its vital lines of supply, but there was little it could achieve against a Continental power. What else was left that could make a British contribution to victory except the RAF?

And how else, except by elaborate bombing attacks, could one reply even half-way credibly to the Russian calls for effective relief? In the end a not unimportant reason was the easing of one's own feelings of guilt towards the ally who was making such heavy sacrifices: are we not obviously doing all we can?[9] That the Soviet leaders were not impressed, that they judged more soberly and insisted on the opening of a land front, is another matter entirely.

Helplessness underlaid by desperation: the situation recalls once again the demands of German admirals for the unrestricted employment of submarines in the First World War, which became all the more insistent the more the battlefleet proved itself to be useless and the land battle got bogged down in the trenches. It even reminds us of the employment of German 'weapons of retaliation' against London in the summer of 1944. Top technology, militarily useless, but still borne up by hope, by a belief in a turn towards a victory for which all other prospects had disappeared. Helplessness apparently must lead to an illusion of which, if only it is technically innovative enough and therefore has the appearance of being a miracle, one can readily convince oneself.

While helplessness does not in any way excuse barbaric war, it at least helps to explain it.

A Community
of Fate

On Sunday 7 December 1941 Churchill spent the evening in Chequers with John Winant, the American Ambassador, and Averell Harriman, President Roosevelt's Special Envoy. The radio reported, quite uncertainly to begin with, a Japanese attack on American shipping off Hawaii. A telephone call to the White House in Washington provided clarification. 'Mr. President,' Churchill asked, 'what's this about Japan?' 'It's quite true,' was Roosevelt's reply. 'They have attacked us at Pearl Harbor. We are all in the same boat now.' 'Ah . . . This certainly simplifies things. God be with you.'

Churchill makes no bones about his feelings:

No American will think it wrong of me if I proclaim that to have the United States at our side was to me the greatest joy. I could not foretell the course of events. I do not pretend to have measured accurately the martial might of Japan, but now at this very moment I knew the United States was in the war, up to the neck and in to the death. So we had won after all! Yes, after Dunkirk; after the fall of France; after the horrible episode of Oran; after the threat of invasion, when, apart from the Air and the Navy, we were an almost unarmed people; after the deadly struggle of the U-boat war—the first Battle of the Atlantic, gained by a hand's-breadth; after seventeen months of lonely fighting and nineteen months of my responsibility in dire stress. We had won the war. England would live; Britain would live; the Commonwealth of Nations and the Empire would live. How long the war would last or in what fashion it would end no man could tell, nor did I at this moment care. Once again in our long Island history we should emerge, however mauled or mutilated, safe and victorious. We should not be wiped out. Our history would not come to an end. We might not even have to die as individuals. Hitler's fate was sealed. . . .[1]

Contemptuously Churchill then brushes aside the claim that the Americans did not know how to fight, and would at best join the war half-heartedly. This idea played a rôle in the Second World War, the importance of which can hardly be underestimated. Time and again Hitler went on about the 'decadence' of the Western democracies and probably actually did believe that they would not be a match for soldierly, determinedly led nations. The same applies to the Japanese, who were led astray by their sword-proud Samurai tradition.[2]

Churchill knew better. He was half-American and he knew American military history, in which the general staffs in Europe — and, obviously, also in Japan — had shown hardly any interest. For his *History of the English-Speaking Peoples*, which was written but had not yet been published, he had studied the largest war of the nineteenth century, which had taken place not in Europe but in America — the conflict between the Union and the Confederacy from 1861 to 1865. And while the military leader of the South, Robert E. Lee, 'had been one of the noblest Americans who had ever lived, and one of the greatest commanders known to history',[3] the civilian society of the North created an army of millions almost out of nothing and then fought on inexorably until the South surrendered unconditionally.[4]

What had been possible once would happen again. In a speech he gave in the Pentagon in 1946 before the American Joint Chiefs of Staff, Churchill said:

> I very much admired how the American Army was built up. It was a masterpiece of organisation and improvisation. There have been many examples of large nations wishing to create large armies for themselves, and with sufficient money, time, discipline and sense of duty this became possible. But the speed with which the small American Army of only a few hundred thousand men which existed before the war was turned into an army of millions is unique in military history, almost a miracle . . . It is an achievement the soldiers of other nations will always regard with admiration and envy.
>
> And this is not the whole story and not even its most important aspect. To create a large army is one thing, to deploy and lead it something else entirely. It will always remain a mystery to me how it was possible from the very small beginnings which existed in the United States during peace, not only to build up an Army and an Air Force, but to find the commanders and to form the huge staffs who were capable of leading such gigantic masses and moving them faster and further than this had ever been done before in a war.[5]

It was exactly this capability of a democratic civilian society to wage war that was completely misjudged by both the political potentates and the generals and staffs, the professional soldiers in Germany and Japan. The pride of the military nations rich in tradition led to their blindness. Churchill, on the other hand, was sure that the United States would take up the Japanese challenge of Pearl Harbor — and Hitler's declaration of war which followed four days later — with the utmost determination. He knew that no one could withstand American economic output once it had been fully mobilised for war:

> I thought of a remark which Edward Grey[6] had made to me more than thirty years before — that the United States is like 'a gigantic boiler. Once the fire is lighted under it there is no limit to the power it can generate.'

Churchill ends his report on 7 December 1941 almost like that of 10 May 1940, the day of his appointment as Prime Minister: 'Being saturated and satiated with emotion and sensation, I went to bed and slept the sleep of the saved and thankful.'

Churchill strove persistently for a war alliance with the United States, and possibly for a close and lasting connection beyond that. He regarded it as vital, not only for the oppressive present but for the future as well. The words with which he began a speech on 9 January 1941 are characteristic and go far beyond the actual event:[7]

> It is not an exaggeration when we say that the future of the world and the hopes of a civilisation based on Christian values depend on the relationships between the British Empire or Commonwealth and the USA. The unanimity of purpose and the firm determination of the whole English-speaking world will, more than any other circumstance, decide the conditions of life for future generations, possibly the centuries which will follow upon our own.

For Churchill the success or failure of political relationships also depended on personal relationships, and here this meant, in concrete terms, on his relationship with Roosevelt:

> Therefore [he remarks a little later in the same speech] it is a highly fortunate circumstance that in this fateful hour a famous statesman stands at the head of the United States, a man with long experience in government, in whose heart burns the fire of resistance against aggression and persecution, and whose nature, whose sympathies, make him an honest and upright protagonist of justice, liberty and all victims of injustice.[8]

This was not extravagant praise; it was Churchill's honest conviction.

One of the important preparatory steps for the war alliance had already been taken when Roosevelt and Churchill met on board the American cruiser *Augusta* and the British battleship *Prince of Wales*[9] in August 1941 in

Placentia Bay, Newfoundland. Here the mutual objectives were formulated and made known to the world as the 'Atlantic Charter'. Its principles later formed the basis for the founding of the United Nations.[10]

After the Japanese attack on Pearl Harbor Churchill was in a hurry to go to America. He set sail on 12 December in the battleship *Duke of York*, which had just recently been placed in service. What was important now was to give the alliance its contours, the right contours. While the winter storms tossed the vessel about, the British Prime Minister and his staff were beset by a worry: would the United States possibly turn in the wrong direction?

> We looked forward with eagerness, but also with some anxiety, to our first direct contact as allies with the President and his political and military advisers. We knew before we left that the outrage of Pearl Harbour [*sic*] had stirred the people of the United States to their depths. The official reports and the Press summaries we had received gave the impression that the whole fury of the nation would be turned upon Japan. We feared lest the true proportion of the war as a whole might not be understood. We were conscious of a serious danger that the United States might pursue the war against Japan in the Pacific and leave us to fight Germany and Italy in Europe, Africa, and in the Middle East.[11]

With their declarations of war on the United States, however, Hitler and Mussolini had already done much to allay these concerns. They were soon to prove to be groundless anyway. The comradeship in war was still brand new and untouched, freshly caught, so to speak, not under pressure anywhere because of reversals, rivalries and disappointments, which inevitably occur with the duration of a partnership. Roosevelt and Churchill appeared to be inseparable. They ate together, even visited each other in their bedrooms. The talks all took place in a hearty atmosphere, all the planning aimed at agreement. The most important decision reached, and for Churchill the crucial one, was expressed in two words: 'Europe first!'

Even the strategic planning was already becoming visible in its outlines. It said, roughly speaking, that a substantial landing operation in France was to be prepared under full power and thereby the 'Second Front' created which the Russians were demanding. But since the preparations would take time—until 1943 as was originally assumed—a campaign in the Mediterranean was to be conducted in the meanwhile. Its importance and strategic objectives were mercifully left hidden for the moment. It was only later that discrepancies, even contrasts, were to appear in the evaluations.

Churchill used the opportunity to speak about the subject closest to his heart. At Christmas a large crowd gathered before the White House and he and Roosevelt gave short addresses. Churchill began with the words:

> I spend this anniversary and festival far from my country, far from my family, yet I cannot truthfully say that I feel far from home. Whether it be the ties of blood on my mother's side, or the friendships I have developed here over many years of active life, or the commanding sentiment of comradeship in the common cause of great peoples who speak the same language, who kneel at the same altars, and, to a very large extent, pursue the same ideals, I cannot feel myself a stranger here in the centre and at the summit of the United States. I feel a sense of unity and fraternal association . . .[12]

Two days later Churchill spoke before Congress and, as he recounts, not without stage fright, because he had never before spoken in another parliament besides the House of Commons. And almost as if to reassure and justify himself after the fact, he points in retrospect to his bloodline, which on his mother's side could be traced back over five generations to a lieutenant in the army of George Washington, and could be based on that. Moreover, '. . . once again I had the feeling, for mentioning which I may be pardoned, of being used, however unworthy, in some appointed plan.'[13]

The stage fright then quickly disappeared:

> I must confess that I felt quite at home, and more sure of myself than I had sometimes been in the House of Commons. What I said was received with the utmost kindness and attention. I got my laughter and applause just where I expected them. . . .

At the close of his speech Churchill said to thunderous applause:

> It is not given to us to peer into the mysteries of the future. Still, I avow my hope and faith, sure and inviolate, that in the days to come the British and American peoples will for their own safety and for the good of all walk together side by side in majesty, in justice, and in peace.[14]

When one looks back at December 1941 from a distance of over half a century, there are many questions. First, was the formation of the Grand Alliance really the turning point of the war? Did it carry within it the assurance of victory as Churchill believed? Yes, with certainty. No matter how great the efforts and sacrifices might become which Germany and Japan were to make, what successes they were still to achieve in the short term, their downfall was only a matter of time. There was no counter to the fully mobilised industrial power and military might of the United States.

Incidentally, for the war in Russia the turning point must also be localised in December 1941, and not only in the Battle of Stalingrad one year later. The Germany Army was taken by surprise by the onset of winter—something that is totally inconceivable. How grotesque does it appear that it was only now, in December, that appeals were made at home for donations of winter clothing! Had there been no foresight? Had no one read and no one taken to heart what had happened to Napoleon's *Grande Armée* on the retreat from Moscow?

The Germans should have dug in for defence in half-way winter-proof positions no later than after the great double victory of Bryansk and Vyazma in the first half of October. But they foolishly continued the advance until everything broke down under the hammer blows of the cold—weapons, engines, supplies. And masses of soldiers, at best equipped for a winter in southern France, suffered frostbite. Withdrawals became necessary, and the losses of men and *matériel* were enormous. What was probably most important of all was that the confidence in victory of the German Army was shattered, while the self-confidence and battle experience of the Red Army grew accordingly. The balance of power shifted substantially and lastingly, and it had to go on shifting with the further duration of the war because the German campaign had been designed only for the short term and for a rapid victory. The reserves in time which large nations and sea powers enjoy were lacking.

To return to Washington and Churchill. How are we to interpret his rapturous hyperbole on destiny and blood-brotherhood? Was there a hopeless romantic hidden somewhere inside the determined warrior? Did he not wager far too much, too enthusiastically and too uncritically on his personal relationship, his friendship with Roosevelt, instead of weighing interests with a cool heart? Did he render Great Britain helpless by delivering her to the United States? Many critics see this as being so, then as now.[15]

But whoever judges romanticism should do so as soberly as possible. To begin with, from 1940, when she mobilised her total economy for war, Great Britain was completely dependent on the United States economically and financially. Civilian exports came to a halt for all practical purposes, foreign currency reserves were quickly exhausted and the country reached the brink of insolvency by the end of the year. The way out was the Lend-Lease Bill which Congress passed on 11 March 1941. It empowered the President to supply states whose defence was—in his judgement—vital to the interests of the United States with war materials and goods.[16] It was clear to everyone involved that this was based on a fiction: very little if any of the 'lent' or 'leased' *matériel* would ever be returned to the United States. Subject to their discretion, they were financing Britain's continuation of the struggle.

This was the situation an economic and financial expert such as Neville Chamberlain had foreseen and always feared. To prevent it he committed all of his strength to the salvation of the peace in 1938. But what other possibilities were there when war came after all and Hitler triumphed over France in the summer of 1940? The alternative to resistance at any price was negotiating with the victor, and this could only lead to something if Great Britain recognised Hitler's hegemony on the Continent and was content to accept her impotent, basically only tolerated position on the sidelines. Anyone who still considers that feasible in retrospect, with the knowledge of all the crimes, in the face of Auschwitz, should stand up and say so, instead of hypocritically complaining about Churchill's having devoted himself completely to the Atlantic Alliance.

The spiritual fronts were of more importance than the material questions anyway: here democracy, which was defending the basic human right to life, liberty and the pursuit of happiness; there tyranny, with its heroically darkened claim for the rule of the chosen and the subjugation or destruction of the inferior. Churchill and Roosevelt both believed in this front, and in this they were, and remained, in complete agreement. Not only the war alliance but also the community of fate of the English-speaking peoples had their foundations here.

This did not, of course, exclude differences of opinion and sometimes even contradictions. For example, Churchill, in his old-fashioned way, still clung to the Empire, as we have already seen by the example of India. For the Americans the British Empire was at best a matter of indifference, but basically something suspicious. On what other claim besides the traditional hegemony of Europe were colonial possessions based? Had the United States themselves not once been a 'colony' that had severed itself from British rule? What else was the Declaration of Independence of 1776 all about? Were the Americans therefore not the first-born, the natural advocates, so to speak, of the desire for liberty of colonies all over the world?

Incidentally, anti-colonial beginnings tend to lead to a penchant towards a moral either/or, which in any given situation preceives only either the children of light or the children of darkness.[17] And so the Americans tended to number the Soviet leaders among the children of light following Hitler's attack on the Soviet Union, so that a limited alliance of convenience appeared to them as being cynical, an expression of that European *realpolitik* — instead of moral politics — they had always mistrusted.[18] What this was to lead to, in the end much to Churchill's despair, will be shown in the next chapter.

When we look at Churchill we come to a surprising conclusion. On the one hand we can actually detect the old-fashioned in him, and in many respects he was and remained a man of the nineteenth century from youth to old age. On the other hand he led forward into the future, into a world already beyond national boundaries. It was not these which were important to him, but the front of liberty against tyranny, and out of this stemmed — in his belief not for the moment but for the duration — the community with the United States which 'destiny' had ordained. Seen from here, it is the critics who accuse him of having sold out the national interests who suddenly find themselves in the position of being old-fashioned.

Churchill's stay in Washington, with an excursion to Ottawa, lasted for almost a month, from December 1941 until January 1942. When it was over a powerful American flying boat took him to Bermuda, where *Duke of York* and her destroyer screen were waiting. But the return home had become pressing. Events, particularly in East Asia, were taking place thick and fast. The question arose whether the flying boat could not be used. Why not, provided it was only loaded with very few people and much fuel?

After a night flight lasting many hours a safe landing was made at Portsmouth. But in parting the captain said that he had never been so relieved in his whole life as at this moment. As it turned out, he had gone off course and almost flown over the German batteries at Brest. The course correction at the last moment had resulted in the aircraft approaching England not from the west but from the south. It was therefore taken for an enemy bomber and Hurricanes were sent up to shoot it down. 'However, they failed in their mission.' One can sense in Churchill's report how much he enjoyed this sort of adventure in his travels. Therefore many, often risky flights were to follow.[19]

Between
Bulls and Bears

'We had won', Churchill cheered after the Japanese attack on Pearl Harbor. A little less prematurely he should have said: 'The road to victory now lay before us.' Yet it, too, was initially paved with defeats.

In the ensuing months the successes by U-boats reached their peak, primarily in American and Caribbean waters to the tacit satisfaction of the British but in any case at the expense of the Allies. The catastrophe in East Asia, on the other hand, was of Britain's making. The Japanese landed in Malaya and sank the battleship *Prince of Wales* and the battlecruiser *Repulse* while they were trying to prevent them. Then the Japanese advanced south. And while in the Philippines the American fortress of Corregidor tenaciously defended itself until 6 May 1942, the supposedly invulnerable Singapore fell on 15 February in a virtual *coup de main*. This was not only one of the heaviest defeats in the long and glorious history of the British military, but also a highly embarrassing one. It was not the Japanese attackers who had been numerically superior, but the British defenders. There were, however, no defences in Singapore on the landward side because no one had thought of building any.

Churchill only learned of this fatal circumstance in January when it was too late to do anything, and he emphasises that he does not intend to excuse himself:

I should have known. My advisers should have known and have told me. I should have asked. The reason I did not is that I could as little imagine fortress Singapore having no defences on the landward side as I could a battleship being launched without deck plates.[1]

The war in North Africa was progressing even more badly. By means of a daring advance in January, Rommel had again destroyed all the temporary progress General Auchinleck had made. At the end of May he began a further offensive. Tobruk surrendered on 21 June. At the end of June the German *Afrika Korps* reached Egyptian soil at El Alamein and stood only 100km from Alexandria. Only the exhaustion of the soldiers and the lack of supplies prevented a further advance. Mussolini, it was reported, was already practising his entry into Cairo mounted proudly on a white horse.

One can feel the horror which still overcame Churchill when he looked back years later. In his history of the Second World War he writes:

> This was one of the heaviest blows I can recall during the war. Not only were its military effects grievous, but it affected the reputation of the British armies. At Singapore eighty-five thousand men had surrendered to inferior numbers of Japanese. Now in Tobruk a garrison of twenty-five thousand (actually thirty-three thousand) seasoned soldiers had laid down their arms to perhaps one-half of their number. If this was typical of the morale of the Desert Army, no measure could be put upon the disasters which impended in North-East Africa . . . It was a bitter moment. Defeat is one thing; disgrace is another.[2]

That criticism arose is readily understandable — criticism, too, of Churchill. 'God knows where we would be without him, but God alone knows where we will get to with him,' noted Sir Alan Brooke, the Chief of the Imperial Staff no less.[3] Churchill himself felt the scepticism which had already met him immediately upon his return from Washington in January. He therefore took the offensive and asked for a vote of confidence in the Commons. In the debate from 27 to 29 January 1942 he unfolded all of his artistry. In the end he even congratulated his critics on their 'excellent speeches'. Was it not a good sign of the vitality of British democracy that such speeches could be held at this moment, at a time of crisis? By this the father Winston also demonstrated to his son Randolph, who had vehemently attacked the critics head on, how really to deal with them — not by inciting them further, but by taking the wind out of their sails. Churchill won the vote of confidence by the triumphant majority of 464 to 1.[4]

A few months later, after the fall of Tobruk, a vote of no confidence was brought in, significantly not by Labour MPs but by the Conservative side, reading that

> . . . this House, while paying tribute to the heroism and endurance of the Armed Forces of the Crown in circumstances of exceptional difficulty, has no confidence in the central direction of the war.

The comprehensive powers the Prime Minister had were to be drastically curtailed. In his reply Churchill said:

> I do not ask for favours, neither for myself nor for His Majesty's Government. After I had defended my predecessor to the best of my abilities I took over the office of Prime Minister and Minister of Defence at a time when the survival of the Empire hung by a thread. I am your servant, and you have the right to dismiss me whenever you like. But you do not have the right to burden me with responsibility without giving me the necessary powers to act . . . Should Parliament today, or at any time in the future, make use of its right of dismissal, I shall step down with a clear conscience and the confidence of having done my duty as it was given to me to do. There is only one thing I would still ask of you in such a case. I would ask you for my successor to give back to him the limited powers you no longer wish to accede to me.[5]

Churchill also won this vote of no confidence, by 475 to 25.

After an appropriate delay the turn of the war then came about after all. In the sea war in the Pacific it was heralded by the Battle of Midway, 4–7 June 1942, when the Americans, themselves numerically inferior, destroyed the core of the Japanese carrier fleet, which was of decisive importance and could not be replaced.

In Egypt the turn began with the Battle of El Alamein. On 23 October, under the command of General Bernard Montgomery and newly equipped with modern American tanks, the British Eighth Army took the offensive.[6] The *Afrika Korps* was threatened with destruction, and during the night of 3 November — against Hitler's order to stand firm — Rommel ordered a withdrawal. Four days later, on 7 November, the Allies landed in Morocco and Algeria. In a counter-move the Axis Powers threw troops into Tunis — very foolishly, because growing Allied superiority at sea and in the air made supply increasingly more difficult and a withdrawal impossible.

The war in Africa ended as might be expected with the Italo-German surrender in Tunis in May 1943; 252,000 men went into captivity. At the end of July the British and Americans landed in Sicily, and in September on the Italian mainland. The Fascist regime collapsed, the *Duce* Benito Mussolini, first arrested, then liberated in a *coup de main*, was from then on merely a puppet in German hands and disappeared into the shadows of history. The King and the new Italian government changed sides. Italy remained a theatre of war until the very end, in which the Allies only gradually advanced from south to north against bitter resistance by the Germans, and only reached the Alps in April 1945.

In Russia the drama of Stalingrad began in November 1942. The German Sixth Army was encircled, but Hitler forbade any attempt at break-out.[7] The lack of supplies, fuel and ammunition, but above all hunger, overcame the army. Of the original 284,000 encircled soldiers, 34,000 wounded were flown out. At the surrender between 31 January and 2 February only 90,000 men remained, most of whom were marked by starvation and disease and did not survive imprisonment. After Stalingrad the Red Army showed itself to be far superior to the German Army in men and *matériel*, and was assured of victory. A final German attempt to regain the initiative failed in the tank battle at Kursk in July 1943. From then on there was nothing to prevent Stalin's armies from advancing further and further westwards, and in the end to Berlin.

The clearer German defeat began to emerge, the more compelling the political questions became. What was to be done with a defeated Germany? Could there be a post-war order in Europe which guaranteed the liberty of the nations and guaranteed peace? Could this be created by agreement between the Western democracies and the Soviet Union? As long as it had been a question of survival everything had been simple. One had to fight at any price and accept allies as they were. To paraphrase Churchill's words: if Hitler were to march into hell, even Satan would be welcome. But what was to become of the alliance without Hitler? And what of Churchill?

The problems with a Free France represented by Charles de Gaulle were rather harmless by comparison and almost amounted to farce. The General and Under Secretary in the Ministry of Defence flew to London shortly before the French surrender in 1940 and there proclaimed the continuation of the war, convinced as he was of the greatness of France — and that he himself embodied it as a sort of 'new Joan of Arc', as he was dubbed. But in the beginning only the distant colonies in equatorial Africa and the even more distant ones in the Pacific joined him. The contrast between his missionary zeal and his lack of power made him react all the more sensitively to any disparagement by the British or the Americans. Churchill was prepared to make allowances for this, but not Roosevelt.

The situation changed with the Allied landings in Morocco and Algeria. Initially the questionable renegade Admiral Darlan took over French leadership there, and after his assassination General Giraud. He outranked de Gaulle by far, and was legitimised by his successful and adventurous escape from German captivity in April 1942. But the two generals did not like each other. With much persuasion — more precisely, by means of massive pressure—the Allies forced the two of them into the marriage bed, in other words jointly to take over the chairmanship of the 'French Committee of National Liberation'. But Giraud was more the soldier than a politician; he resigned in November 1943 because of the constant disagreements with de Gaulle and left the field and the fame to his rival. De Gaulle's great moment came on 25 August 1944 with his triumphant entry into Paris.

Another great moment came two and a half months later, on 11 November 1944, the anniversary of the armistice and victory in the First World War. As the provisional head of state of a provisional government, de Gaulle received the British state guest in the liberated capital, and republican France was again displaying all its royal pomp. Churchill reports:

> . . . At eleven o'clock on the morning of November 11 de Gaulle conducted me in an open car across the Seine and through the Place de la Concorde, with a splendid escort of Gardes Républicains in full uniform with all their breastplates. They were several hundred strong, and provided a brilliant spectacle, on which the sun shone brightly. The whole of the famous avenue of the Champs Élysées was crowded with Parisians and lined with troops. Every window was filled with spectators and decorated with flags. We proceeded through wildly cheering multitudes to the Arc de Triomphe, where we both laid wreaths upon the tomb of the Unknown Warrior. After this ceremony was over the General and I walked together, followed by a concourse of the leading figures of French public life, for half a mile down the highway I knew so well. We then took our places on a dais, and there was a splendid march past of French and British troops. Our Guards detachment was magnificent. . . .
>
> [Afterwards] De Gaulle entertained me at a large luncheon at the Ministry of War, and made a most flattering speech about my war services. . . .[8]

'What a spectacle! But woe! A spectacle only!' one is tempted to quote from Goethe's *Faust*. Churchill recalled his last visit to the Quai d'Orsay in May 1940 with Prime Minister Reynaud and Commander-in-Chief General Gamelin, when papers were being burnt out in the garden because everyone was expecting the Germans to march in. Now the past appeared to have flown away 'like a bad dream'.

It had not: it loomed ever more menacingly the more clearly military victory revealed itself. This was particularly true of the Polish problem. Great Britain had pawned its honour for the independence of Poland, and had gone to war for it. There was a Polish government-in-exile in London, and throughout the whole war Polish soldiers fought side by side with their British comrades. But geography, and therefore the fate of history, had placed Poland in the neighbourhood of Russia, in every sense far removed from

Great Britain. In the complicity between Hitler and Stalin, Germany and Russia had—yet once again in history—divided the Polish spoils between them in the autumn of 1939.

During the final years of the war the dispute involving the Soviet Union, Great Britain and the United States about the fate of Poland ran like a red thread through all the diplomatic discussions, particularly the conferences between Stalin, Churchill and Roosevelt. Here are some of the key data necessary to keep track.

On 4 December 1941 the Polish government-in-exile led by General Sikorski concluded a treaty of friendship and support with the Soviet Union and re-established the diplomatic relations broken off in 1939. In April 1943 the mass graves of 4,413 Polish officers who had been shot were discovered near Katyn to the west of Smolensk. The Soviet Union denied having anything to do with this, of course, but it is obvious that these were members of the army who fell into Russian hands in 1939.[9] The government-in-exile in London demanded an investigation by the Red Cross. To this was added a dispute about the future border. The Soviet Union broke off relations with the government-in-exile.

On 4 July Sikorski was killed in an air crash. His successor was Mikolajczyk. At the conference in Teheran from 28 November to 1 December 1943 Churchill and Roosevelt conceded the 'Curzon Line'—which had already been drawn in 1919 by the British Foreign Secretary Curzon—to the Soviet Union as its western border.[10] For her losses in the east, Poland was to be compensated in the west by German territory.

In the summer of 1944 the Red Army advanced into Poland. At the end of July the 'Polish Committee of National Liberation'—the so-called 'Lublin Committee'—was created. As the government-in-exile in London declared, this was a 'creation by unknown Communists'. But on 2 August the Soviet Union formally recognised the Committee as the provisional government, while Britain held fast to the Mikolajczyk government. On 1 August an uprising by the Polish Undergound Army against the German forces of occupation began in Warsaw. While the British attempted to provide aid by night flights, the Red Army watched the destruction of the national forces of resistance from the proximity of the eastern bank of the Vistula without lifting a finger.

On 1 January 1945 the 'Lublin Committee' formally declared itself to be the government. The government-in-exile in London protested in vain. With the winter offensive by the Red Army, which began on 12 January, western Poland also fell under Communist rule.

At the conference in Yalta from 4 to 11 February 1945 the Western Powers demanded democratic elections and an extension of the government 'to include democratic leaders who live in the country, and Poles who live abroad'. The Soviets made promises but did not keep them. Western observers were not permitted into the country. On 27 March sixteen leaders of the national resistance were arrested and later sentenced to long prison terms. The 'democratic' government which the Western Powers finally recognised developed on the model of enforced block formation under Communist predominance which then soon turned into domination.

These notes show that what Stalin always wanted was to prevent the establishment of an independent Poland and to create a satellite state under Communist — in other words, Soviet — rule. He was prepared to employ any means to achieve this, including criminal acts.

And what did Churchill do? He has been accused of having 'betrayed' Eastern Europe, the Baltic states, the Balkans, and especially Poland.[11] But the question is: how could he have prevented what happened? Wherever the Red Army marched in, the might of its bayonets decided the issues, and against this no amount of persuasion, no diplomacy, no protest on paper were of any help. Furthermore, in his American ally the British Prime Minister found only half-hearted support at best, not to say that he was left in the lurch by the President of the United States. The most important thing for Roosevelt was building a good personal relationship with Stalin, the apparently kind-hearted 'Uncle Joe', even at Churchill's expense, in the hope of thereby being able to solve the political problems and securing the road to a lasting peace. This was dramatically demonstrated at the meeting of the 'Big Three' in Teheran. During the conference the President lived, almost symbolically, in the Soviet Embassy. Churchill claims that this had been solely for Roosevelt's security and comfort, but his unease becomes apparent when he reports:

> Shortly after the President's move into . . . the Soviet Embassy Stalin came to greet him, and they had a friendly talk. . . . He [Roosevelt] cautioned Stalin against bringing up the problems of India with Churchill, and Stalin agreed that this was undoubtedly a sore subject. Roosevelt said that reform in India should begin at the bottom, and Stalin replied that reform from the bottom would mean revolution.[12]

The American President obviously had nothing to say to that.

A far more serious incident occurred during an intimate dinner. Stalin declared that after the war 50,000 German engineers and technicians would have to be shot in order to remove the foundations of German militarism once and for all. Churchill protested:

> The British Parliament and public will never tolerate mass excecutions. . . . they would turn violently against those responsible after the first butchery had taken place. The Soviets must be under no delusion on this point.

Stalin repeated: 'Fifty thousand must be shot.' Churchill in reply:

> I would rather be taken out into the garden here and now and be shot myself than sully my own and my country's honour by such infamy.

Churchill continues:

> At this point the President intervened. He had a compromise. Not fifty thousand should be shot, but only forty-nine thousand. By this he hoped, no doubt, to reduce the whole matter to ridicule. Eden also made signs and gestures intended to reassure me that it was all a joke. But now Elliott Roosevelt [the President's son] rose in his place at the end of the table and made a speech, saying how cordially he agreed with Marshal Stalin's plan and how sure he was that the United States Army would support it. At this intrusion I got up and left the table . . .

Stalin himself, suddenly at his most charming, brought his guest back to the table with the assurance that it really had only been a joke. But could one be sure? Had the game of words not possibly been kite-flying? Churchill in any case was overcome by doubts.[13] And when we recall Katyn, then the laughter dies out with a shudder.

Once again the question arises: What should, what could Churchill have done to prevent the 'betrayal' of Poland, of Eastern Europe? The Soviet Union had a gigantic military machine which by now was moving irresistibly foward, and the United States was seeking close ties with the Soviet Union. Great Britain was economically and now also militarily dependent on the United States. Among the 'Big Three' it was by far the weakest partner, almost a dwarf between two giants. Or to put it into Churchill's terms: after the conference in Teheran he had learned

> . . . what a small nation we are. I had got myself between the Russian bear with his claws extended on the one side, and the huge American bull on the other, and between them sat the poor little English donkey . . .[14]

Whoever speaks about a 'betrayal' of Poland and Eastern Europe should at least add that it was impossible for Churchill to prevent it.

Incidentally, he suffered greatly under his insight. He was seized by depression during the conference in Teheran — on 30 November 1943, his 69th birthday, of all days. To his personal physician Lord Moran he spoke about the looming catastrophe, about a further war which could follow: 'Vast problems unfold themselves before our eyes and we are only the specks of dust which settle down at night on a map of the world.' Then the question to the doctor: 'Do you think my strength will last for as long as the war lasts? I sometimes feel as if I were finished.' And: 'I would like to sleep for a billion years.'[15]

On the trip back from Teheran Churchill first stopped over in Cairo, then in Tunis, in order to meet General Eisenhower. A serious attack of pneumonia laid him low. Significantly enough, the title of the chapter in which he talks about this is 'In Carthage Ruins . . .'[16] A longer period of recuperation in Marrakesh became necessary. But

> Physical weakness oppressed me at Marrakesh following my illness at Carthage. All my painting tackle had been sent out, but I could not face it. I could hardly walk at all. Even tottering from the motor-car to a picnic luncheon in lovely weather amid the foothills of the Atlas was limited to eighty or a hundred yards. I passed eighteen hours out of the twenty-four prone. I never remember such extreme fatigue and weakness in body. . . .[17]

But is the body not the mirror of the spirit and the soul? Is it absurd to deduce that the physical weakness was an outcome of the political weakness, of the bitter realisation that the bull and the bear were playing their own game without any regard for the poor little donkey?

179

The Military Finale

In January 1943, at the end of the summit meeting in Casablanca, President Roosevelt went before the Press and caused worldwide excitement with the demand for the unconditional surrender of the enemy powers. Churchill, too, heard this 'with some surprise', but he agreed in order to avoid any impression of disunity. It is now believed that Roosevelt introduced this formula unilaterally, and deliberately before the Press in order to cut off any discussion and objections.

Churchill, however, recalled the old professor who, having been asked for a final piece of advice by his students, sums up the total wisdom gained in a lifetime by saying: 'Check your sources and quotations!' When checking, Churchill — to his genuine surprise — found that 'unconditional surrender' appeared in the conference papers days before and also in his own report to the War Cabinet in London, only he had forgotten it. From then on he defended the formula accordingly.[1] But was this not a mistake, possibly even one of the greatest committed by the Allies during the Second World War? Did it drive the Germans to continue to fight in desperation? Was the war unnecessarily extended, with all of the sacrifices that the final phase, in particular, demanded? Many critics see it that way, then as now.[2]

But it is not the critics, it is Churchill who has the better arguments on his side. What would the alternative have been? Should one have offered Hitler negotiations, made concessions to him? Would he himself have agreed to such negotiations? No, certainly not.[3] He had always been determined to fight to the end, to his own destruction, which was expressly to include the destruction of Germany. And he knew only too well — as his British oppo-

180

nent had known in 1940—that with the beginning of negotiations the will to go on fighting would break down, from the field marshals to the common soldiers, and with the people.

The claim that the demand for unconditional surrender united nation and *Führer* and discouraged resistance is of greater weight. However, there is no proof that this is true. At the core of the resistance we must take seriously, the issue was not opportunism but the moral revolt against tyranny and its crimes. In this sense General Henning von Tresckow, for years one of the leaders of the military resistance, declared:

> The assassination attempt [on Hitler] must be carried out *coûte que coûte*. Should it not succeed action must still be taken in Berlin, because it is no longer a matter of the practical purpose, but that the German resistance movement dared the decisive throw before the world and before history. Compared to that everything else is unimportant.[4]

When Stauffenberg then failed on 20 July 1944 and Tresckow chose death, he said to his confidant Fabian von Schlabrendorff:

> Now the whole world will come down on us and vilify us. But I am still firmly convinced that we acted rightly. I hold Hitler not only to be the arch-enemy of Germany, but also the arch-enemy of the world. When in a few hours I stand before the throne of God to give account for my acts and omissions, I believe I can stand up for what I have done with a clear conscience. If God once told Abraham that he would not destroy Sodom if only ten righteous men could be found there, I hope that God will not destroy Germany for our sake. None of us can complain about his death . . . The moral value of a human being only begins when he is prepared to give his life for his convictions.[5]

We do not know what would have happened after a successful assassination attempt—what if Field Marshal Rommel, uninjured, had opened the way out of Normandy to Germany for the Allied armies—and it does not really make much sense to speculate. But any possible answer has little or nothing to do with Roosevelt's demanding unconditional surrender at the Casablanca summit and Churchill's agreeing with him.

In 1942 and 1943 there were conflicts between the British and the Americans about the strategy which was to lead to victory and the unconditional surrender of Germany. Not only the Soviets but the Western Allies too regarded it as crucial to create a Second Front in France as quickly as possible. Their preparations, however, required time, much time, and because of the calls for help from Russia, to remain idle in the meantime was not permissible. It was therefore agreed that the war in North Africa must be brought to a close and Italy forced to surrender.

Churchill, however, went further. He emphasised the singular importance of the Mediterranean theatre. His idea was to make a really strong drive north through Italy and simultaneously to make an appropriate offer to persuade Turkey to join the war. From this some far-reaching, not to say extravagant conclusions have been drawn. Churchill writes:

> It has become a legend in America that I strove to prevent the cross-Channel enterprise called 'Overlord', and that I tried vainly to lure the Allies into some mass invasion of the Balkans . . . Much of this nonsense has already [earlier in his book] . . . been exposed and refuted . . .'[6]

But legends have tough lives, and not only in America. In Sebastian Haffner, for example, we can read:

> Churchill . . . believed he saw a way Britain, although the smallest partner, could dominate and direct the coalition—he felt confident he could wag the dog with the tail, so to speak. He did not want to leave the victory half won, let alone deliberately cripple it, he did not want to simultaneously embody both Marlborough and his opponent Bolingbroke, who concluded a useful but quite shabby special peace with Louis XIV behind the Generalissimo's back. That was against his nature. Yet he wanted not only to destroy Hitler, but with the same move also cut out Stalin and tie in Roosevelt—tie him in so tightly that America would never again be able to separate from Britain.
>
> For this he needed a course of the war which would physically keep Russia out of Europe, and this required making Eastern, not Western Europe the objective of the main Anglo-American offensive. The same blow which broke Germany's power was to push a barrier of steel between Russia and Europe. That meant, however, that it would have to be delivered from the south, and not the west, not based on England, but based on North Africa, not across the Channel, but across the Mediterranean, not with a direction of advance Paris–Cologne–Ruhr Basin, but with a direction of advance Trieste–Vienna–Prague, and then on to Berlin or even Warsaw.
>
> If that were to succeed, at the end of the war the united armies of Britain and America would be the only ones in Europe and they alone would rule Europe. Russia would not get beyond its borders. France would not again become a theatre of war, it would re-emerge untouched and unscathed—liberated and a little shamed. And Churchill felt confident that he could remain the one to call the shots within the Anglo-American combination which would then give liberated and occupied Europe a new character.[7]

If ever there was a democratic statesman in the twentieth century capable of imaginative planning, this was certainly Winston Churchill. And if what Haffner is describing here had been only half-way true, the accusation that he had even considered 'betraying' Poland and other eastern European countries would collapse of itself. Unfortunately this is a dream image without any foundation in reality. Time and again Churchill quite rightly defended himself against the accusation that he had wanted to sabotage the landing operation in France, and all the documents speak in his favour.

Most of this can already be put aside by a few simple questions. How were modern motorised armies to cross the Alps from Italy? How would they move in the Balkans, incidentally through Communist-controlled — in other words, in all likelihood hostile — territory held by partisans?[8] How were the huge quantities of supplies they required to be shipped over long distances at sea and then transported over the poor roads in the Balkans? Where, outside England, were there bases for gigantic air fleets? Were the British and Americans even capable of beating the *Wehrmacht* on their own, without the help of the Red Army? Who was going to justify the additional, probably huge blood sacrifices which would have been required? And what power on earth could have made the Russians sit idly by and watch themselves being shut out? No. Churchill had imagination, but he was not a woolly-headed dreamer. His operation in the Dardanelles in the First World War had had much in its favour in principle, and he now had something similar in mind, only in an alliance with, instead of a war against, Turkey. However, his poor reputation as a strategic planner, gained in 1915, still clung to him.

Churchill describes the differences of opinion which actually did exist between the British and the Americans using the discussions during the Teheran Summit as his example. The issue under consideration was whether Turkey should be urged to join the war, or at least to provide air bases and to open the Dardanelles to the Allies. If that were to succeed, said Churchill, control of the Black Sea could be established without any trouble, and Russia could be supplied with aid much more quickly and in larger amounts than via the Arctic ports or the Persian Gulf. (This had been a major reason for the Dardanelles operation in 1915.)

Churchill doggedly presented his arguments several times, and was not afraid of repeating himself, and he says:

> I could have gained Stalin, but the President was oppressed by the prejudices of his military advisers and drifted to and fro in the argument, with the result that these subsidiary but gleaming opportunities were cast aside unused. Our American friends were comforted in their obstinacy by the reflection that 'at any rate we have stopped Churchill entangling us in the Balkans'. No such idea had ever crossed my mind. . . .[9]

We must add, however, that Churchill had counted his chickens before they were hatched. At the meeting in Adena on 30 and 31 January 1943 between Churchill and the Turkish President Inönü, Turkey refused to join the Allies, as she did again at the conference in Cairo which followed the summit in Teheran on 2–6 December. It was only on 23 February 1945, long after the military decision in the Balkans had been reached — and in the Soviet Union's favour if we except Greece — that Turkey declared war on Germany without any risk of having to make a contribution to the fighting, in order to be on the side of the victors and join the United Nations.

What ulterior motives Churchill might have had in formulating his plans may be disregarded. It would certainly have been all right with him if, after an entry into the war by Turkey, for example, Bulgaria could have been occupied and drawn into the Western camp, even at the expense of tensions with the Soviet Union. The conflict with the Americans was therefore not without import. It also played a rôle in the campaign in Italy. The issue was whether the invasion in Normandy was to be supported by a landing in southern France, even if this meant that the armies in Italy would lose much of their offensive power. The Americans prevailed. The landing on the Riviera began on 15 August 1944 and quickly led to extensive advances against weak German opposition.

We must state that, as far as possible, Churchill plays down the Anglo-American disputes, so we must be careful of following him blindly in this area. He always had the community of the English-speaking peoples at heart, and as a politician, after 1951 even as Prime Minister again, the writer of memoirs after the war remained tied to diplomatic considerations. To tell the truth and nothing but the truth is one thing; to bring the whole truth to light is something else. We will now see how, with approaching victory, the contrasts grew and could be kept hidden less and less.

On D-Day, 6 June 1944, the long discussed landing always demanded by the Soviets began in Normandy under the command of American General Dwight D. Eisenhower. It had been postponed several times because this or that was still lacking. But now the technically perfected, materially most elaborate operation in the history of war began. Included in the preparations was deliberate misinformation. The Germans were to be made to believe that the landing in Normandy was only a feint, and that the main attack would follow against the Channel coast near Calais. Thus, during the early, critical days, when it was crucial to drive the still weak invasion troops back into the sea, important divisions were instead held back in idleness. And even surprise was achieved. The weather on 6 June was fairly rough — unsuitable for landing craft, according to the German experts. The Commander-in-Chief in Normandy, Field Marshal Rommel, was therefore not at his headquarters but at home with his wife when Operation 'Overlord' began.

Altogether 6,400 landing craft were employed, under the protection of six battleships, 23 cruisers and 103 destroyers, which began by bombarding German coastal positions. The Allied air forces disposed 3,100 bombers and 5,000 fighters as against 165 bombers and 185 fighters on the German side. The Allies even brought their own artificial harbours along, and laid pipelines from England to France for the supply of fuel. By 12 June 326,000 men had been landed, by the end of July more than one and a half million. The Americans broke through the Cotentin peninsula and took Cherbourg on 30 June. While the defenders did make an effort to destroy the port facilities, they were put back into operation within a matter of weeks so that ocean-going ships could sail in and be unloaded.

The German soldiers fought with the courage of desperation and took heavy losses. But there was little they could do against the enemy's superiority. On 14 July Rommel prepared a situation report for Hitler at the end of which he said:

> The troops are fighting heroically everywhere, yet the unequal battle is drawing to a close. It is necessary in my view that the political consequences be drawn. As the Commander-in-Chief of the Army Group I feel obliged to state this clearly.[10]

Rommel was determined to end the battle himself if necessary. On 17 July he was severely wounded in an attack by low-flying aircraft and after his recovery forced to commit suicide on 14 October. A state funeral, the last and most mendacious of the crumbling *Reich*, saw him off to Valhalla.

On 31 July the Allies broke through the German defensive front and went over to a war of movement. In only a few weeks they had overrun France and Belgium. On 17 August Chartres and Orléans were occupied. Three days later the Americans reached the Seine on both sides of Paris. On 25 August General de Gaulle made his entry there. On 3 September the Allies marched into Brussels, on the 4th into Antwerp and on the 6th into Liège, close to the German border. Only the *coup de main* against Holland failed in the Battle of Arnhem.

In the meantime the Red Army had also begun its great summer offensive. It shattered the German eastern front, took several hundred thousand prisoners and advanced into East Prussian border regions, deep into Poland and into the Balkans. Germany's eastern European allies, Rumania and Finland, changed sides. In the end, after advances of several hundred kilometres, problems of supply brought the Allied and Russian armies to a temporary halt. But this was only to catch their breath for the final attack.

The only rôle left for Churchill with regard to military events was that of an observer. But he wanted, of course, to be as close to the events as possible. The King had stopped him from sailing off to France on D-Day, but he did so four days later. In his report he writes:

> Montgomery, smiling and confident, met me at the beach as we scrambled out of our landing-craft. His army had already penetrated seven or eight miles inland. There was very little firing or activity. The weather was brilliant. We drove through our limited but fertile domain in Normandy. It was pleasant to see the prosperity of the countryside. The fields were full of lovely red and white cows basking or parading in the sunshine. The inhabitants seemed quite buoyant and well nourished and waved enthusiastically. Montgomery's headquarters, about five miles inland, were in a château with lawns and lakes around it. We lunched in a tent looking towards the enemy. The General was in the highest spirits. I asked him how far away was the actual front. He said about three miles. I asked him if he had a continuous line. He said, 'No.' 'What is there then to prevent an incursion of German armour breaking up our luncheon?' He said he did not think they would come.

Churchill then learned that the château had been heavily bombarded the night before and urged his general to change quarters because 'Anything can be done once or for a short time, but custom, repitition, prolongation, is [sic] always to be avoided when possible in war.'[11]

Nine months later a similar and quite characteristic situation occurred on the lower Rhine. Montgomery's troops crossed the river at Wesel on 24 March 1945. Churchill showed up the very next day, first as a guest of General Eisenhower. From a house protected by sandbags they observed the other bank together, believed to be still occupied by the enemy. But everything appeared to be quiet:

> The the Supreme Commander had to depart on other business, and Montgomery and I were about to follow his example when I saw a small launch come close by the moor. So I said to Montgomery, 'Why don't we go across and have a look at the other side?' Somewhat to my surprise he answered, 'Why not?' After he

had made some inquiries we started across the river with three or four American commanders and half a dozen armed men. We landed in brilliant sunshine and perfect peace on the German shore, and walked about for half and hour or so unmolested.[12]

In these texts one can sense how much fun these excursions to the front were for Churchill. In this by now corpulent man leaning on his cane, who had meanwhile reached and exceeded the biblical age of three score and ten, there was still something of the young lieutenant of Hussars whom romanticism and the lust for adventure had driven into the Sudan against all normal orders so as not to miss the last notable cavalry charge in history at Omdurman.

Or does something else become apparent here, something unspeakably sinister — a premonition of a death wish? Or at least a wish to escape from the oppressive present for a few hours, for a day, so as not to have to look into the future? This now shows itself to be sinister enough, despite — or because of — the prospect of victory. The overpowering Soviet military machine was moving inexorably into central Europe. What would it do? In Poland it already ruled as it liked with a harsh hand and without bothering about Allied protests. Terrible tales began circulating about the conduct of the Russian soldiers towards the German civilian population. And who was going to stop the Red Army? Who was going to stop Stalin if he were to take over Hitler's legacy and reach out for hegemony over Europe? The Americans were already declaring that after the war they intended sending their soldiers home as quickly as possible. What would then be left except the poor little donkey against the big bear with the extended claws?

During the summit meeting in Cairo in 1943, after Teheran, a strange conversation took place about which Harold Macmillan told Randolph Churchill:

Churchill suddenly said to him late one night: 'Cromwell was a great man, wasn't he?' 'Yes, sir, a very great man.' 'Ah,' he said, 'but he made one terrible mistake. Obsessed in his youth by fear of the power of Spain, he failed to observe the rise of France. Will that be said of me?' He was, of course, thinking of Germany and Russia.[13]

And for 'Cromwell' we must, of course, read 'Churchill'.

A series of conferences, the last one in Yalta from 4 to 11 February 1945, had decided that the western border of Poland was to be advanced to the Oder and Neisse rivers, and that while Germany was to be divided into zones of occupation, it was to be jointly administered. But the fate of Poland appeared to be more uncertain than ever. The Soviets did whatever they wanted in Warsaw, and did not give a damn about what they had previously promised. Churchill therefore bombarded the American President with urgent messages imploring him to take part in determined joint action. A telegram of 13 March, for example, said:

> At Yalta also we agreed to take the Russian view of the frontier line. Poland has lost her frontier. Is she now to lose her freedom? That is the question which will undoubtedly have to be fought out in Parliament and in public here. I do not wish to reveal a divergence betwen the British and United States Governments, but it would certainly be necessary for me to make it clear that we are in [the] presence of a great failure and an utter breakdown of what was settled at Yalta, but that we British have not the necessary strength to carry the matter further and that the limits of our capacity to act have been reached. . . .[14]

Roosevelt replied three days later with evident displeasure:

> I cannot but be concerned at the views you expressed in your message of the 13th. I do not understand what you mean by a divergence between our Governments on the Polish negotiations. From our side there is certainly no evidence of any divergence of policy. We have been merely discussing the most effective tactics, and I cannot agree that we are confronted with a breakdown of the Yalta agreement until we have made the effort to overcome the obstacles incurred in the negotiations at Moscow.[15]

No, Roosevelt did not want to be forced, not even by Churchill, to give up his idea that with a bit of goodwill 'Uncle Joe' could be made to see the light and that the structure of a peace which would deserve the name could be created together. Churchill in his turn did not want to give up his belief in a personal and indestructible friendship. Perhaps everything could be explained in terms of Roosevelt's (hopefully temporary) exhaustion and weakness, which had already become apparent at Yalta:

> Although I had no exact information about the President's state of health I had the feeling that, except for occasional flashes of courage and insight, the telegrams he was sending us were not his own. I therefore sent him a message in a personal vein to ease the uphill march of official business.[16]

Two old men who were clinging to their illusions?

But Churchill did not permit himself any illusions with regard to the future. He described with complete clarity what the issues were for him during the final weeks of the war:

First, that Soviet Russia had become a mortal danger to the free world.

Secondly, that a new front must be immediately created against her onward sweep.

Thirdly, that this front in Europe should be as far east as possible.

Fourthly, that Berlin was the prime and true objective of the Anglo-American armies.

Fifthly, that the liberation of Czechoslovakia and the entry into Prague of American troops was of high consequence.

Sixthly, that Vienna, and indeed Austria, must be regulated by the Western Powers, at least upon an equality with the Russian Soviets.

Seventhly, that Marshal Tito's aggressive pretensions against Italy must be curbed.

Finally, and above all, that a settlement must be reached on all major issues between the West and the East in Europe *before the armies of democracy melted*, or the Western Allies yielded any part of the German territories they had conquered, or, as it could soon be written, liberated from totalitarian tyranny.[17]

There was still hope. After the Allied armies had crossed the Rhine — first in a *coup de main* on 7 March 1945 at the railway bridge in Remagen, the destruction of which failed at the last moment, then on a broad front — they were advancing east at a fast pace. They reached Magdeburg on 18 April, and Leipzig a day later. The Red Army only began its big offensive on the Oder river on 16 April and because of the desperate German resistance needed several days before it could unfold its advance on Berlin. Churchill implored General Eisenhower not to call a halt and to keep advancing. But he was receiving his instructions from Washington, and did not even dream of jeopardising his position and his fame as a commander by acting against orders. He halted his troops on the Elbe and Mulde rivers, and prevented the self-willed and energetic army commander George Patton from crossing the Czech border and marching on Prague.[18] Thus did the great opportunities which had offered themselves almost unexpectedly remain unused, because, in the end, the Germans generally still fought only in the East and not in the West, and secretly hoped almost as much for occupation by the Anglo-American forces as they feared it by the Soviets.

Triumph
and Tragedy

On 12 April 1945 Franklin Delano Roosevelt died. He was 63 years old. In Warm Springs, Georgia, where he had gone to recuperate, he suddenly collapsed, lost consciousness and did not regain it. The end came after only a few hours.

In Berlin, in the bunker underneath the crumbling *Reich* Chancellery, Dr Joseph Goebbels had been reading to his *Führer* from Carlyle's epic *Frederick the Great* in order to cheer him up. Now he hurried to Hitler with the news and declared: this was the hoped-for miracle, salvation at the last moment, just as it had been granted to the Prussian King by the death of the Russian Tsarina.[1] That was nonsense, of course. Modern democracies react very differently, and in the majestically flowing stream of public opinion far more sluggishly, from the absolute rulers of the eighteenth century.

Churchill was deeply moved because he had still counted on the relationship man to man, and put his faith in the friendship and hoped-for agreement:

> When I received these tidings early in the morning of Friday, the 13th, I felt as if I had been struck a physical blow, My relations with this shining personality had played so large a part in the long, terrible years we had worked together. Now they had come to an end, and I was overpowered by a sense of deep and irreparable loss. . . .[2]

The President and the Prime Minister had exchanged more than seventeen hundred messages and had spent 120 days together at nine meetings.

And who knew anything about the successor, the former Vice-President Harry S. Truman? He did not stem from one of the élite families of the

East Coast like Roosevelt, but came from humble origins and the deepest provinces—from Missouri. It was to be demonstrated later that he possessed firmness and the will to act, and of course Churchill immediately also addressed him with his most urgent messages. But until now he had been a shadow, excluded from much information and hardly involved in important decisions. It was therefore only natural that in the beginning he listened to his—in other words Roosevelt's—foreign policy and military advisers. And they had sworn themselves to the alliance with the Soviet Union:

> We can now see the deadly hiatus which existed between the fading of President Roosevelt's strength and the growth of President Truman's grip of the vast world problem. In this melancholy void one President could not act and the other could not know. . . .[3]

But what did the dark thoughts of a lonely old man in 10 Downing Street matter any more? The moment of victory, of triumph had arrived. At Torgau on the Elbe river American and Russian soldiers met on 25 April 1945 and celebrated the victory together they had so dearly fought for separately and yet in common.[4] The sight of the crimes which now lay open to the eye also promoted unity. The Red Army had liberated Auschwitz, the Americans moved into Dachau and Buchenwald, and the British discovered horror in Bergen-Belsen.

On 30 April Hitler committed suicide in the bunker under the *Reich* Chancellery, together with Eva Braun whom he had married the day before, with his Alsatian bitch Blondi acting as a sort of fore-taster of death.[5] In his book *Mein Kampf* he had written: 'Diplomacy has to take care that a nation does not go under heroically, but that it is preserved in practice.'[6] But he had done everything he could to achieve exactly the opposite.

All that was left for the successor, Grand Admiral Dönitz, was to end the war as unconditionally as the Allies had been demanding ever since the summit meeting in Casablanca in 1943. Partial surrenders had already taken place in the south on 2 and 4 May, and in the north on 5 May. The complete surrender became effective on 9 May at 0.01 a.m. Millions of German soldiers went into captivity, with a very different fate depending on whether they were taken by the Russians, the Americans or the British. This will be discussed later.

If we leave out the vanquished, the triumph united the peoples, the nations, in Europe, in Russia and in America. In London normal British reticence exploded into foaming enthusiasm after Churchill announced the German surrender and the British victory on the afternoon of 8 May. When he left his office to go to Parliament he was moved to tears by the members of his staff who formed a double line to the garden gate and applauded him. There was an even greater double line on the street. Hordes of people crowded around, applauded, cheered and shouted 'Good old Winnie!' And so, too, in the Commons. The members 'shouted and shouted and waved their order papers'.[7]

It was a long time before the Prime Minister could make himself heard. He first read out the declaration he had already made over the radio, and then pushed his notes aside, quite in breach of his normal procedure. As the parliamentarian he had always been and remained, he thanked 'the House' and all its Members for their patient, lenient, critical, trusting and dependable support during the years of tribulation. Then, at his suggestion — and following the example Lloyd George had set on a similar occasion in 1918 — everyone went to St Margaret's church to 'humbly and with reverence thank God the Almighty for his deliverance from the menacing German danger'. Finally Churchill stepped out on a balcony to show himself to the crowds with his famous 'V for victory' sign — and experienced probably the most thrilling contradiction one could imagine. When he called to the crowd 'This is your victory!' the chorus came echoing back: 'No, no, it is your victory!'

What is strange however, is that in Churchill's history of the Second World War, in six volumes with a total of about four thousand, mostly closely filled pages, the report about the enthusiasm of victory only occupies eleven lines. And he was certainly not the man to hide his light under a bushel. *Triumph and Tragedy* is the title of the final volume, but almost the only thing treated is the tragedy. Immediately after the eleven lines it says:

> When in these tumultuous days of rejoicing I was asked to speak to the nation I had borne the chief responsibility in our Island for almost exactly five years. Yet it may well be there were few whose hearts were more heavily burdened with anxiety than mine. After reviewing the varied tale of our fortunes I struck a sombre note which may be recorded here.
>
> 'I wish,' I said, 'I could tell you to-night that all our toils and troubles were over. Then indeed I could end my five years' service happily, and if you thought that you had had enough of me and that I ought to be put out to grass I would take it with the best of grace. But, on the contrary, I must warn you, as I did when I began this five years' task — and no one knew then that it would last so long — that there is still a lot to do, and that you must be prepared for further efforts of mind and body and further sacrifices to great causes if you are not to fall back into the rut of inertia, the confusion of aim, and the craven fear of being great. . . .

'On the continent of Europe we have yet to make sure that the simple and honourable purposes for which we entered the war are not brushed aside or overlooked in the months following our success, and that the words 'freedom', 'democracy', and 'liberation' are not distorted from their true meaning as we have understood them. There would be little use in punishing the Hitlerites for their crimes if law and justice did not rule, and if totalitarian or police Governments were to take the place of the German invaders. . . .

'. . . I told you hard things at the beginning of these last five years; you did not shrink, and I should be unworthy of your confidence and generosity if I did not still cry: Forward, unflinching, unswerving, indomitable, till the whole task is done and the whole world is safe and clean.'[8]

Cleansed of what? The Soviet Union is not mentioned as the new danger, but the allusions are unmistakable. The only question was: did people still want to hear that now? Did they not want to lean back, forget, enjoy their having survived — and rather close their eyes to a road into the future which again was obviously, as in 1940, to be marked by blood, sweat and tears? Then, after Dunkirk, the danger was tangible for everyone. Now it was hidden somewhere off in the distance, only recognisable by the initiated. One can therefore hardly speak of 'cowardly flight' before greatness. And who can fault the people for reacting as mere humans who were tired of having to be heroes after five years of war?

The question is twofold, in terms of both domestic and foreign politics. General elections were long overdue, and after some discussion they were set for 26 July. The whole world, at least outside Great Britain, expected a victory for the Conservatives, in other words Churchill. The triumph over Hitler's *Reich* had actually been his victory, and he indisputedly stood at the peak of his fame. Who could be a match for him? Clement Attlee, of all people, the leader of the Labour Party? He was not a colourful but a drab personality, so that many underestimated his abilities, in keeping with the malicious remark often attributed to Churchill but never proved that 'an empty taxi drove up and out stepped Attlee'.

Churchill reports how he was seized by a dark premonition:

However, just before dawn [on election day] I woke suddenly with a sharp stab of almost physical pain. A hitherto subconscious conviction that we were beaten broke forth and dominated my mind. All the pressure of great events, on and against which I had mentally so long maintained my 'flying speed', would cease and I should fall. The power to shape the future would be denied me. The knowledge and experience I had gathered, the authority and goodwill I had gained in so many countries, would vanish. . . .[9]

193

Churchill speaks of the 'dissatisfaction' which overcame him. More appropriate, but un-British, would probably be to speak of desperation. And the premonition did not lie: Labour won an overwhelming victory. Churchill resigned and Clement Attlee was his successor.

At first this reversal in the power structure caused astonishment. Then people spoke with admiration about democratic maturity: where else in the world would people have let themselves be so little blinded by fame, and turned out the saviour in need, the victor in the war, so soberly? Churchill himself once quoted Plutarch: 'Ingratitude towards its great men is the sign of a strong people.'

Yet the British were not ungrateful. The were well able to appreciate historic greatness. The reverence and the gratitude which were Churchill's at the end of the war were genuine, lasting and borne up by deep convictions. With much justification, but sometimes rather weepishly, the destroyers of monuments were to complain even years or decades later that there was hardly any progress to be made against these feelings.

But the British took a clear decision between the man for war and the man for peace. The war was over, and it should stay over. If Churchill were to remain in office one could never be sure. In his address to the nation already cited he had said:

> Though holiday rejoicing is necessary to the human spirit, yet it must add to the strength and resilience with which every man and woman turns again to the work they have to do . . .

No, people did not want to just take a few days off: they wanted peace and security for the duration, and above all social security. What else had they fought for? And what could be expected from Churchill, what from the Conservatives, in this field? The Socialists, on the other hand, had a clear-cut programme. Their objective was the Welfare State. What they promised in the election campaign therefore fit in exactly with the mood of the nation. Incidentally, they kept their promise – with, however, doubtful consequences for the development of the economy and of wealth. Ten years after the unconditional surrender the Federal Republic of Germany was well on the way to her *Wirtschaftswunder* (economic miracle) while Great Britain was stagnating. After a further ten years the Federal Republic was developing into a world power in exports, and the West German skilled worker was earning twice as much as his British counterpart.

On 8 May 1945, however, this all still lay in the unknown future, and anyone who might have predicted it would have been laughed out of court. Churchill, in the meantime, was occupied with a future which in his eyes was already as clearly discernible as the menace of Hitler had been in 1933:

> The main bond of common danger which had united the Great Allies had vanished overnight. The Soviet menace, to my eyes, had already replaced the Nazi foe. But no comradeship against it existed. At home the foundations of national unity, upon which the war-time Government had stood so firmly, were also gone. Our strength, which had overcome so many storms, would no longer continue in the sunshine. How then could we reach that final settlement which alone could reward the toils and sufferings of the struggle? I could not rid my mind of the fear that the victorious armies of democracy would soon disperse and that the real and hardest test still lay before us. I had seen it all before. I remembered that other joy-day nearly thirty years before, when I had driven with my wife from the Ministry of Munitions through similar multitudes convulsed with enthusiasm to Downing Street to congratulate the Prime Minister. Then, as at this time, I understood the world situation as a whole. But then at least there was no mighty army that we need fear.[10]

Churchill did what he could to meet the danger. On 12 May he sent a telegram to Truman in which he said:

> . . . An iron curtain is drawn down upon their front. We do not know what is going on behind. There seems little doubt that the whole of the regions east of the line Lübeck–Trieste–Corfu will soon be completely in their hands. To this must be added the further enormous area conquered by the American armies between Eisenach and the Elbe, which will, I suppose, in a few weeks be occupied, when the Americans retreat, by the Russian power. . . .
> . . . Meanwhile the attention of our peoples will be occupied in inflicting severities upon Germany, which is ruined and prostrate, and it would be open to the Russians in a very short time to advance if they chose to the waters of the North Sea and the Atlantic.
> . . . Surely it is vital now to come to an understanding with Russia, or see where we are with her, before we weaken our armies mortally of retire to the zones of occupation. . . .[11]

A stream of directives was issued from Downing Street. Captured German aircraft and weapons were not to be destroyed. Bomber Command, in fact the Royal Air Force as a whole, was not to be reduced. If necessary the crews could be sent on leave, but the number of squadrons had to be maintained. And while the German prisoners of war in British hands were to be released, they were also to be registered by the military authorities so that they remained available.[12]

This, incidentally, led to the prisoners in British hands receiving generous treatment as a rule. To mention only one detail: for their move out which lasted until June, the various units in Denmark were allowed to retain some of their weapons to protect themselves from possible acts of revenge by the population or the resistance movement. Only after crossing the border were the weapons laid down and the units disbanded. The Americans, on the other hand, bunched their prisoners together in large assembly camps, often without bothering about supplies. After that they handed many prisoners over to the French or Belgians. The Red Army took its prisoners to Russia as forced labour under harsh, sometimes inhuman conditions. Officers and generals were condemned in droves to long terms in prison as war criminals, and without any trial worthy of the name. The last prisoners were freed by Konrad Adenauer during his visit to Moscow in 1955, more than ten years after the end of the war, when he stubbornly insisted on making their return home a condition for the establishment of diplomatic relations.

But to return to Churchill's directives. All in all, we are dealing with an astonishing and hardly known chapter of the post-war period.[13] How can it be explained? Must we speak of hysterics? It would at least appear reasonable to assume a loss of reality. Not only the American President and his advisers wanted peace instead of the continuation of the war against a different opponent, but also the people of the West. The Soviet Union was the ally who had made the greatest sacrifices, and the verdict on the Germans was never more severe than during the initial weeks and months after the surrender, because what had gone on in the concentration and extermination camps was now no longer hearsay but lay open to everyone's eyes. No one would have been able to understand it if the Allies had now suddenly gone to war against Russia together with a resurrected German Army. It was therefore no coincidence that the Americans remained deaf to Churchill's appeals.

But another way of looking at things is at least conceivable: Churchill was only reacting to changed circumstances more quickly and with more foresight than the normal statesmen who went swimming along with the turgid stream of public opinion. Only a few years later what he was demanding and anticipating was no longer considered to be odd but quite natural.

To give a few clues: In his speech in Stuttgart on 6 September 1946 US Secretary of State Byrnes announced a change in policy towards Germany. On 7 March 1947 President Truman declared that the United States would aid the nations who 'were free, but menaced in their freedom'. This aid was soon supported economically by the European Recovery Program, abbreviated ERP and popularly known as the Marshall Plan. Western Germany received her share as well. In June 1948 the Soviets blocked the Allies' access routes to West Berlin. The Air Lift began, and the Allies stood side by side with German citizens in the defence of freedom. On 4 April 1949 the North Atlantic Treaty was signed in Washington. As early as 1950 discussions began in the Federal Republic about German rearmament. In 1954 the Federal Republic's membership in NATO was decided, and on 2 January 1956 the build-up of the *Bundeswehr* began with the call-up of the first volunteers.

The world turned on its head when looking back at the situation in 1945! Churchill remarked ironically:

> A few years later it was Britain and Western Europe who were urged in many quarters to play the 'moderating rôle' between the U.S.A. and the U.S.S.R. Such are the antics of fortune.[14]

We have recounted earlier how passionately Churchill took on any office entrusted to him, and how this led to fissures which put off his contemporaries. The young Minister of Economics wanted to develop the Welfare State and, to finance this, reduce arms expenditures. The First Lord of the Admiralty demanded ever more and always more expensive battleships, and for this he painted the danger of war which he had formerly denied. The Chancellor of the Exchequer of the 1920s again fought with the Navy, which wanted new construction, only to complain about insufficient British armaments a few years later. But what was more important was what Churchill himself always emphasised: changing situations require different, possibly even contradictory views. In war one must fight with all harshness in order to throw down the enemy; after victory one must reach out a hand to him and help him. It is no coincidence that the motto, 'the moral of the story' of Churchill's history of the Second World War which precedes not just one but all six volumes is: 'In war, Resolution. In defeat, Defiance. In victory, Magnanimity. In peace, Goodwill.'

Here we find the key to understanding: with the victory of 1945 the situation changed, and therefore behaviour also had to change. Hitler's tyranny had been destroyed, and Germany was a field of ruins. To kick the nation already on the ground would not only have been unfair, it would have been unwise. It had to be helped to a new start. As a man with the experience of history, Churchill had always respected German abilities and achievements in times of peace and feared them in times of war. What was called for now was to use them for freedom.

And if a new tyranny now stood in central Europe, armed to the teeth, then it had to be opposed with the same determination as the recently vanquished one. Churchill attempts to show that the necessary conversion did not succeed, or only after such a delay as human sluggishness demands. And it is in this, superficially in the triumph of victory, in the feeling of being in the right and remaining so, that in Churchill's view the tragedy he is talking about is founded.

There is a final note to be added on Churchill's last important official act, his participation in the summit meeting at Potsdam which took place in Cäcilienhof Castle between 17 July and 2 August 1945. The group taking part had changed since Teheran and Yalta. Instead of Roosevelt, Truman now sat among the 'Big Three', and because of the uncertain outcome of the General Election, Churchill brought Attlee along, who replaced him after 29 July and also signed the closing documents.

Churchill concentrates his portrayal of the conference on the discussion about the atomic bomb whose employment against Japan was imminent, and on the westward extension of Poland to the Oder and Neisse rivers. He emphasises that he and his Foreign Secretary Anthony Eden had always had the eastern Neisse in mind, and would never have agreed to a shift forward to the western Neisse. And he says:

> Moving three or four million Poles was bad enough. Were we to move more than eight million Germans as well? . . . For the future peace of Europe here was a wrong beside which Alsace-Lorraine and the Danzig Corridor were trifles. One day the Germans would want their territory back, and the Poles would not be able to stop them.[15]

But it did not end that way. In 1990, on the way to reunification, Germany officially recognised the border drawn in 1945 as being final, and this border turned into a bridge of reconciliation. After everything the two nations have done to each other—first in 1939 with the German reign of terror in Poland, then in 1945 with the expulsion of the Germans—it appears to be succeeding to a degree which raises hopes for a common future. But who could have known that then, when the issues were the border lines and the expulsions? Churchill's sinister prediction appeared to be far more realistic, and it was also claimed that Stalin hoped for what the British Prime Minister feared: Poland and Germany would be fixed to their hostility in the long term so that the Soviet Union could all the more easily dominate them both.

From the German perspective we must add, unfortunately, that Churchill is washing his hands of all blame in vain. He and his Foreign Secretary—as well as Roosevelt—had already agreed at Yalta to the principle of shifting the borders, and thereby to the expulsion of the Germans from the territories east of the Oder and Neisse. Whether this was to be the eastern or the western Neisse is only a minor detail.

The Potsdam summit meeting decided that northern East Prussia, with Königsberg, was to fall to the Soviet Union. Poland took the rest of East Prussia, Danzig and West Prussia, eastern Pomerania, the Brandenburg Neumark and Silesia—'under administration until a final ruling by a peace conference', as it was phrased in diplomatic obfuscation. But the expulsion of the population aimed at finality. How was this ever to be reversed? By a counter-expulsion of the Poles who had moved in meanwhile? Incidentally, the decision of Potsdam also applied to the Germans in Czechoslovakia and Hungary. A total of 12.4 million people were affected. It said, further, that the 'resettlement' was to take place in an 'orderly and humane form'. But is it not inhumane when people are driven from their hereditary home no matter in what form? In the better times for war and peace of the eighteenth and nineteenth centuries, the mere thought of such an act of violence would have been considered barbaric. What then took place in practice flew in the face of the wording. For shipment out the 'resettlers' were only permitted to take with them what they could carry—and, as an evil rule, were then attacked and stripped clean, often literally down to their last shirt, by professionally organised gangs operating without any interference.[16]

With the coldness of heart of economic calculation we could add something more. In the east, Germany lost agrarian problem areas which had placed a heavy burden on the Weimar Republic, and the Federal Republic gained very much. The refugees and those expelled did not want to remain paupers and wished to escape from their threatening social declassification at any price. They developed a unique willingness to achieve that made a decisive contribution to the material rise of the Federal Republic, to her *Wirtschaftswunder*. This unexpected outcome of the Potsdam decisions is one of the ironic gambits history loves. But what does it count compared to the loss of home and of historic ties?

October Sun
and November Fog

> It only remains for me to express to the British people, for whom I have acted in these perilous years, my profound gratitude for the unflinching, unswerving support which they have given me during my task, and for the many expressions of kindness which they have shown towards their servant.

These are the words with which Churchill ended a message to the nation on election night, 26 July 1945, and with them his report on the Second World War also ends.[1] And why did he not leave it at that? Why did he not really retire? He had now passed the line to which the Bible points in Psalm 90:

> The days of our years are threescore years and ten: and if by reason of strength they be fourscore years, yet is their strength labour and sorrow; for it is soon cut off, and we fly away.

And did the war years, with their enormous pressures, not count double? The curse of people in retirement – not having anything to do – need hardly have been feared. The great summary of the past years would have provided normal writers or historians with enough work for half, or the whole of, a lifetime.

Churchill stood at the zenith of his reputation. He was a famous man the world over, possibly the most famous of all the men of his times if we disregard the organised adulation of Stalin in the cathedrals and foyers of Communism. Honours simply rained down upon him, from doctor's mortar boards to the Nobel Prize for Literature in 1953, the *Karlspreis* of the city of Aix-la-Chapelle in 1956 and honorary citizenship of the United States in 1963. And His Majesty King George VI would have liked nothing better than to elevate him to a dukedom with the full concurrence of the government and Parliament, just as Queen Anne had once elevated John Churchill to become Duke of Marlborough. He could then have spoken in the House of Lords just as he liked, and have stood far above the lowly spheres of party politics. He could have travelled and given speeches the world would listen to, as he did in 1946 in Fulton and Zürich, in 1948 in Amsterdam and in 1949 in Strasburg. And he was personally able to afford anything he liked, because he was now not just a nationally but an internationally best-selling author. The financial worries of the pre-war period were long past and were never to return again. The rich of this world already counted it an honour to receive him as their guest and to surround him with all the luxury they could offer him, for example in their villas on the Riviera or on their yachts. A sunny autumn lay before him, such as is given only to a few chosen ones.

But Churchill would not even consider stopping. He took on the position of Leader of the Opposition in the Commons and sank his teeth into the party political fight against the coalition partner of the war years, not infrequently in petty, not to say quarrelsome, polemics. He fought for his return to the highest office of state with all his energy. He threw himself into the election campaigns of 1950 and 1951 with full commitment. In February 1950 he lost by a whisker; in October 1951 the Conservatives won a majority of 26 seats and Churchill, now approaching his 77th birthday, was again Prime Minister.

Why? The answer must be given on several levels. To begin with, there is the rule that a person who has enjoyed political power to the fullest measure can no longer give it up—just as an addict cannot give up his heroin. One can find proof of this everywhere—in Germany from Bismarck to Konrad Adenauer to Helmut Kohl. Only wisdom or laziness—preferably both combined—lead to the exceptions, as with Stanley Baldwin who resigned voluntarily in 1937. But Baldwin belonged to a dying breed: he was still an amateur, not a professional, politician. After Roosevelt, therefore, wisdom in the United States limited the term in office of the President to eight years. Unwise regimes must reckon with the senility of their leaders in office—like those of the Communist states until their collapse.

Secondly, in an earlier chapter we discussed the rankings of human passions and discovered that for Churchill political passion was the dominating one. Be it in Parliament or in the political arena of the world, only the challenge to fight provoked his commitment, and the greater the challenge the greater also the commitment, the better, the more joyful. One need only recall the war year 1940. What else was worth living for? What was left after quitting politics? 'It is all so boring' were, allegedly, the last words the dying man spoke.

Thirdly, Churchill actually did believe that he was better qualified to lead the country than anybody else. But what challenge was there in the early 1950s which could have made the commitment worthwhile? The defence of the Empire? No: its core — India — had already been released into independence, and it could be foreseen that other countries would follow. That the days of colonial rule were over was drastically demonstrated in 1956 when the Americans and the Russians joined together in rare unanimity to stop British and French military action against Egypt over the Suez Canal.

Or was it economic renewal? Churchill was not an expert on the economy and did not have any inspiring visions such as Ludwig Erhard had in the Federal Republic of Germany. This applies to the Conservatives in total. To stop the creeping decline which had been going on for half a century would have required a radical cure, not just the doctoring of symptoms or a little pruning of one or other of the shoots of socialist growth. No again, therefore. The destruction of encrusted but traditional conditions — all the way to the order or anarchy of the unions — was not a job for the old élites. It required an upstart lacking in respect like Margaret Thatcher. But she, half a century younger than Churchill, only entered Parliament in 1959, becoming party leader in 1974 and Prime Minister in 1979.

Or should we mention the unification of Europe? This actually was on the historic agenda after 1945. Churchill provided stimuli and gave inspiring speeches.[2] But by Europe he meant the Continent — France, Germany, the Netherlands, Belgium, Italy and whatever other countries there might be — not Great Britain. She was to assume a special rôle, possibly as the joint or link between Europe and the United States. This was the reason why Churchill, while belonging to the instigators, did not belong to the architects of Europe, like Alcide de Gasperi, Konrad Adenauer, Robert Schumann and Jean Monnet.

Something important, or fateful, must be added: Churchill's strength now began to fail noticeably. He was only able to concentrate and work for a few hours a day. Behind closed doors he was called the 'part-time Prime Minister'. In the summer of 1949 he suffered a mild stroke, though without any visible effects, and the public did not learn about it because he had been away on holiday on the Riviera at the time. Then, on 27 June 1953, the British newspapers reported that the Prime Minister was overworked and 'had to reduce his commitments for a while'. In actual fact he had suffered a further stroke, this time a heavy one which paralysed one side of his body and removed his powers of speech. The doctors were reckoning with his death, his colleagues in the Cabinet with his resignation.

But the tough old man did not give up. Once again he fought a great battle, this time literally for his life—or one like a child for the way into life, to sit upright, to grasp something, to stand up, to take the first faltering steps, to say the first stammering words, to learn to speak. Like a child he burst into tears when he could not do what he wanted and tried to do, and commented on this with the irony of old age: 'I was always rather weepy, but now I have turned into a real cry-baby. Is there nothing to be done about it?'[3] Progress led from the wheelchair to walking with a stick, and in September Churchill could once again be seen in public. The summer holidays and the Parliamentary recess proved to be a piece of luck in adversity: everyone was away on holiday between July and September, the professors and students, the Members, the Ministers and the Queen. Why not the Prime Minister as well?

The acid test came in October. As Party Leader Churchill had to speak at the annual Conservative conference. Was that at all possible, and would he succeed? Would he be able to stand on his feet for long enough and speak forcefully, as inspiringly as the audience expected of him? Or would he begin stammering, lose his train of thought, have to sit down and bury his face in his hands as once before, almost half a century ago, as a young MP? Nothing can be more challenging than a Party Conference. The delegates insist on their right to be inspired and if they are disappointed they demand bitter recompense. The expression 'battle with words' assumed a very special meaning here. Churchill fought it against himself and won—an almost unbelievable achievement of the will.

All in all, however, the second term in office as Prime Minister was a disappointment. There is only one further initiative to report. On 5 March 1953 Jossif Wissarionovitch Dshugashwili—Stalin—died. Was this not the opportunity for a new beginning in world politics? On 11 May that year Churchill made a very surprising speech.[4] He demanded an end to the Cold War, overcoming the bloc formation into East and West, the organisation of togetherness instead of expensive and dangerous confrontation. Whoever wishes to may talk once again of the irony of history. Churchill made a turn-about of 180 degrees compared to the position he had taken and demanded in vain from the Americans in 1945. There was enthusiasm in Great Britain; Washington was displeased; and in Bonn Konrad Adenauer threw up his hands in horror.[5]

The initiative led to no practical results. While Churchill was able to make himself heard, there was little he could achieve. The decisions were taken by the world, or by the superpowers, and in Moscow people were primarily occupied with the power struggle for the succession to Stalin, from which Nikita Khrushchev emerged as the victor. It was only in February 1956, at the Twentieth Party Convention of the CPSU, that he initiated 'de-Stalinisation' with his famous secret speech, but without giving up the objective of convert-ing the world to Communism. In the United States anti-Communism was approaching its apogee. John Foster Dulles, Secretary of State since January 1953, practised it with a firm and harsh hand,[6] and by his persecution of Communists Senator McCarthy created the climate of a witch hunt, particu-larly against intellectuals and artists who fell under suspicion of behaving in a way that was 'un-American'. To this must be added that Churchill himself lost much of his power because the stroke paralysed him for months.

What remains, nevertheless, is admiration for the willpower of the old man. The born warrior recognised that in the atomic age war had changed its appearance and could no longer be permitted as a clash between the world powers if humanity was to have a chance for survival. Once more his thoughts, his worries, led him into the future, far ahead of most of his contemporaries.

The end of the story is quickly told. Despite the astonishing climb out of the depths of the stroke, the decline of Churchill's physical and mental powers continued. 'For a few hours he is still great, better than ever,' his associates said, 'but then everything suddenly stops and for a long time he is simply mentally not there.'[7]

Yes, the autumn fogs were descending on him and the depressions were oppressing him. He had always had them, possibly as a legacy from his father. He called them my 'black dog'. Now they became stronger and stronger. Other people, his colleagues in the Cabinet, urged him to resign from office. On 4 April 1955 Her Majesty Queen Elizabeth II visited the Prime Minister in Downing Street, a royal favour that had never before been bestowed. On 5 April he resigned.

This separation from office was not yet, not quite, the end of his political career. Churchill still clung to Parliament with every fibre of his heart. He felt more at home there than in any other place, and therefore the Member for Woodford continued to take his seat in the Commons, a corner seat on the centre aisle which was reserved for him in reverence. Actually, according to long tradition, this seat belonged to the prominent rebels, and Churchill had been one often enough during his long parliamentary career – between 1929 and 1939 for a whole decade. But now he no longer embarrassed his own government. Until 1959 he occasionally still spoke outside Parliament, but no longer in the Commons. He sat there, listened and remained silent.

Was he really listening? Did he still understand what was being said? Doubts are permissible. One of the complaints of Churchill's old age was a growing, in the end almost total deafness. But twice more, in 1955 and 1959, he let himself be elected to the House of Commons. To give it up appeared to him to be impossible. Here, on 18 February 1901, he had made his first speech; here he had spent his life, with all the ups and downs of a chequered career. For him saying goodbye to the House of Commons would be like saying goodbye to life itself. After having resigned as Prime Minister he had therefore again stoutly resisted the temptation of being elevated to a dukedom and transferred to the House of Lords.

Churchill also fell silent as an author. While his four-volume *History of the English-Speaking Peoples* did appear between 1956 and 1958, the manuscript had been written before the war and was thereafter hardly changed. Anyway, it already ends before the era with which *The World Crisis* and *The Second World War* deal.

Increasingly less remained. Conversations failed because of deafness, and hand and eye failed before the easel. Only this was left: a very old man is sitting in a chair wrapped in blankets because he feels cold even in the sun, he is sunk in reflections or in absence, and with his stick he draws shaky signs in the sand which no one can interpret.

Death came to Churchill after a cruel delay.[8] There were further strokes. In 1962 he fell and fractured the neck of a femur. When he was carried out of the hospital again, wasted and wrinkled, he hesitatingly lifted his hand in the V-for-victory sign to the crowd that was waiting for him. He lived to see – or suffer through – his 90th birthday and died on 24 January 1965.

His country gave him the sort of splendid funeral of which only states with traditions, possibly only ancient monarchies, are capable. Why not?

With him a glorious period of British history was carried to the grave. Some would have preferred to entomb him in the vaults of fame of Westminster Abbey or St Paul's Cathedral. But his last will prohibited this. His grave can be found in the unspectacular village cemetery of Bladon in Oxfordshire, next to the grave of his father whom he had always wanted to be close to, and whom he survived by seventy years to the day.

Attempt at a Summary

There is the story of the German, the Frenchman and the Englishman who are celebrating the turn of the nineteenth to the twentieth centuries together by going on a cruise around the world. Somewhere along the way the German, keen as usual, is looking out to sea with his binoculars and points: 'There is an island out there!' The Frenchman suspiciously: 'Is it British?' 'It usually is', murmurs the Englishman sleepily without even bothering to look up.

Yes, as in a fairy tale we can say: once upon a time that is the way it was. The size, the power and the glory of the British Empire, spanning the globe as no other before it, had reached its zenith. England was the precursor of the Industrial Revolution, a constitutional model, the leading power in economy and trade; her Navy ruled the seas, and to her colonial possessions belonged not only islands but parts of and even whole continents.

Winston Spencer Churchill was born into this glory, and on the sunny side of life at that, as a descendant of the tradition-conscious and unshakably self-confident upper class that had ruled Britain and the Empire since time immemorial. Two years after Churchill's birth Benjamin Disraeli crowned Queen Victoria Empress of India. The child saw his own grandfather, the Duke of Marlborough, surrounded by a brilliant court as Viceroy of Ireland. The young man learned something about the pride of power, adventure and victory in India, the Sudan and South Africa.

And why should it not remain as it was, only with continuing progress towards liberty and wealth? The most famous social philosopher of the age, Herbert Spencer (1820–1903), described the historic dimensions and the future perspectives of this progress with great optimism, almost as if it were a law of nature.[1]

There were social problems, of course, from which Karl Marx and Friedrich Engels drew their radical conclusions, hardly by coincidence in London and Manchester. Because in Britain, too, or especially there, the gap between wealth and poverty was crass, and class barriers appeared almost 'like Indian castes'.[2] But something could be done about that. The hour, not to say the glorious century, of the social democrats and social reformers had arrived.[3] They could be found in all the camps, even among the Liberals and the Conservatives. The still young Minister for Economic Affairs, Churchill, was one of them, driven onwards by the persuasiveness and enthusiasm of his teacher David Lloyd George. Churchill admired the achievements of the German social state, whose foundations had been laid by the latter-day Bismarck, and tried to transfer them to Britain. And in fact, despite all the ups and downs, wars and catastrophes, in Great Britain, in Germany and in other European countries the development of the social state was to continue without interruption. It is only at the end of the twentieth century that it is being increasingly called into question. That is why meanwhile we talk, perhaps prematurely, about 'the end of the social democratic age'.[4]

There was also Imperialism, which found its expression in the race and struggle for colonies by the European powers, finally and particularly in Africa. Germany spoke about 'her place in the sun' that she intended to gain, and began to build a battlefleet so that words might possibly be followed by deeds. But was the war really inevitable? The clash can at least not be attributed to the struggle for markets, quite in contrast to the theories Lenin was later to expound.[5] Disputes were settled,[6] and the nations and states were basically directed far more towards co-operation than towards conflict. Economic development was not a game of zero end result, in which one side always had to lose what the other gained; it brought advantages to everyone taking part. When, for example, the United States and Germany began to catch up with Great Britain, this may have been uncomfortable for the home of the steam engine and the railway, the steel and the textile industries, but the figures show that the new economic powers were not in any way replacing the old. Exports and imports increased reciprocally, and Great Britain only fell back in relative terms. The give-and-take of world economics has rarely been so well balanced as it was on the eve of the First World War.[7]

Even war—if there was to be one after all—appeared to be losing its horrors. The nineteenth century had civilised it. The soldiers paid a blood toll, as it was their professional duty to do, and were feared and honoured for this, and the civilian population was hardly affected. Furthermore, the newer European wars one could recall only lasted a few weeks, or at worst months, like the war of Sardinia and France against Austria in 1859 and Bismarck's wars against Denmark in 1864, Austria in 1866 and France in 1870–71. No, there was only little to fear and still much to gain. Any sensible consideration pointed, as with Herbert Spencer, to further progress towards freedom and wealth, to the road towards sunny uplands that Great Britain had paved for Europe and the world.[8] Incidentally, even in the days of crisis, on the very brink, for example in the 'Blood, Sweat and Tears' speech in 1940, the hope returned in Churchill that 'humanity is moving forward towards its goal'.[9] In the sense of this hope for—if no longer an unerring belief in—progress, he always remained a son and heir of the nineteenth century.

The question is, however, whether the people and the nations permit themselves always and safely to be governed by reason leading to the uplands. Are there not also the dark depths in which envy and hatred, the thirst for revenge and the lust for power lie hidden? Or, possibly even more effective, the longing to prove oneself, for fame and heroics, to which only appropriate 'idealistic' reason need be added to unleash it unto death and destruction beyond any rational reason? What else does the history of the world teach us? What were the Crusades fought for? Why were the faggots of the stakes ignited? Is it a coincidence that immediately after the expulsion from the Garden of Eden, the Bible tells us the horror story of the first fratricide?

In retrospect, in any case, the belief in progress appears to have been foolish. It only lights up the surface. It says farewell to both history and the nature of man, sinful 'old Adam', in favour of a future which should belong to the designers, including the designers of a new, in the end only boringly 'good' human being.[10] Here cultural pessimism, which always accompanied the belief in progress like its shadow, plumbed deeper, especially in Germany.

The start of the First World War tore the veil of illusion asunder. Europe stumbled into catastrophe—and not in horror but with great enthusiasm. Had the process of civilisation perhaps demanded too much from man in the way of a renunciation of his basic drives, and given him too little in return—in the end only a surfeit of what existed? Before the start of the war the philosopher Max Scheler wrote:

... [the objective, the] reconstruction of the view of the world we envisage [will be] like the first step into a blooming garden by someone who has been kept in a dark dungeon for many years. And this dungeon will have been our human environment with its 'civilisation', limited as it is by a mentality only directed towards what is mechanical or can be mechanised ... And the prisoner will have been European man of yesterday and today, who with sighs and groans goes striding along under the burden of his own mechanisms and, with only the earth in his eye and heaviness in his limbs, has forgotten his God and his world.[11]

Liberation through the destruction of civilisation, salvation through war, a new meaning of life through the encounter with death? In 1914 the gentle poet Rainer Maria Rilke, the sensitive friend of France and Russia, spoke for millions — and not only in Germany — when he said

> Hail me, that I see those who are moved. For long
> has fate for us not been true
> and the contrived picture did not appeal seriously to us.
> Beloved, now time speaks like a prophet
> blind, out the most ancient spirit.
> Hark ye. You do not hear it yet. Now you are as trees
> the powerful current thrums through ever louder:
> Over the levelled years it comes storming across
> from the emotions of the fathers, from higher deeds, from the high
> peaks of heroism, who nightly under the fresh snows
> of your joyful fame shine more purely, closer ...

War, however, had a very different character from that which the people and the nations had expected. It was stamped by the achievements of an industrial society. The age of the machine created the machine gun as the terrible, dominating weapon, and the chemical industry provided the poison gas. Battles of *matériel*, and the soldiers only disposable *matériel*, dirt instead of purity, miserable death instead of the peaks of heroism. At best the chivalrous duels of the fighter pilots still offered in modern trappings a reflection of what may once have been — and that only because their weapons were too new to be as horribly effective as they were later on in the Second World War. The fall from enthusiasm into disappointment could not have been greater. In the end the only thing discovered was not a new meaning, but the senselessness of it all. For what except self-destruction had the war been fought at all?

This result split Europe. On one side stood the victors, who had achieved little or nothing that promised to be lasting. What they imposed on the vanquished was submission without the prospect of reconciliation — commented upon with perspicacity by the Allied Commander-in-Chief Marshal Foch: 'This is not Peace. It is an Armistice for twenty years.'[12] And what followed, to use Churchill's words, was 'a sad story of complicated idiocy'.[13] Very understandably the experience of senselessness led to the conclusion: 'Never again war!' Pacifism developed into a political power in the nations in the West.

At the opposite pole stood the Soviet Union, 'the fatherland of the worker', with its claim to be able to convert the evil of this world into good, founded by Lenin and then led by Stalin. It, too, had been created by the war, and not only in the sense that military failure, the collapse of Russia, had made the October Revolution of 1917 possible. What was far more important was that the experience of senselessness demanded being given a new sense: the creation of the classless, model society for mankind, which, according to Marxist teachings, alone offered a guarantee that exploitation, violence and war could be brought to an end truly and for ever. For such a high goal any means appeared to be justified, even demanded. It justified dictatorship, violence for the abolition of violence, the idealism of the willingness to sacrifice and the destruction of the class enemies.

Those actually vanquished could be found, as it were, in the shattered centre between the poles — first and foremost Germany. On the one hand they gambled on a democratic republic — as an experiment, so to speak, and rather half-heartedly — and thereby on the contact with Western civilisation.[14] On the other hand they swore themselves to hatred and revenge, initially in many mutually competing ideologies and organisations.[15] For the determined individuals, here too any means appeared to be justified. In the end the most determined missionary of hatred and revenge triumphed — Adolf Hitler.

Churchill's historic rôle begins with the results of the First World War, which already carried the seeds of future evil in them. What had gone on before — the young parliamentarian who crossed the floor, the speaker and writer, the minister in varying offices, the successes and failures — certainly made him into an interesting figure, but only one among many. Recent British history is rich in interesting figures. But the age of violence the First World War initiated finds its echo, its counter-player, not to say its appropriate expression in the nature, complicated as it is to the point of contradiction, of a Churchill.

He was first a dyed-in-the-wool liberal from the beginning, the man of liberty and law, born into the belief in progress of the nineteenth century and into the conviction of the 'mission of civilisation' of Great Britain, its Dominions and the United States of America — in brief, the English-speaking peoples. In their 'history', written before the Second World War and published in old age almost like a political testament, this conviction finds its expression — naïve if you like, but reasoned with all the more self-confidence. In the picture, and as part of the issue, we also have the parliamentarian, for whom the British House of Commons was not just an institution like many others but the epitome of political wisdom, and which provided him with a home in a deeper sense, touching both the heart and the head. Therefore the defence of the parliamentary system against all vicissitudes and foes was for him only natural.

At the same time Churchill was something else entirely — a born warrior. The young man had already been magically attracted by military adventure on the Indian border, in the Sudan and in South Africa, and the two great wars of the twentieth century set free all his energies and passions.

Of course, he did not let himself be surpassed by anyone in his criticism of the stupid butchery of the First World War, in his condemnation of the statesmen and strategists who could think of nothing better than driving the youth of Europe against the enemy wire and machine guns in senseless attacks. But one has to look closely: The World Crisis we read about is basically a crisis of war.[16] Churchill's intent and purpose is to salvage war, to preserve it as the possible continuation of politics by other means. The narrow-minded military leaders are being chastised because they spoil war and deliver it into the hands of its detractors.

Herein lies the foundation for the admiration of imaginative generals and important strategists, even among the enemy, as, in the Second World War, Erwin Rommel and Erich von Manstein. It is even more the basis for his own interference, the restless search for ways out by the amateur strategist, beginning with the Dardanelles operation of 1915, whose failure almost breaks him. Only the old man was able to see his way clear — in the light of the atomic bomb — to taking leave of war. It was more than taking leave of war as a traditional instrument of politics and a civilisation which also included war as if it were natural,[17] but, possibly even more important and contradictory, taking leave of a human possibility for seeking adventure and not being stifled by a boredom which ends in self-destruction.[18]

Finally, but not less importantly, Churchill was a man of history. He lived from it, and it is not by chance that he turned to it both as a reader and a writer. He knew that it included violence and the abysses of human passions one might be able to tame but never overcome — and that one required power in order to oppose violence. That was why he experienced his finest and most happy hour when power fell to him in 1940.

In far more than a party political sense, his being rooted in history branded Churchill as a conservative, in other words as an opponent of all ideologies and utopias. Woe to the false prophets who want to create a new man — no matter under what auspices — and woe even more the the peoples and nations who succumb to the false prophets! Under the spell of the ideological designers reality turns into insanity. Any attempt to create a new world, the new man, out of the ruins of what exists unleashes the violence of insanity, which ends in destruction and nothing else. Edmund Burke had already taught Churchill this, and, guided by him, he recognised the great movements of violence of the twentieth century with all their fearful implications. And so he recognised Hitler as well, in contrast to his contemporaries who only longed for peace and a reasonably calculating politician of peace like Neville Chamberlain, and was ordained to become his counterplayer.

In retrospect there is reason for astonishment. Churchill was actually an heir of the nineteenth century, spoiled by the circumstances of his birth, and his old-fashioned traits are visible clearly enough. Yet he proved himself to be fit for the future because he was able to grasp that Western civilisation was no longer self-evident, as Herbert Spencer still believed, but an artificial product of history, based on many conditions, and as easily shattered as any noble vessel. And this is what made him into a conservative, into the determined defender of liberty and law.

None of the three elements could be lacking. The belief in progress was important, so as not to lose heart, but it knew too little about the dark depths and the powers of destruction. Therefore it proved itself to be quicksand, and its adherents betrayed it when it was no longer able to support them. Without the determination to wage war, if necessary at any price, liberty and law could not have been upheld in the hour of danger. Historic insight identified the enemy, the power of destruction of those forces which are driven by hatred when they proclaim paradise on earth or promise absolute rule. And out of insight grew the strength to resist.

The question now is, what did Churchill actually achieve or what did he fail to achieve? Must we in summary speak of the triumph or the tragedy of his life? Before we judge summarily and prematurely we must differentiate.

To begin in the negative: there can be no doubt that Churchill enmeshed himself in guilt. One need only recall the unleashing of the air war against the German civilian population. It turned out to be barbaric—and ineffective for the purpose of bringing Hitler's regime down. It was both a crime and a mistake. The expulsion of millions of people from their hereditary homes looks only marginally less bad. While Churchill might not have been able to prevent these deportations, he was involved in them at least through carelessness. As far as Poland and other countries in eastern Europe are concerned, however, it was hardly in his power to prevent their subjugation by Stalin. The same applies to the territories in central Germany which the Western Allies first occupied and then evacuated again.

An important question is whether Churchill could have pursued a different policy from that he actually followed. Would it have been better to seek a negotiated peace instead of insisting on victory at any price? There are voices that claim this. Erich Schwinge, for example, writes:

> When on 28 May 1940 the British Cabinet again discussed the question whether it was not advisable to seek negotiations with Hitler, Churchill sharply replied to those in favour that Hitler would demand the handing over of the British Fleet and the occupation of all British naval ports. According to the report by Labour Minister Dalton, this claim immediately made the opposing side fall silent. There was not a shred of evidence that Hitler would make such demands. Here Churchill had—as he so often did—exaggerated the German danger. And if in the further course of the war a negotiated peace did not come about, then Churchill bears the majority of the blame for this. Millions of people's lives could have been spared if he had given up this inflexible position.[19]

Exaggeration of the danger, negotiations, agreement with Hitler? Neville Chamberlain tried it. He had gone to the extreme in order to save the peace, and had failed. At the end of the meeting in Bad Godesberg in September 1938 stood his bitter sentence: 'I must say with great disappointment and deep regret, *Herr Reichskanzler*, that you have not given me even the smallest support in my efforts to preserve the peace.' After Hitler's entry into Prague in March and his attack on Poland in September 1939, Chamberlain could have modified his words: '*Herr Rechskanzler*, I must state in horror and outrage that your promises and signatures are worth nothing.'

We remarked earlier that the mere attempt to open negotiations would probably have irrevocably broken the British will to resist. Apart from that,

Hitler wanted to rule Europe and to destroy everyone who stood in his way. His programme included the extermination of the Jews and the conquest of *Lebensraum* in the East and the enslavement of the peoples who lived there. Only with horror can we imagine the fate that would have been theirs after 'final victory' by Germany. Thanks to Churchill's steadfastness millions of lives were saved.

For Hitler any means were justified for the achievement of his objectives. Why not also a negotiated peace which was just bearable for Great Britain? For him this would only have been a temporary tactical measure, like the treaty of non-aggression with the Soviet Union in August 1939. There would never again have been a way out of dependence for Great Britain. No one would have been left to defend Western civilisation from the onslaught of tyranny. In other words, the critics stare at Churchill and completely lose sight of Hitler. In the worst cases they seem to regard him as a gentleman who remains unbesmirched by a few peccadillos.

If this is now clear, if there were no promising, and certainly no honourable, alternatives to Churchill's position and behaviour, then the consequences become unmistakable, especially the dependence on the United States into which Great Britain first fell financially and economically, and then militarily and politically. Many critics take Churchill to task about this, but without stating what other alternatives there were.[20]

Churchill himself never hesitated to let himself in for this dependence, and he defined it as the community of fate in the battle against tyranny that it actually was. Of course he was confident that he could continue to play a leading rôle and — to use Haffner's metaphor — wag the dog with the tail. This, however, could not succeed in the long run and even the cornerstone of his friendship with Roosevelt turned out to be brittle in the end. Here we must speak of over-confidence, of illusion, and in 1945 Churchill's disappointment was appropriately great.

What, then, did he achieve, and what remains in retrospect? History must constantly be rewritten because perspectives change as time passes. If we start with the fateful year of 1945, we can easily speak of a tragedy, as Churchill himself did. Hitler's regime had been destroyed and Germany had become a field of ruins over which the Allies ruled as they pleased. But, in place of Hitler, Stalin now stood at the apogee of his power and the Red Army in central Europe. Behind the Iron Curtain which separated East from West there was no liberty for the people and nations, but again tyranny and violence. No one could know what further threat the Soviet empire posed now that the armies of the West were melting away. Had the struggle been worth it? Looked at from a pessimistic point of view it could well be appropriate to say with Goethe's Mephisto: 'A great effort, shamefully! has been wasted.'

But history does not end in 1945. Only a few short years later things looked quite different. Western Europe began with its unification, and an alliance under the patronage of the United States protected its freedom. If Soviet power stood on the Elbe and Werra rivers, immovable as it appeared, then the borders of the West had also been moved forward by a decisive span—from Aix-la-Chapelle to Helmstedt. The major part of Germany now belonged to the West, with two-thirds, and soon—because of the movement of refugees from east to west—almost four-fifths of the population. The economic development of the West outdistanced that of the East even further, and West Berlin formed an outpost of freedom.

At the close of the twentieth century the situation has again changed, and dramatically so. The Soviet Union has fallen apart and its empire has dissolved. Not even the Red Army still exists, only the Russian Army, which has moved far away and is no longer feared by anyone. Germany has been resurrected as a national state, no longer as an unfathomable military power but as a civilian society, a democracy that is no longer a danger, integrated into Europe. The Poles, Czechs and other peoples again live as they themselves want, and are preparing themselves for membership in NATO and the European Union.

A better balance sheet is hardly conceivable. It can be summarised in one sentence: liberty and peace reign in Europe. In a centennial look back at a blood-soaked era full of horror there is cause for gratitude. And as to no other, our gratitude is owed to the man who in the hour of need, of the triumph of tyranny, when everything appeared to be lost, seized the banner of freedom and carried it unwaveringly onwards to victory.

Notes

The Shudders of Childhood and Youth

1 Whoever would like an entertaining example should go to see the film *Kind Hearts and Coronets* starring Alec Guinness. A young man murders his way through his relatives with great charm in order to inherit the ducal title and the fortune that goes with it.

2 Winston Churchill, *My Early Life: A Roving Commission*, London, 1930, pp. 12–13.

3 Possibly for reasons of discretion, Churchill wrote about St James' School, also in the text cited here, and this has led to much confusion. Many biographers have allowed themselves to be misled. In actual fact, the school was named after St George.

4 Churchill, *op. cit.*, pp. 18–21. That Churchill's horror story is hardly an exaggeration is confirmed by Maurice Baring, who attended the school a little later and wrote in his book *The Puppet Show of Memory* (1922): 'Terrible stories were told about Winston Churchill, who had been taken from school. His bad behaviour appears to have broken all bounds. He was beaten because he took some sugar, and far from displaying repentance, he trampled the Head Master's hallowed straw hat which hung above the door. His stay at this school was one long battle with authority, and in this the other boys were not on his side.'

5 See Randolph S. Churchill, *Winston S. Churchill*, London, 1966–88, vol. I, p. 60. The great biography by Churchill's son comprises eight volumes (from vol. III onwards by Martin Gilbert) and is exhaustingly long-winded. But the richness of its material is unsurpassed. It is complemented by thirteen volumes which primarily contain a collection of letters by and to Churchill. Here the work is cited as Official Biography.

6 The liberal deputy Ludwig Bamberger has vividly described the situation: 'The German parliament is the only one in the world in which the Ministers and their deputies appear with a sabre at their side and give their speeches with one hand on the pommel. When emotions rise in the heat of debate it can occur that this

hand on the pommel of the sword turns into a characteristic gesture. This singularity of our conditions of representations does not lack a deeper significance.' See L. Bamberger, *Gesammelte Schriften* (Collected Works), vol. 5, Berlin, 1897, p. 333.

7 *My Early Life*, p. 46. There are a number of books dealing with Churchill's childhood and youth. To mention a few: E. D. W. Caplin, *Winston Churchill and Harrow*, Harrow, 1941; Richard H. Davis, *The Young Winston Churchill*, New York, 1941; Stanley Nott, *The Young Churchill*, New York, 1941; John Marsh, *The Young Churchill*, London, 1955; Peter de Mendelssohn, *Churchill: Sein Weg und seine Welt* (Churchill: His Way and His World), vol. I: *Erbe und Abenteuer: Die Jugend Winston Churchills 1874–1914* (Heritage and Adventure: The Youth of Winston Churchill 1874–1914), Freiburg im Breisgau, 1957 (only this first volume was published); Ted Morgan, *Churchill: Young Man in a Hurry, 1874–1915*, New York 1982.

8 Here—in *The River War*, published in 1899—Churchill is talking about the Mahdi who unleashed the (initially successful) uprising against the British. But behind the portraits there are, of course, always elements of a self-portrait. Decades later, in the biography of his ancestor Marlborough (published 1933–38), one can read: 'It is said that famous men are usually the product of unhappy childhood. The stern compression of circumstances, the twinges of adversity, the spur of slights and taunts in early years, are needed to evoke that ruthless fixity of purpose and tenacious mother-wit without which great actions are seldom accomplished.'

Life as an Adventure

1 *My Early Life*, p. 69.
2 Robert Rhodes James, *Churchill : A Study in Failure, 1900–1939*, London, 1970, p. 14.
3 During the summit meeting in Yalta in February 1945 Churchill visited the battlefield of Balaklava near Sevastopol, where the Light Brigade had made its famous charge in 1854. In his conversation with the accompanying Soviet officer a nice misunderstanding occurred. Churchill pointed in the direction from which the attack had come. The officer nodded and began to give explanations—but 90 years out of date. Churchill had meant the British cavalry charge against the Russians; the officer was talking about the Russian tank attack against the Germans.
4 There had been uprisings since 1868. In 1898, after the explosion of the American warship *Maine* in the harbour at Havana, the United States declared war on Spain and forced the cession of the island. With this, the chequered and tension-filled relationship between the USA and Cuba began.
5 Official Biography, vol. I, p. 271.
6 *Ibid.*, vol. I, p. 275.

7 Churchill's later literary allusions mainly stem from the education he managed to acquire by reading during his time in India and in the years thereafter. See Darrell Holley, *Churchill's Literary Allusions: An Index of the Education of a Young Soldier, Statesman, and Litterateur*, Jefferson, Ohio, 1987.

8 *My Early Life*, p. 165.

9 *Ibid.*, p. 197.

10 *Ibid.*, p. 203.

11 For literature on the history of the Boer War see F. Maurice, *History of the War in South Africa*, 4 vols, London, 1906–1910; E. Holt, *The Boer War*, London, 1958; and J. S. Marais, *The Fall of Kruger's Republic*, Oxford, 1961.

12 Official Biography, vol. I, p. 451.

13 Winston Churchill, *A History of the English-Speaking Peoples*, 4 vols, London, 1956–58, vol. IV, *The Great Democracies*, p. 358.

14 During his visit to New York Churchill also met an American namesake, and asked him: 'Why don't you go into politics? I mean to be Prime Minister of England: it would be a great lark if you were President of the United States at the same time.' See Official Biography, vol. I, p. 353.

An Aside on Human Passions

1 Pamela Plowden later married the Earl of Lytton. Possibly with a trace of regret about the connection with Churchill which did not come to pass, she said in retrospect: 'When you meet Winston for the first time you only see his faults – and you then spend the rest of your life discovering his good qualities.'

2 Official Biography, vol. II, p. 249.

3 G. A. Riddell, *The Riddell Diaries 1908–1923*, pub. by J. M. McEwen, 1986, p. 20.

4 For more detail see Mary Soames, *Clementine Churchill*, London, 1979. Also by Mary Soames, a daughter of Churchill: *A Churchill Family Album*, London, 1982. See also Richard Hough, *Winston and Clementine: The Triumph of the Churchills*, London, 1990; A. L. Rowse, *The Early Churchills: An English Family*, London, 1959; and the same, *The Later Churchills*, London, 1958.

5 A whole book could be written on this subject; one need only recall Goethe's son August. Even worse than Randolph Churchill's was the fate of Bismarck's son Herbert. See Christian Graf von Krockow, *Bismarck: Eine Biograpie* (Bismarck: A Biography), Stuttgart, 1997, p. 279.

6 Sebastian Haffner, *Winston Churchill mit Selbstzeugnissen und Bilddokumenten* (Winston Churchill with Self-Avowals and Pictorial Documents), 14th edn, Reinbeck bei Hamburg, 1997, p. 39.

7 See, for example, John Lukacs, *Churchill und Hitler: Der Zweikampf* (Churchill and Hitler: The Duel), Munich and Zürich, 1995, p. 67.

8 Churchill himself paid tribute to painting when he first explained how an amateur too can learn to see through painting and then said: 'When I get to heaven I mean to spend a considerable portion of my first million years in painting, and

so get to the bottom of the subject.' See *Thoughts and Adventures*, London, 1932, p. 325 *et seq.*; and Winston Churchill, *Painting as a Pastime*, London, 1948.

9 Sebastian Haffner said quite rightly: 'Like Thomas Mann, Churchill wrote a totally unmistakable and inimitable style, a high style polished by the classics in his language, and, as with Thomas Mann, Churchill's linguistic orchestra resembled the gigantic instrumental assemblies of the times — the orchestras of a Gustav Mahler, for example, or a Richard Strauss, or, to stay in Churchill's England, an Edward Elgar. He used words the way a composer uses instruments, and they were all at his disposal, from the trombone to the piccolo flute, from the triangle to the organ, and how well he knew how to play on this gigantic orchestra! Like a composer he also knew how to deal with great masses of subject matter. He was a master of the great form, knew how to make something complicated transparent, something abstract vivid and tangible, and everything he touched exciting.' See 'Winston S. Churchill: Vom Krieger aus Leidenschaft zum Friedenspolitiker' (Winston S. Churchill: From the Warrior out of Passion to the Politician of Peace), in *Im Schatten der Geschichte: Historisch-politische Variationen* (In the Shadow of History: Historical-Political Variations), Stuttgart, 1985, p. 259.

10 Official Biography, vol. II, p. 54. There are, of course, exceptions to the rule. In the 1930s the American reporter Edgar Snow discovered a man named Mao Tse-tung in a loam cave in China and made him known to the world in his book *Red Star over China*. He also taught Mao and his followers how to play bridge, and one of Mao's great successors, Deng Xiao-peng, has remained a passionate life-long bridge player — and a good one, according to reports.

11 For more details see Krockow, *Bismarck*, p. 261 *et seq.*

12 See *Das Tagebuch der Baronin Spitzemberg: Aufzeichnungen aus der Hofgesellschaft des Hohenzollernreiches* (The Diary of Baroness Spitzemberg: Recordings from the Court Society of the Hohenzollern Empire), pub. by Rudolf Vierhaus, 4th edn, Göttingen, 1976, p. 238.

The Parliamentarian

1 *My Early Life*, p. 380.

2 *Ibid.*, pp. 381–2.

3 John Charmley, *Churchill: The End of Glory: A Political Biography*, London, 1993, p. 207. To interject a recollection of my own here: as a young exchange student I attended one of Churchill's campaign rallies in 1951. It took place in a football stadium and was perfectly staged. It was dark and the moon was just rising when Churchill stepped out on the podium. During his speech he stumbled over the name of the local Labour candidate. He tried again — and muddled it up again. The result was a storm of laughter and applause. Everyone had got the point: if the man's name is that unpronounceable, one can obviously not vote for him. Even the celestial staging was perfect: the moment the speech was over, the moon disappeared behind some clouds.

4 See Carl Schmitt, *Der Begriff des Politischen* (The Definition of Politics), 3rd edn, Hamburg, 1933, p. 48.

5 *Ibid.*, p. 12.

6 See Carl Schmitt, *Politische Theologie* (Political Theology), 2nd edn, Munich and Leipzig, 1934, p. 54.

7 See Carl Schmitt, *Die geistesgeschichtliche Lage des heutigen Parlamentarismus* (The Intellectual-Historical Situation of Contemporary Parliamentarism), 2nd edn, Munich and Leipzig, 1926, p. 22. For more detail see Christian Graf von Krockow, *Die Entscheidung: Eine Untersuchung über Ernst Jünger, Carl Schmitt, Martin Heidegger* (The Decision: A Study on Ernst Jünger, Carl Schmitt, Martin Heidegger), Frankfurt-am-Main and New York, 1990.

8 C. Northcote Parkinson, 'The Will of the People, or Annual General Meeting' in *Parkinsons's Law and Other Studies in Administration*, New York, 1968, p. 28 *et seq.*

9 Winston Churchill, *The Second World War*, vol. I, bk I, ch. 5, London, 1948–54. Since there have been several editions of this work and the page numbers differ, all quotations from *The Second World War* are cited only according to volume, book and chapter.

Stages of a Political Career

1 Official Biography, vol. II, p. 135.

2 On Smith see J. Campbell, *F. E. Smith, First Earl of Birkenhead*, 1994.

3 See R. Hyam, *Elgin and Churchill at the Colonial Office*, 1968.

4 Official Biography, vol. II, pp. 320–1.

5 On Botha see H. Spender, *General Botha*, 2nd edn, London, 1919; and S. C. B. Buxton, *General Botha*, London, 1924. On Smuts see W. K. Hancock, *Smuts*, 2 vols, Cambridge, 1962 and 1968.

6 Churchill wanted to send ships with food to Hamburg immediately after the armistice of 11 November 1918. Nothing came of this, of course.

7 Churchill repeatedly cited this motto, and in his history of the Second World War it is the motto of every one of the volumes.

8 *My Early Life*, pp. 345–6.

9 On the Fabian Society see E. R. Peasant, *History of the Fabian Society*, London, 1925; and A. M. McBriar, *Fabian Socialism and English Politics, 1884–1918*, Cambridge, 1962. On 27 February 1900 the Independent Labour Party (active since 1893), the unions, the Social Democratic Federation and the Fabian Society founded the Labour Representative Committee. In 1906 this was renamed the Labour Party.

10 Here is an example of the catchy way in which Lloyd George spoke: 'The House of Lords has long ceased to be the watchdog of the Constitution. It has become Mr Balfour's poodle. It barks for him. . . .' See Official Biography, vol. II, p. 318. At the time Balfour was the leader of the Conservative opposition.

11 *Thoughts and Adventures*, p. 60.

12 Conservative Prime Minister Stanley Baldwin once made a nicely malicious statement about Churchill: 'I would like to say that at his birth fairies poured gift upon gift over his crib: imagination, the art of rhetoric, diligence, talent. But then one fairy came along and said that no one could claim so many gifts. So she picked him up and shook and rattled him so hard that he lost judgement and wisdom.' Quoted in Thomas Jones, *A Diary with Letters*, 1954, note of 22 May 1936.

13 *The Second World War*, vol. I, bk II, ch. 38, 'The Fall of the Government', final passage of the book.

14 Winston Churchill, *Great Contemporaries*, London, 1937, p. 149.

15 Official Biography, vol. II, p. 313.

16 *Ibid.*, p. 512.

17 *Ibid.*, pp. 513–4.

18 During the First World War David Beatty (1871–1936), Earl of the North Sea and of Brooksby, commanded the British battlecruiser squadron in the Battles of Heligoland Bight (28 August 1914), Dogger Bank (24 January 1915) and Jutland (31 May 1916). He became Commander-in-Chief of the Fleet and was First Sea Lord from 1919 to 1927. Churchill had first met him in 1898 in the Sudan, where the young naval officer commanded a gunboat. On Beatty see W. S. Chalmers, *The Life and Letters of David Earl Beatty*, London, 1951. For Churchill's time as First Lord of the Admiralty see Robert M. Dawson, *Winston Churchill at the Admiralty, 1911–1915*, Oxford, 1940; and, somewhat more broadly, Peter Gretton, *Winston Churchill and the Royal Navy*, New York, 1969.

19 The rates of increase were relatively even greater in France, Russia, Italy and Austria-Hungary. Readers who would like to know more about the navies, maritime trade and the merchant marine of the nations before the First World War should refer to *Taschenbuch der Kriegsflotten* (Handbook of Navies), XV edn, 1914, pub. by B. Weyer, reprinted Munich, 1978.

20 *The World Crisis*, vol. I, p. 100.

21 Michael Stürmer, *Das ruhelose Reich* (The Restless Reich), 2nd edn, Berlin, 1983, p. 320. As a standard work on German battlefleet construction see Volker R. Berghahn, *Der Tirpitzplan: Genesis und Verfall einer innenpolitischen Kriegsstrategy unter Wilhelm II.* (The Tirpitz Plan: Genesis and Decline of Domestic War Strategy under Wilhelm II), Düsseldorf, 1971. On the dream of becoming a world power see Christian Graf von Krockow, *Die Deutschen in ihrem Jahrhundert 1890–1990* (The Germans in Their Century 1890–1990), Reinbeck, 1990, p. 80 *et seq.*

22 For comparison, German battleships launched up to 1906 — the last being *Schlesien* and *Schleswig-Holstein* — had a displacement of 13,200 tonnes, a main battery of four 28cm guns and a speed of about 19 knots. The British dreadnoughts of the *Queen Elizabeth* class, launched only a few years later in 1913 and 1914, displaced 28,500 tonnes (according to information of 1914; in reality probably more). They had a speed of 25 knots and were armed with eight 38.1cm guns.

The weight of a broadside from *Schleswig-Holstein* was 1,690kg, that from *Queen Elizabeth* 7,442kg.

23 Official Biography, vol. II, p. 546.

24 For a biography see R. H. S. Bacon, *The Life of Lord Fisher*, 2 vols, London, 1929.

25 Churchill describes Fisher in *The World Crisis*, 5 vols, London, 1923–31, in vol. I, p. 64 *et seq.*

26 *Ibid.*, p. 67.

27 Alfred Thayer Mahan, *The Influence of Sea Power upon History 1660–1783*, 1890.

28 *Thoughts and Adventures*, pp. 182–3.

29 The first ships of the *Queen Elizabeth* class converted to oil were 3–5 knots faster than their German and British counterparts running on coal. The maximum range for these ships, at reduced speed to conserve fuel, was given at 20,000 nautical miles, whereas for German battleships it was 5,500nm.

30 Even in the Second World War the lack of fuel developed into a problem for the heavy naval units of the German, Italian and Japanese fleets. Thus while the modern German battleships spent most of the time lying at Brest or in a Norwegian fjord, the British battleships launched in 1913–14 — *Queen Elizabeth*, *Barham*, *Malaya*, *Valiant* and *Warspite* — went right on performing their duties, be it in protecting convoys against surface attack or bombarding coastal installations.

31 *The World Crisis*, vol. I, p. 187.

The First World War

1 Quoted in Robert Rhodes James, *op. cit.*, p. 52.

2 Adolf Hitler, *Mein Kampf*, 190th/194th edn, Munich, 1936, p. 177.

3 *The World Crisis*, vol II, p. 515.

4 Quoted in John Charmley, *op. cit.*, p. 180.

5 *The World Crisis*, vol. III, p. 16. For an evaluation of Churchill's book as a history of the First World War see Robin Prior, *Churchill's 'World Crisis' as History*, London, 1983. Defoe's famous story *The Life and Strange Adventures of Robinson Crusoe* appeared in 1719.

6 *The World Crisis*, vol. III, p. 65.

7 *Ibid.*, p. 39. The losses for both sides are listed and compared on p. 37 *et seq.*

8 *Ibid.*, p. 59.

9 Without looking at any alternatives, the German General Staff had committed itself to the Schlieffen Plan, which foresaw an attack through Belgium without regard to the political and military consequences in order to seek a quick decision in the West. This led to a fatal automatism: to avoid falling behind schedule, mobilisation by Russia immediately required a declaration of war against France. If one wanted to be sarcastic one could say that generals — if they have been victorious — do not prepare for the next war but for the one just past. The Schlieffen Plan only repeated, in mirror image and in gigantically expanded

form, the 'Sedan strategy' of 1870, which encircled the French Army, pushed it against the Belgian border and destroyed it there. Developments in weapons technology which, with the firepower of the repeating rifle and the machine gun, favoured the defender, were not taken into consideration at all. The same with the French later on: not taking into consideration what implications the newly developed armoured forces had for the attackers, they built their Maginot Line based on the myth of their defence of Verdun, and thereby set their defeat in 1940 in concrete.

10 *The World Crisis*, vol. III, p. 57.

11 *Ibid.*, vol. IV, p. 53.

12 *Ibid.*, p. 4.

13 *Ibid.*, vol. II, p. 432.

14 *Ibid.*, p. 500.

15 B. E. C. Dugdale, *Arthur James Balfour*, 1936, p. 184. Fisher, from 1909 Baron Fisher of Kilverstone, was 'reactivated' by Churchill as First Sea Lord in 1914. He, like Churchill, was forced to resign in May 1915 because of the failure of the Dardanelles venture.

16 G. A. Riddell, *op. cit.*, p. 115.

17 Lord Birkenhead, *Churchill 1874–1922*, 1989, p. 393.

18 Churchill to his wife. See Official Biography, vol. III. sup. vol. II., p. 1467, letter of 28 March 1916. On Clementine's fears see Mary Soames, *Clementine Churchill*, London, 1979, p. 122.

19 Lloyd George, *War Memoirs*, 6 vols, London, 1933–36. Cited here according to the revised and abbreviated new 1938 edition in one volume, p. 637.

20 *Ibid.*, p. 638.

21 *The World Crisis*, vol. IV, pp. 541–2.

22 *Ibid.*, vol. V. pp. 20–1. For Churchill's position during the post-war years see Donald G. Boadle, *Winston Churchill and the German Question in British Foreign Policy 1918–1922*, The Hague, 1973.

23 The allusion is to the *Dolchstosslegende*, the claim that the Army had remained steadfast and basically invincible until the end, and that defeat had been brought about behind its back by the subversive undermining activities of pacifist or Bolshevist agents. Unfortunately even Hindenburg, as a German patriot, also contributed to this shallow and rather poisonous blather when he wrote in his memoirs: 'We were finished! Like Siegfried under the treacherous spear of grim Hagen, our exhausted front collapsed. In vain had it tried to drink new life out of the drying spring of the vitality of home.' See *Aus meinem Leben* (My Life), Leipzig, 1920, p. 403. This was deliberately phrased as a lie: it had been Hindenburg and Ludendorff who had surprised the still steadfast home front with their demand for an immediate armistice, and in those days it was the commanders who were accused of betrayal. When an officer who had been sent to Berlin to explain the reasons for the demand for an armistice finished with his unvarnished description of the military situation before state secretaries and representatives of the *Reichstag*, a journalist describes the reaction: 'I heard half-

smothered exclamations, I saw welling tears. An awakening out of narcosis, anger, rage, shame, accusation: for a long time we have been lied to by the military, and we believed in them like in the gospel!' See Johannes Fischart, *Das alte und das neue System* (The Old and the New System), vol. I, Berlin, 1919, p. 246. That not only a small circle of (finally) initiated but public opinion in general saw things in this way has been confirmed by Ernst Troeltsch: 'No one at the time believed in the lie of the "stab in the back" or "undefeated in the field". Instead everyone, unless he had long had his suspicions, felt betrayed by the explanations and emotional incitements of those in power.' See *Spektator-Briefe* (Spectator Letters), pub. by Hans Baron, Tübingen, 1924, p. 14. Churchill explains the unexpected collapse of German power with the sobriety of an engineer: 'When the great organizations of this world are strained beyond breaking point, their structure often collapses at all points simultaneously . . . The mighty framework of German Imperial Power, which a few days before had overshadowed the nations, shivered suddenly into a thousand individually disintegrating fragments.' See *The World Crisis*, vol. IV, p. 540.

24 *Ibid.*, pp. 543–4
25 The copies of *The World Crisis* in the university library in Göttingen are covered with pencilled marginal notes of outrage by former readers: 'Sheer nonsense!' — 'Not true!' — 'Totally absurd!'

Vladimir Ilyitsh Lenin and Edmund Burke

1 On this topic see Stéphane Courtois, Nicolas Werth, Jean-Loius Panné, Andrzej Paczkowski, Karel Bartosek and Jean-Louis Magolin, *Das Schwarzbuch des Kommunismus: Unterdrückung, Verbrechen und Terror* (The Communist Black Book: Oppressions, Crime and Terror), Munich, 1998.
2 Official Biography, vol. IV, sup. vol. I, p. 531; Kerr's note is dated 15 February 1919. See also Alex P. Schmidt, *Churchills privater Krieg: Intervention und Konterrevolution im russischen Bürgerkrieg, November 1918–März 1920* (Churchill's Private War: Intervention and Counter-Revolution in the Russian Civil War, November 1918–March 1920), Zürich, 1975.
3 G. A. Riddell, *op. cit.*, p. 267, note of 11 April 1919.
4 Quoted in John Charmley, *op. cit.*, p. 142.
5 Edmund Burke, 'Speech on Moving Resolutions for Conciliation with the Colonies', *The Works*, Boston, 1839, vol. II, p. 80.
6 *Reflections on the French Revolution*, vol. III, p. 252.
7 The most important stems from Thomas Paine, *The Rights of Man: Being an Answer to Mr. Burke's Attack on the French Revolution, 1791/92.*
8 *Freiherr vom Stein: Briefwechsel, Denkschriften und Aufzeichnungen* (Freiherr vom Stein: Correspondence, Memoranda, Notes), pub. by E. Botzenhart, Berlin, 1931–37, vol. III, p. 617.
9 Letter to B. Vaughan, 1791.

10 *Thoughts and Adventures*, p. 40. Churchill also talks about Burke in his *History of the English-Speaking Peoples*, London, 1956–58. See vol. III: *The Age of Revolution*, p. 176 *et seq*. On Churchill's connection to Burke (and Disraeli) see Stephen R. Graubard, *Burke, Disraeli, and Churchill: The Politics of Perseverance*, Cambridge, Mass., 1961.

11 Burke, 'Thoughts on French Affairs', *op. cit.*, vol. IV, p. 10.

12 'Remarks on the Policy of the Allies . . .', *ibid.*, p. 114.

13 'A Letter . . . to a Noble Lord, 1796', *ibid.*, p. 282.

14 Georg Friedrich Wilhelm Hegel, *Philosophie der Geschichte* (Philosophy of History), pt 4, sect. 3, ch. 3: 'Die Aufklärung und die Revolution' (Enlightenment and Revolution).

15 Burke, 'Observations of a Late Publication, entitled The Present State of the Nation, 1769', *op. cit.*, vol. I, p. 294.

16 Aldous Huxley, *Eyeless in Gaza*, ch. 35.

17 Jules Monnerot, *Soziologie des Kommunismus* (The Sociology of Communism), Cologne and Berlin, 1952, p. 356.

18 Robespierre, 'Habt ihr eine Revolution ohne Revolution gewollt?' (Did You Want a Revolution Without Revolution?), *Speeches*, Leipzig, undated, p. 321 *et seq*.

19 *Ibid.*, p. 329

20 Burke, 'Three Letters, Addressed to a Member of the Present Parliament, on the Proposals for Peace with the Regicide Directory of France', *op. cit.*, vol. IV, p. 329 *et seq*. Normally cited (as in Churchill) as *Letters on a Regicide Peace*.

21 Lenin's older brother was executed in 1887 as a co-conspirator in an assassination attempt on Tsar Alexander III. Lenin had loved and admired this brother, whose death gave him possibly the decisive push towards becoming a professional revolutionary.

22 *The World Crisis*, vol. IV, pp. 73–4

23 *Great Contemporaries*, p. 107.

Ireland and India

1 When the representatives of the Estates met in Paris in May 1789 they even differed according to dress. The nobility wore black velvet coats trimmed with gold and lace and plumed hats, the normal citizens plain black coats and hats without feathers. But since clothing always also has a symbolic value, it changed during the course of the Revolution. The *sansculotte*, who wore pantalons as opposed to the culottes of the nobility, soon began to set the trend. In the nineteenth century the uniformly sombre bourgeois dress with frock coat or tails and top hat prevailed, in marked contrast to the more colourful dress of the aristocratic courtly society of the eighteenth century. Only the military preserved their colourful splendour until the First World War. To mention a more

modern and charactaristic development in Germany: with the chant of *'Unter den Talaren – Muff von tausend Jahren'* (Under the robes – the fug of a millennium), the rebellious students of 1968 caused the robes with which the professors had set themselves apart on festive occasions to disappear.

2 Gandhi studied law in London. Nehru attended Harrow (like Chuchill, only with better results), studied in Cambridge and worked as a solicitor in London before he returned to India.

3 *The World Crisis*, vol. IV p. 296.

4 Burke, 'Speech on Presenting to the House of Commons a Plan for the Better Security of the Independence of Parliament and the Economic Reformation of the Civil and Other Establishments, 1780', *op. cit.*, vol. II, p. 163.

5 *Thoughts and Adventures*, p. 224.

6 *Ibid.*, p. 225.

7 *The World Crisis*, vol. IV, pp. 305–6.

8 For literature on the history of modern, finally independent Ireland see P. Baeslai, *Michael Collins and the Making of a New Ireland*, 2 vols, London 1926; N. Mansergh, *The Irish Question 1840–1921*, London, 1965; and J. C. Beckett, *The Making of Modern Ireland*, London, 1966.

9 *Churchill Speaks. Collected Speeches 1897–1963*, pub. by Robert R. James, 1974, p. 514 *et seq*. See also *India: Speeches and an Introduction*, London, 1931.

10 James, *op. cit.*

11 See John Charmley, *Duff Cooper: The Authorized Biography*, 1986, p. 78.

12 *The Empire at Bay: The Leo Amery Diaries 1929–1955*, pub. by J. Barnes and D. Nicholson, 1988, p. 395.

13 There is an anecdote full of symbolic meaning. Two troop transports pass each other in the Suez Canal. One is bringing French troops to Vietnam, the other British troops from India back to Britain. The British call out to the French: 'Comrades, you are going in the wrong direction!'

14 *Taschenbuch der Kriegsflotten*, p. 507 *et seq*.

15 Even as late as the post-Second World War years, the German scholar Hans Freyer wrote a book entitled *European World History* (2 vols, 1948).

16 From the other side, two books throw an interesting light on Churchill's errors: Hira Lal Seth, *Churchill on India*, Lahore, 1942; and Narayan Gopal Jog, *Churchill's Blind Spot: India*, Bombay, 1944.

The Return of the Prodigal Son

1 See Lord Beaverbrook, *The Decline and Fall of Lloyd George*, 1963. Beaverbrook, born in Canada in 1879 as William Maxwell Aitken, came to England in 1910 and built up a press empire there. He was a Conservative MP, and, as a Lord, a member of the Upper House from 1916 onwards. A friend of Lloyd George and Churchill, he served as the first British Minister of Propaganda towards the end

of the First World War, and during the Second World War first as Minister of Aircraft Production, then as Minister of Supply and finally as Lord Privy Seal.

2 For more detail on the elections see *British Parliamentary Election Results 1918-1949*, pub. by F. W. S. Craig, new edn, 1977.

3 For Goschen's letter of 5 August 1924 to Churchill see Official Biography, vol. V, sup. vol. I, p. 172 *et seq.* For Churchill's reply on 11 August see *ibid.*, p. 174 *et seq.*

4 Quoted in D. Dilks, *Neville Chamberlain*, vol. I: *Pioneering and Reform, 1869-1929*, 1984, p. 398.

5 Quoted in M. Cowling, *The Impact of Labour*, Cambridge, 1971, p. 59.

6 Robert Boothby, *Recollections of a Rebel*, 1978, p. 46. Boothby was Churchill's private parliamentary secretary from 1926.

7 William Bridgeman, *The Modernization of Conservative Politics: The Diaries and Letters of William Bridgeman, 1904–1935*, pub. by P. Williamson, 1988, p. 233 *et seq.*

8 *Thoughts and Adventures*, p. 39.

9 For a similar reason the same sort of political crisis—albeit a far more serious one—occurred in Germany in 1928 concerning the construction of 'Battleship A'. Construction was permissible within the framework of the Treaty of Versailles, and had been approved in 1927. The government of the Great Coalition under Social Democrat Hermann Müller confirmed the decision. But the SPD faction in the *Reichstag* forced their own Ministers to retract—which had no effect on the decision but only destroyed the reputation of the government and the *Reichstag*, as the *Frankfurter Zeitung* wrote on 17 November 1928: 'The Chancellor must decide whether in his heart he feels more sorrow about the parliamentary defeat of his party or joy at the salvation of his government. By the events of the past few days, about which we have reported with great reluctance, the reputation of Parliament has been brought low. One should make every effort seriously to grasp this, and if there is a small consolation in this shameful situation, then this may be the observation that a general mood of depression reigns . . .' By such means are democratic institutions not rooted in history like those in Britain made ripe for storming.

10 Letter of 28 April 1925 from Baldwin to King George V. See Official Biography, vol. V, sup. vol. I, p. 472 *et seq.*

11 Keynes (1883–1946)—from 1942, Baron Keynes of Tilton—wrote *The Economic Consequences of the Peace* (1920) and advocated *A Revision of the Treaty* (1922). In 1936 his principal work appeared—*The General Theory of Employment, Interest and Money*. Keynes advocated an anti-cyclic financial policy and was one of the fathers of the agreement of Bretton Woods in 1944, by which the post-war economy was revived. His theories were generally accepted for a long time, but then came under increasingly harsh criticism by the liberal 'neo-classics'. On the re-introduction of the gold standard, Keynes wrote *The Economic Consequences of Mr. Churchill*, London, 1925.

12 Churchill called the first volume of his history of the Second World War—in which he describes the road to disaster—*The Gathering Storm*.

A Long Way Through the Desert

1 *The Second World War*, vol. I, bk I, ch. 12, p. 197.
2 That Churchill's life was a failure — at least up to 1939 — was also claimed later. See, for example, Robert Rhodes James, *op. cit.*
3 Quoted in Sebastian Haffner, *Winston Churchill mit Selbstzeugnissen und Bilddokumenten*, p. 93.
4 See Charles Macmoran Wilson Moran, *Churchill: Der Kampf ums Überleben. Aus dem Tagebuch seines Leibarztes Lord Moran* (Churchill: The Fight for Survival. From the Diary of his Personal Physician Lord Moran), Munich and Zürich, 1967.
5 *My Early Life*, p. 111.
6 *The Second World War*, vol. I, bk I, ch. 5, p. 71.
7 *Ibid.*
8 See John Charmley, *op. cit.*, p. 283.
9 *The Second World War*, vol. I, bk I, ch. 5.
10 *Ibid.*
11 *Ibid.*
12 On Churchill the painter see Mary Soames, *Winston Churchill: His Life as a Painter. A Memoir by his Daughter*, London, 1990. See also Churchill's own portrayals in *Thoughts and Adventures*; and *Painting as a Pastime*.
13 *Thoughts and Adventures*.
14 After the German collapse of November 1918 Max Weber gave his famous presentation on *Politics as a Profession*, and then published a greatly extended version in October 1919. See Max Weber, *Gesammelte Politische Schriften* (Collected Political Writings), 2nd edn, Tübingen, 1958, p. 493 *et seq*. The discussion is still going on today about the differentiation between the 'ethics of principles' and the 'ethics of responsibility' Weber made. Hardly taken into consideration, however, are the tangible practical implications: with the conversion of the former German *Reich* into the Weimar Republic the erstwhile ruling political élite was replaced by a new élite which depended to a far greater extent on politics as a profession, in other words as a source of income and security, than had the former. To this was added a radical expropriation of large segments of the population due to inflation. Not so in Great Britain: there the traditional upper classes had always been wealthier then those in Germany, and therefore depended even less on income from political office. Furthermore, there was no drastic change in the system of government, so that the transition to new career patterns proceeded much more slowly, even though it had already announced itself with the formation of the Labour Party.
15 Half a century before Churchill, Bismarck's *Gedanken und Erinnerungen* (Thoughts and Memories) — which appeared in November 1898 almost immediately following the death of the founder of the *Reich* — became a German centennial best-seller: within only one month 300,000 copies were sold. But that was an exception in those days. Even after the First World War, the attempts by

Alfred Tirpitz, *Kaiser* Wilhelm II, Hindenburg and Ludendorff to sell their memoirs turned out rather sadly. Nowadays large initial editions are guaranteed
when a politically prominent person (or his ghostwriter) picks up the pen after
having left office. One need only recall Helmut Schmitt, Hans-Dietrich Gen-
scher, Charles de Gaulle or former American Presidents and generals. And the
trend continues. In the age of mass media it is already sufficient to belong to the
prominent moderators on television.

16 *The Second World War*, vol. I, bk I, ch. 5.
17 *Ibid.*, ch. 14.
18 *My Early Life*, p. 224.
19 Sebastian Haffner, *op. cit.*, p. 7.
20 *History of the English-Speaking Peoples*, vol. I, p. 206. On Churchill the historian
    see Frederick William Dampier Deakin, *Churchill, the Historian*, Zürich, 1969.
21 *History of the English-Speaking Peoples*, vol. II, p. 288.
22 *Ibid.*, vol. III, p. 231.
23 Churchill admired Thomas Edward Lawrence (1888–1935), who had been influ-
    enced by his encounter with the desert, and said that Lawrence's *The Seven
    Pillars of Wisdom* was one of the greatest books ever written in the English lan-
    guage. Had Lawrence achieved nothing else except to write this book as a mere
    creation of his imagination, his fame would still have lasted 'as long as the Eng-
    lish language is still spoken in some corner of the world' (to cite Macaulay's
    well-worn phrase). See *Great Contemporaries*, op. cit., p. 115. This taking of a
    break before the test also reminds us of Adenauer, who was dismissed from
    his office as Lord Mayor of Cologne by the Nazis in 1933 and returned in
    1945 — only to be 'dismissed' once again by the British and thereby freed for 'big
    politics'.

Neville Chamberlain, Adolf Hitler and Winston Churchill

1 Like Chamberlain, others too dreamed of a German-British-American community — Cecil Rhodes (1853–1902), for example, another social riser who made his
   fortune in South Africa and acquired some rather problematic political influence. In order to do something practical for the fulfilment of the dream, he created the Cecil Rhodes Foundation, which provided annual scholarships for two
   oustanding German and two outstanding American students to go and study at
   Oxford. One such German Rhodes Scholar was Adam Trott zu Solz, who was
   execcuted in 1944 as a member of the resistance against Hitler. Churchill's meeting with another such Rhodes scholar will be recounted later in this chapter.
2 For a biography see J. L. Garvin, *Life of Joseph Chamberlain*, 3 vols, London,
   1932–34; continued with vols 4 and 5 by J. Amery, 1951–53.
3 For literature on Neville Chamberlain see K. Feiling, *The Life of Neville Chamberlain*, London, 1946; W. N. Medlicott, *Neville Chamberlain*, London, 1953; I.
   Macleod, *Neville Chamberlain*, London 1962; and C. B. Pyper, *Chamberlain and his*

Critics, London 1962. In general for the subject dealt with in this chapter see M. Cowling, *The Impact of Hitler: British Politics and British Policy 1933–1940*, Cambridge, 1975.

4 The wording of the oath read: 'I swear by God this holy oath, that I will give unconditional obedience to the *Führer* of the German *Reich* and nation and Commander-in-Chief of the *Wehrmacht* Adolf Hitler, and be prepared as a brave soldier to risk my life for this oath.' Before then the soldiers had sworn on the constitution and not on the *Reich* President. When regarded with the degree of attention to specifics nobody is apparently prepared to pay any longer, it is seen that the new oath was based on a breach of the former one.

5 The expenditure for the *Wehrmacht* and its equipment rose from four per cent of the budget in 1933 to about fifty per cent in 1938. In 1938 public expenditure (excluding local administration and social security) was already high, namely at 35 per cent of the gross national product, as compared to 23.8 per cent in Great Britain and 10.7 per cent in the United States.

6 Beck then took over a leading rôle in the resistance against Hitler. He died on 20 July 1944 after the failure of Stauffenberg's attempted assassination. Beck's successor as Chief of the General Staff, Franz Halder, claimed that he had been determined to prevent the war and to arrest Hitler but that the Munich Accord prevented this. The whole subject remains controversial because it loses itself in a hypothetical 'what would have happened if . . .'. After the war Halder naturally had a vital interest in underlining his determination to intervene. But the fact is that he remained in office until his dismissal on 24 September 1942. He was arrested after 20 July 1944 and held in a concentration camp until the end of the war. What has been proved, however, is that men of the resistance like Adam Trott zu Solz and Ewald von Kleist-Schmenzin went to England in order to try, via their contacts, to persuade the British government not to give in to Hitler's demands.

7 *The World Crisis*, vol. IV, p. 45.

8 *The Second World War*, vol. I, bk I, ch. 5, p. 77. Churchill does not state when the question and answer session took place in Oxford, but from the context we can deduce that it must have been around 1933.

9 The importance of these casualties should not be underestimated. After the First World War Great Britain counted 947,000 killed, whereas the figure after the Second World War was 388,000, including 62,000 civilians. After the First World War France mourned 1,385,000 dead — in relationship to the population the highest casualty rate of all.

10 In the so-called *Seeberg Adresse*, named after the Berlin professor of theology Reinhold Seeberg who wrote it, and signed by a total of 352 university professors, we read: 'We intend to place ourselves firmly and broadly on secured and extended home territory so that our existence will be secured for generations to come. The nation is unanimously united in these fundamental objectives. The most genuine of truths, and one which applies in general everywhere, is that there is only one fear in all segments of the people — particularly widespread

and profound in the most humble circles—namely the fear that out of a mistaken illusion of reconciliation, or even out of nervous impatience, a premature and therefore false and never durable peace might be concluded; that, as happened one hundred years ago [i.e. at the Congress of Vienna in 1815], the pen of the diplomat could spoil what the sword won victoriously ... Let it be understood that while we do not want world domination, we do want the full measure of world recognition that is commensurate with the greatness of our cultural, economic, and military power.' The demand was then made, among other things, that Belgium was to become a German protectorate and that France should cede important territories from Belfort in the south to the Channel Coast in the north. Even more important were conquests in the east: 'But the foundation for the growth of our nation will be land that Russia must cede. It must be land suitable for agricultural settlement. Land that will give us healthy farmers, that fountain of youth of all national strength and state power.' This already anticipates Hitler's programme, almost to the choice of words. For the complete text see *Aufrufe und Reden deutscher Professoren im Ersten Weltkrieg* (Proclamations and Speeches by German Professors in the First World War), pub. by Klaus Böhme, Stuttgart, 1975, p. 125 *et seq.* In 1917 as many as 1,100 university professors signed a declaration against the peace resolution of the *Reichstag* which aimed at reconciliation.

11 See Christian Graf von Krockow, 'Von der Versöhnung' (On Reconciliation) in *Vom lohnenden Leben: Ein Wegweiser für junge und ältere Leute* (On a Worthwhile Life: A Guide for Young and Older People), Stuttgart, 1996, p. 98 *et seq.*

12 *The Second World War*, vol. I, bk I, ch. 7, p. 109.

13 See Herbert Michaelis and Ernst Schraepler (pub.), *Ursachen und Folgen. Vom deutschen Zusammenbruch 1918 und 1945 bis zur staatlichen Neuordnung in der Gegenwart* (Causes and Results. From the German Collapse in 1918 and 1945 to National Restructuring in the Present), a collection of documents on contemporary history, vol. IX *et seq.*, Berlin, 1964 *et seq.*, here vol. XI, p. 674.

14 We can read in Stefan Zweig what the downfall of a European 'world of yesterday' in his home town of Vienna looked like: 'Since the other nations openly showed their fear, brutality no longer needed to have any moral scruples, it no longer used—what was England still worth, what France, what the rest of the world?—any hypocritical excuses about 'Marxists' who had to be eliminated politically. Now there was no longer just rape and theft, free rein was given to every personal lust for revenge. University professors were made to scrub the streets with their naked hands, pious white-bearded Jews were dragged into the temple and forced by howling adolescents to do sit-ups and shout 'Heil Hitler' in chorus. Innocent people were rounded up in the streets like rabbits and dragged off to clean the latrines in the barracks of the SA. Everything that sick, dirty fantasies of hatred had orgiastically conceived during many dark nights was now being practised in broad daylight. When they broke into private homes and tore the earrings from trembling women, that was something which may also have occurred already hundreds of years ago during the plundering

of cities in the wars of the Middle Ages. But what was new was the shameless lust of public torment, the spiritual tortures, the refined degradations. All this has been recorded not by one, but by thousands who suffered it, and a calmer age, not one as morally exhausted as our own, will one day read with shudders what one single individual full of rage and hatred was able to commit in the twentieth century in this city of culture.' See Stefan Zweig, *Die Welt von Gestern: Erinnerungen eines Europäers* (The World of Yesterday: Memories of a European), pocket book edn, Frankfurt-am-Main, 1970 *et seq.*, p. 460 *et seq.*

15 Nuremberg War Crimes Trials: The Trial of the Principal War Criminals Before the International Military Court, Nuremberg, 14 November 1945 to 1 October 1946, 42 vols, Nuremberg 1947–49, vol. XXXIV, p. 368 *et seq.*

16 Count Ciano, *Tagebücher 1937/38* (Diaries 1937/38), Hamburg, 1949, p. 124.

17 Nuremberg War Crimes Trials, vol. XXXVII, p. 634.

18 See *Foreign Relations of the United States: Diplomatic Papers*, vol. I, 1938, p. 500 *et seq.*

19 Nuremberg War Crimes Trials, vol. XXXV, p. 415 *et seq.*

20 F. Wiedemann, *Der Mann, der Feldherr werden wollte* (The Man Who Wanted to Become Commander). The experiences of Hitler's superior in the First World War who later became his personal adjutant. Velbert-Kettwig, 1964, p. 171.

21 Quoted in Max Domarus, *Hitler: Reden und Proklamationen* (Hitler: Speeches and Proclamations), Munich, 1965, here vol. I, pt II, p. 932.

22 Paul Schmidt, *Statist auf diplomatischer Bühne 1923–1945* (Bystander on the Diplomatic Stage 1923–1945), Bonn, 1949, p. 401.

23 *Ibid.*, p. 405.

24 Quoted in Gerhard Ritter, *Carl Goerdeler und die deutsche Widerstandsbewegung* (Carl Goerdeler and the German Resistance Movement), Stuttgart, 1954, p. 198.

25 Cooper (1890–1954), from 1952 Viscount Norwich, was a politician, diplomat and like Churchill, also an important writer. Among his better-known books are *Talleyrand* (1932), *Haig* (2 vols, 1935–36) and the autobiography *Old Men Forget* (1953).

26 Daniel 5, xxvii. Here Churchill is alluding to the *menetekel*, the writing of fire on the wall. The prophet deciphers it and predicts King Belshazzar's downfall.

27 The complete speech is reprinted in (among other places) *Blood, Sweat, and Tears: Churchill's Speeches*, pub. by Randolph Churchill, New York, 1941, p. 55 *et seq.* The quotations are from pp. 58, 60 and 66.

28 *Hitlers Politisches Testament: Die Bormann-Diktate vom Februar und April 1945* (Hitler's Political Testament: The Bormann Dictations of February and April 1945), pub. by H. Trevor-Roper, Hamburg, 1981, p. 99 *et seq.* In actual fact Hitler's view is highly questionable. The economic and military integration of Austria required time, and the *Wehrmacht* was still far from being prepared for war. And what would a victory over Czechoslovakia have brought? The 'drive towards the East' would not have been satisfied and exactly the same situation would have occurred as that which actually came about in 1939.

29 Domarus, *op. cit.*, p. 974.

30 Speech before the election to Chairman of the Conservative Party on 9 October 1940. Reprinted in *Blood, Sweat, and Tears*, p. 395.

31 Quoted in Hans-Ulrich Thamer, 'Verführung und Gewalt: Deutschland 1933–1945' (Seduction and Violence: Germany 1933–1945) in *Die Deutschen und ihre Nation* (The Germans and Their Nation), Berlin, 1986, vol. V, p. 760.

32 *Ibid.*

33 Sebastian Haffner, *Anmerkungen zu Hitler* (Remarks on Hitler), Munich, 1978, p. 59 *et seq.*

34 Letter to Ida Chamberlain on 10 September 1939, Neville Chamberlain Papers, Birmingham University Library. Quoted in John Charmley, *op. cit.*, p. 345.

35 Letter to Hilda Chamberlain on 15 October 1939, *ibid.*

36 We should recall that the first and only things Churchill knew about Hitler, and which put him off and prevented a personal encounter in 1932, were his racial delusions and his hatred of the Jews.

37 Heinrich Heine, *Zur Geschichte der Religion und Philosophie in Deutschland* (On the History of Religion and Philosophy in Germany), 1835, vol. 3, final passage.

'Winston is Back'

1 *The Second World War*, vol. I, bk II, ch. 22.

2 *Ibid.*, ch. 23.

3 *Ibid.* Franklin Delano Roosevelt, born in 1882 on the family estate, Hyde Park near New York, had been Under-Secretary of the (US) Navy since 1913. He contracted poliomyelitis in 1921 and from then was able to walk only with great difficulty.

4 *Ibid.*, ch. 22.

5 *Ibid.*, vol. II, bk I, ch. 1

6 *Scharnhorst* and *Gneisenau* each had nine 28cm guns whereas the older British battleships which had been built or planned during Churchill's first tenure as First Lord of the Admiralty—and of which some had taken part in the Battle of Jutland in 1916—had eight 38cm guns. This was the type on which *Bismarck* and *Tirpitz* were modelled, except that they were faster and had far heavier armour.

7 Churchill gives numbers in *The Second World War*: during the first week in September 1939 U-boats sank 11 ships of 64,595 tonnes, in the fourth week only one of 4,646 tonnes.

8 The importance this success had for British prestige can be gauged from the fact that Churchill devotes a separate chapter to it (*The Second World War*, ch. 8). *Graf Spee*'s commander, Captain Langsdorff, decided to scuttle his damaged (though still battleworthy) ship because, on the basis of deliberate British misinformation, he believed that an overwhelmingly superior enemy force was blocking the exit into the Atlantic and that he had no chance of escape. He then shot him-

self. He was a man respected by friend and foe alike; Churchill calls him 'a high class person'. The incident illustrates a fundamental problem of German naval operations both in the First and in the Second World War: the British cruiser *Exeter*, which had been heavily damaged in the engagement, was able to run to her base in the Falklands, but for damaged German ships there were no repair facilities outside their North Sea or Baltic home ports.

9 Churchill took over this term and used it as the title for Book II of Volume I of his history of the Second World War.

10 There was, however, a bitter battle raging behind the scenes: Hitler wanted to attack in the West as early as possible, but the generals talked about bad weather, soggy roads and other difficulties. The date kept being postponed, finally to 10 May 1940. The only visible event which could have given an unexpected turn — not only to the history of the war but to that of all Europe — was Georg Elser's assassination attempt on 8 November 1939. This withdrawn Swabian, hardly literate in the conventional sense, had manual talents: without any model or instructions, he constructed a perfect bomb and in many weeks of night work built it into the pillar of the Munich *Bürgerbräukeller* before which Hitler gave his annual speech to his 'old fighters' in commemoration of the 'march to the *Feldherrnhalle*' . No other assassination attempt came so close to succeeding, and only a ridiculous circumstance led to failure — fog. The aircraft for the return to Berlin could not take off and Hitler had to take the train. He therefore spoke more briefly than usual and, without staying for the customary get-together, hurridly left the spot. The bomb exploded only minutes later and caused a bloodbath. During his interrogation Elser said: 'I was convinced last year at this time that the Munich Accord would not be the last word, that Germany would make further territorial demands of other countries and annex other countries, and that therefore a war was inevitable.' Apparently the insight of a simple mind is sometimes deeper than the wisdom of statesmen. Elser also admitted: 'When you ask me whether I consider my deed to be a sin in the sense of Protestant teaching, I would like to reply "in a deeper sense, no!" . . . By my deed I intended to prevent a far greater bloodbath.' Quoted in Lothar Gruchmann (pub.), *Autobiographie eines Attentäters: Johann Georg Elser, Aussagen zum Sprengstoffanschlag im Bürgerbräukeller, München, am 8. November 1939* (Autobiography of an Assassin: Johann Georg Else, Testimony on the Bomb Attempt in the Bürgerbräukeller, Munich, on 8 November 1939), Stuttgart, 1970, pp. 81 and 75.

11 *The Second World War*, vol. I, bk II, ch. 15.

12 The whole debate can, of course, be found in the appropriate annual edition of *Hansard's Parliamentary Debates*. Specifically on Amery, see his diary: Leo S. Amery, *The Empire at Bay: The Leo Amery Diaries 1929–1955*, p. 592, entry for 7 May 1940.

13 Harold Nicolson, *Diaries and Letters*, vol. II: *The War Years, 1939–1945*, pub. by N. Nicolson, London, 1967, diary entry for 7 May 1940.

14 *The Second World War*, vol.I, bk II, ch. 38.

15 *Ibid.* This is the final passage of vol. I, *The Gathering Storm.*

16 *The Second World War,* vol. II, bk I, ch. 1.

17 I have been unable to find any information as to the duration, but, based on the printed text, the speech cannot have lasted for more than five to six, or at most seven minutes.

18 It is remarkable that even linguistic artists of note often do not find the most memorable phrasing straight off, so that the mysterious process which turns a phrase into a 'familiar quotation' must be added on. Another such example can be found in Bismarck's famous 'blood and iron'. In the original text he had said 'iron and blood': 'It is not by speeches and majority votes that the great issues of the times are decided — that was the mistake made in 1848 and 1849 — but by iron and blood.'

19 *Blood, Sweat, and Tears,* pub. by Randolph S. Churchill, New York, 1941, p. 276.

The Player and his Counter-Player

1 Göring's conduct during the September crisis in 1938 indicated that, whereas Ribbentrop demanded 'a sure and strong language on the Czech Question', only then himself beginning to consider a postponement of the war in view of the objections by the military, Göring wished to avoid a military conflict with Great Britain under any circumstances. To the great surprise of the conservative diplomats in the Foreign Ministry, Hitler's 'paladin' was suddenly to be found 'on the side of the military' in the camp of the 'pacifists'. See Hans-Ulrich Thamer, *op. cit.,* p. 586. Göring behaved similarily on the eve of the outbreak of the war in 1939. Through Swedish mediation he sought a contact to Chamberlain and Halifax in order to prevent disaster.

2 *Mein Kampf,* p. 44. While Hitler is speaking here about the propaganda of the Social Democrats, what he says applies not so much to theirs as to his own.

3 *Ibid.,* p. 530 *et seq.*

4 Quoted in Herbert Michaelis and Ernst Schraepler (pub.), *op. cit.,* vol. XIII, p. 115.

5 Ernst Jünger, *Das abenteuerliche Herz* (The Adventurous Heart), Berlin, 1929, here 2nd edn, p. 92.

6 This is particularly (but not exclusively) true for John Charmley, whom we have repeatedly quoted, who intends by his biography, as the title of his book indicates, to bring about 'the end of glory' for Churchill. 'From a Continental point of view', Erich Schwinge writes: 'If a negotiated peace did not even come about during the later course of the war, then Churchill must bear the major part of the blame. The lives of millions of people would have been saved if he had given up this obdurate position. But as he rule he did not give a thought to the human lives his great political decisions cost.' See Erich Schwinge, *Churchill und Roosevelt aus kontinentaleuropäischer Sicht* (Churchill and Roosevelt from a Continental European Point of View), 4th edn, Marburg, 1986, p. 21. We shall return to this criticism at the end of this book.

His Finest Hour

1 Official Biography, vol. VI, p. 314.

2 One can even recognise the actual situation by looking at organisational structures. The majority of the French tanks — and there were more than 2,000 — were not concentrated into armoured divisions or armies but split up into battalions and attached to the infantry. With this they lost the ability to attack, which was their main strength: when tanks are employed in small numbers they really are only good for defence. If they still try to attack, the defensive weapons of the enemy are normally sufficient to destroy them. It is only in a mass that armour assumes a different quality. On the tactics for employing armour see the excellent book by Heinz Guderian: *Achtung! Panzer* (Attention! Tanks), published in 1937. In France Charles de Gaulle vainly attempted to achieve something similar. But as initially in his political career after 1940, here too he was an outsider no one listened to. It remains true: the victors of yesterday prepare for the last war, the vanquished for the next war.

3 By way of comparison, in the Franco-Prussian War of 1870–71 the Prussian-German Army lost 49,000 killed — in other words substantially more than in the campaign of 1940 — and in 1870 the population was only half that in 1940.

4 *The Second World War*, vol II, bk I, ch. 2.

5 *Ibid.*, ch. 3.

6 For an overview of numbers, types and losses of ships, as well as the daily number of soldiers evacuated between 27 May and 4 June, see *The Second World War*, ch. 5.

7 The speech is reproduced in *Blood, Sweat, and Tears*, p. 289 *et seq.*, here pp. 290, 291, 292 *et seq.*, 296 *et seq.*

8 *The Second World War*, vol. II, bk I, ch. 10.

9 *Ibid.*

10 For more details see *ibid.*, ch. 9.

11 The complete speech is reproduced in *Blood, Sweat, and Tears*, p. 305 *et seq.*, here p. 314.

12 When the Allies landed in North Africa in November 1942 Darlan happened to be in Algeria. He went over to the Allies and again tried to play a leading rôle. On 24 December 1942, however, he was killed by a fanatical Gaullist. Shortly before this, on 4 December, he wrote Churchill a letter in which he tried to justify himself. See *The Second World War*, vol. II, bk I, ch. 11. His promise, incidentally, was kept. When German troops marched into Unoccupied France in reply to the Allied landings in North Africa, the warships collected in Toulon scuttled themselves.

13 *Ibid.*

14 See Henry Channon, *Chips: The Diaries of Sir Henry Channon*, pub. by R. R. James, 1967, p. 252. See also Harold Nicolson, *Diaries and Letters*, pub. by N. Nicolson, vol. I. Churchill himself also alludes to the matter: see *The Second World War*, vol. II, bk I, ch. 1.

15 John Colville, *The Fringes of Power: Downing Street Diaries, 1939–1955*, London 1985, p. 122.

16 Alexander Calder, *The People's War: Britain 1939–45*, London, 1969, p. 106.

17 Frederick Edwin, Earl of Birkenhead, *Halifax: The Life of Lord Halifax*, 1965, p. 548, entry for 27 May 1940.

18 Philipp Bell, *A Certain Eventuality: Britain and the Fall of France*, London, 1974, p. 48.

19 We must recall that the *Reichstag* had lost all legislative powers and no longer even served as a forum for discussion but only to provide Hitler with an appropriate stage for his 'historic' speeches, for example at the start of the war on 1 September 1939. It was mocked as being 'the most expensive choir in the world' because at the end, after the required applause, it sang the national anthem and the *Horst Wessel* song.

20 The complete text of the speech is reproduced in *Der Grossdeutsche Freiheits-kampf: Reden Adolf Hitlers* (The Greater German Battle of Liberation: Adolf Hitler's Speeches), Munich, 1941, vol. II, pp. 47–81.

21 The most important book on this subject is: John Lukacs, *The Duel, 10 May–31 July 1940: The Eighty-Day Struggle Between Churchill and Hitler*, New York, 1990.

22 A standard work is: Karl Klee, *Dokumente zum Unternehmen 'Seelöwe'* (Documents on Operation 'Sealion'), 2 vols, Göttingen, 1959. Important in a broader context are Andreas Hillgruber, *Hitlers Strategie: Politik und Kriegsführung 1940–1941* (Hitler's Strategy: Politics and Waging War 1940–1941), Düsseldorf, 1965; and, on the British side, P. Fleming, *Invasion 1940*, London, 1957, and Kenneth Macksey, *Invasion: The German Invasion of England, July 1940*, London, 1980; Another important book was written by the American Rear-Admiral W. Ansel: *Hitler Confronts England*, Durham, NC, 1960.

23 *The Second World War*, vol. II, bk I, ch. 15.

24 The most famous of all fighter pilots, the 'Red Baron' Manfred von Richthofen, became a legend during and after the First World War—like Field Marshal Erwin Rommel in the Second World War—even though he was killed at age 26.

25 See the list in *The Second World War*, vol. II, bk II, ch. 16.

26 *Ibid.*, app. C.

27 *Ibid.*, ch 16.

Alone

1 The dismissals began in the winter crisis of 1940/41 and became all the more hectic the more hopelessly the *Wehrmacht* approached its impending defeat. Increasingly strategists (like Erich von Manstein) were replaced by brutal proponents of hanging on at all costs (like Ferdinand Schörner).

2 Sebastian Haffner, *op. cit.*, p. 59.

3 Churchill recounts a characteristic episode. In August 1941 he sailed in *Prince of*

Wales to the meeting with Roosevelt in the Atlantic and the ship had to steer a zig-zag course and make a detour in order to avoid German submarines which had been reported. In addition, radio silence had to be maintained. 'Thus there was a lull in my daily routine and a strange sense of leisure which I had not known since the war began. For the first time for many months I could read a book for pleasure. Oliver Lyttelton, Minister of State in Cairo, had given me *Captain Hornblower, R.N.*, which I found vastly entertaining. When a chance came I sent him the message, "I find *Hornblower* admirable." This caused perturbation in the Middle East Headquarters, where it was imagined that "Hornblower" was the code-word for some special operation of which they had not been told.' See *The Second World War*, vol. III, bk II, ch. 23. In his preference for films, Churchill was again much like Hitler. During the trip in *Prince of Wales* he had *Lady Hamilton* shown and was deeply moved even though he was seeing the film for the fifth time. For an interesting view of this topic see D. J. Wenden and K. R. M. Short, 'Winston S. Churchill: Film Fan' in *Historical Journal of Film, Radio and Television*, 1991, vol. 11, p. 197 *et seq.*

4 On 2 June 1944 the King wrote to Churchill: 'I want to make one more appeal to you not to go to sea on D-Day. Please consider my own position. I am a younger man than you, I am a sailor, and as King I am the head of all these Services. There is nothing I would like better than to go to sea, but I have agreed to stay at home; is it fair that you should then do exactly what I should have liked to do myself? You said yesterday afternoon that it would be a fine thing for the King to lead his troops into battle, as in old days; if the King cannot do this, it does not seem to me right that his Prime Minister should take his place. . . . I ask you most earnestly to consider the whole question again, and not let your personal wishes, which I very well understand, lead you to depart from your own high standard of duty to the State.' Churchill reproduces this letter in *The Second World War*, vol. V, bk II, ch. 35.

5 See Churchill's portrayal in *The Second World War*, vol. VI, bk I, ch. 1.

6 *Ibid.*, vol. II, bk II, ch. 17.

7 Albert Speer, who was probably closer to Hitler than anybody else, wrote: 'During his walks Hitler's attention was mostly not directed towards his companions but to his German shepherd Blondi . . . This dog probably played the most important rôle in Hitler's private life. It was more important than even his closest associates.' See Albert Speer, *Erinnerungen* (Memoirs), Berlin, 1970, p. 400. Blondi kept this rôle until the end: her master had the poison Eva Braun later took tested on her and her litter.

8 Churchill describes these attempts in a separate chapter: *The Second World War*, vol. VI, bk I, ch. 19.

9 In the sinking of *Scharnhorst* the superiority of British radar played a rôle, in the sinking of *Tirpitz* the absence of air cover against British air attacks. What remains incomprehensible in the sortie made by *Bismarck* is that after the destruction of *Hood* her commander, Admiral Lütjens, did not turn back while this was still possible but continued his advance into the Atlantic. He had to

assume that British cruisers were shadowing him and that the whole British fleet would hunt for him. Perhaps we shall have to call it fanaticism: in the end, all that was left for him was to send Hitler a message of devotion before going under. It is all the more strange, therefore, that the *Bundesmarine* has named one of its ships after Lütjens. Why, too, was the impending campaign against Russia left out of all considerations? Was it impossible to foresee that British convoys would bring vital aid in terms of war materials to Murmansk or Archangel? *Bismarck*, together with *Tirpitz*, could have posed an effective threat to such convoys. The war in the Pacific proved that it was no longer the battleship but the aircraft carrier that was the most important type of warship, and the latter also played its rôle in the Atlantic. *Bismarck*'s fate was sealed by British carrier aircraft. Had she been accompanied by *Graf Zeppelin* with fighter aircraft on board this fate might have been averted.

10 *The Second World War*, vol. VI, bk I, ch. 30.

11 A total of 1,170 U-boats were put into service, of which 863 were sent into combat. Losses comprised 630 on combat patrol and 123 by bombs, mines and accidents in home waters; 215 boats scuttled themselves, 38 were taken out of service and 153 handed over to the victors after the surrender. A further eight boats were given to Japan and three were interned.

12 *The Second World War*, vol. II, bk II, ch. 20.

13 *The Second World War*, vol. VI, bk II, ch. 13.

14 *The Second World War*, vol V, bk I, ch. 1.

15 Of the 39,000 men who served in U-boats during the war, 33,000 lost their lives.

16 There are many books on the war at sea and the Battle of the Atlantic. See, for example, Friedrich Ruge, *Der Seekrieg 1939–1945* (The War at Sea 1939–1945), 4th edn,1963; Jürgen Rohwer, *Die U-Boot-Erfolge der Achsenmächte 1939–1945* (Submarine Successes of the Axis Powers 1939–1945), Munich, 1968; Donald Macintyre, *The Naval War Against Hitler*, London and New York, 1971; John Creswell, *Sea Warfare, 1939–1945*, revised edn, Berkeley, Ca., 1967; Léonce Peillard, *Geschichte des U-Boot-Krieges 1939–1945* (History of the Submarine War 1939–1945), Vienna and Berlin, 1971; Martin Middlebrook, *Convoy*, Berlin, 1977; Brian B. Schofield, *Geleitzugschlacht in der Hölle des Nordmeeres* (Convoy Battle in the Hell of the Arctic Sea), with an introduction by Jürgen Rohwer, Herford, 1980; Peter Padfield, *Dönitz: Des Teufels Admiral* (Dönitz: The Devil's Admiral), Berlin, 1984; Lothar-Günther Buchheim, *Das Boot* (The Boat), a novel portraying the submarine war, first published in 1973 and now also a film.

17 *The Second World War*, vol. II, bk II, ch. 26.

18 *Ibid.*

19 *The Second World War*, vol. II, bk I, ch. 6.

20 *The Second World War*, vol. II, bk II, ch. 27.

21 Churchill writes: 'An ironic touch is imparted to this event by the fact that on this very day the Italian Air Force at the express wish of Mussolini had taken part in the air attack on Great Britain.' But many machines were shot down, and

so 'This was their first and last intervention in our domestic affairs. They might have found better employment defending their fleet at Taranto.' See *The Second World War*, vol. II, bk II, ch. 27.

22 *The Second World War*, vol. II, bk II, ch. 31.

A Hell of a Mess

1 *The Second World War*, vol. III, bk I, ch. 11. What Churchill is describing led to British as well as German authors interesting themselves in Rommel. As examples see Lutz Koch, *Erwin Rommel: Die Wandlung eines grossen Soldaten* (Erwin Rommel: The Metamorphosis of a Great Soldier), Stuttgart, 1950; Desmond Young, *Rommel*, Wiesbaden, 1959; Hans Speidel, *Invasion 1944: Ein Beitrag zu Rommel und des Reiches Schicksal* (Invasion 1944: A Contribution to Rommel and the Fate of the Reich), 5th edn, 1961; Ronald Levin, *Rommel*, 2nd edn, Stuttgart, 1971; David Irving, *Rommel: Eine Biographie* (Rommel: A Biography), Hamburg, 1978; and David Fraser, *Knights Cross: A Life of Field Marshal Erwin Rommel*, London, 1993.

2 Under the title *Crete: The Advent*, Churchill reports critically about the preparations but puts the blame for the omissions on the overworked Command Headquarters in Cairo. See *The Second World War*, vol. III, bk I, ch. 15.

3 King Pyrrhus I of Epirus went to war against Rome and won three battles in 280 and 279 BC in which he suffered such heavy losses that he reputedly said, 'One more such victory and we are lost!'

4 *The Second World War*, vol. III, bk I, ch. 16.

5 *Ibid.*

6 *The Second World War*, vol. II, bk II, ch. 31.

7 *The Second World War*, vol. III, bk I, ch. 20.

8 Churchill is quoting from a note by his private secretary. See *ibid.*

9 At the conference in Casablanca in January 1943 Roosevelt demanded the unconditional surrender of Germany and her allies, and Churchill agreed. This will be discussed later. In principle, however, this demand is already implied in the sentence just cited.

10 *The Second World War*, vol. III, bk I, ch. 20.

11 In addition to the 13.6 million military dead there were about seven million civilians who were killed or starved to death. In contrast Great Britain lost 388,000 killed, including 62,000 civilians.

12 As an example, in September 1942 the British convoy PQ.19/QP.14 lost seventeen ships totalling 94,791 tonnes in the Arctic Ocean against German losses of four submarines and 41 aircraft. In total about four million tonnes of goods were shipped to Russia and about 300,000 tonnes were lost. The British merchant marine lost 829 men and the Royal Navy 1,840 men and nineteen ships, including two cruisers. A good impression can be gained from the book by Brian B. Schofield, *op. cit.*

13 *The Second World War*, vol. III, bk II, ch. 21.

14 See, for example, Erich Schwinge, *op. cit.*, p. 27 *et seq.* Field Marshal Lord Alan-brooke wrote in his war diary: 'My personal feeling is that our policy towards the Russians was wrong to begin with. We kowtowed to them, did all we could for them, and never asked them for information about their production, strength, plans etc. The result is that they despise us and were only out to get as much from us as possible.' See *Triumph in the West: A History of the War Years Based on the Diaries of F. M. Lord Alanbrooke*, pub. by Arthur Bryant, 1959, entry for 13 August 1943. A critic such as John Charmley is even capable of alternately accusing Churchill of too much and of too little co-operation with the Soviet Union. See John Charmley, *op. cit.*

The Barbaric War

1 A 'classic' on this subject was published in 1946: Eugen Kogon, *Der SS-Staat: Das System der deutschen Konzentrationslager* (The SS State: The System of German Concentration Camps), new edn, Munich, 1974. For more recent works see Wolfgang Sofsky, *Die Ordnung des Terrors: Das Konzentrationslager* (The Structure of Terror: The Concentration Camp), Frankfurt-am-Main, 1993; Christian Graf von Krockow and Dirk Reinartz, *Totenstill* (Dead Silence), Göttingen, 1994.

2 As an example, when Tilly's Imperial troops took Magdeburg by storm on 10 May 1631 two-thirds of the inhabitants were slaughtered and the city was put to the torch. Only the *Liebfrauenkirche* and the cathedral remained intact, so the victors were able to celebrate their *Te Deum* above the smell of blood and smoke.

3 For examples see Helmut Krausnick and Hans-Heinrich Wilhelm, *Die Truppe des Weltanschauungskrieges: Die Einsatzgruppen der Sicherheitspolizei und des SD 1938–1942* (The Troops of the War of Ideologies: The Task Forces of the Security Police and the SD 1938–1942), Stuttgart, 1981. In his introduction Martin Broszat writes: 'In view of the fact that the Task Forces could not have carried out their special assignments without appropriate concessions by the *Wehrmacht*—and especially by the Army Command—Helmut Krausnick explores the relationship between security police and Army Command in detail and comes to depressing conclusions with regard to the rôle played by the *Wehrmacht*.' A further depressing example is provided by Christian Streit, *Keine Kameraden: Die Wehrmacht und die sowjetischen Kriegsgefangenen 1941–1945* (They Were Not Comrades: The Wehrmacht and the Soviet Prisoners of War 1941–1945), Stuttgart, 1978. See also Arno J. Mayer, *Der Krieg als Kreuzzug: Das Deutsche Reich, Hitlers Wehrmacht und die 'Endlösung'* (War as a Crusade: The German Reich, Hitler's Wehrmacht and the 'Final Solution'), Reinbeck, 1989; Jörg Friedrich, *Das Gesetz des Krieges: Das deutsche Heer in Russland 1941–1945. Der Prozess gegen das Oberkommando der Wehrmacht* (The Law of War: The German Army in Russia 1941–1945. The Trial of the Supreme Command of the Wehrmacht), Munich, 1995; and Walter Manoscheck, *Die Wehrmacht im Rassenkrieg: Der Vernichtungskrieg hinter der Front* (The Wehrmacht in the Racial War: The War of Extermi-

nation behind the Front), Vienna, 1996. For the pre-war events see Manfred Messerschmidt, *Die Wehrmacht im NS-Staat: Zeit der Indoktrination* (The Wehrmacht in the NS State: Time of Indoctrination), Hamburg, 1969; and Klaus-Jürgen Müller, *Das Heer und Hitler: Armee und nationalsozialistisches Regime 1933–1940* (The Army and Hitler: The Army and the National Socialist Regime 1933–1940), Stuttgart, 1969.

4 Gordon A. Craig, *Die preussisch-deutsche Armee 1640–1945, Staat im Staate* (The Prussian-German Army 1640–1945, a State within the State), Düsseldorf, 1960, p. 543.

5 The standard work on the British air war against Germany is Sir Charles Webster and Noble Frankland, *The Strategic Air Offensive Against Germany 1939–45*, 4 vols, London, 1961 *et seq.* An order to attack German cities was issued on 11 May 1940, the day after Churchill's appointment as Prime Minister. The directive of 14 February 1942 then became key, in which the switch to area bombing was expressely stated: 'It has been decided that the principal target of the operation is the morale of the enemy civilian population, especially of the industrial workers.' For the complete wording of the directive see: Webster and Frankland, *op. cit.*, vol. IV, p. 143 *et seq.* For a portrayal from the German point of view see Olaf Grohler, *Bombenkrieg gegen Deutschland* (Bomb War Against Germany), Berlin, 1991.

6 See, for example, his two chapters 'The Blitz' and 'London Can Take It' in *The Second World War*, vol. II, bk II.

7 *The Second World War*, vol VI, bk II, ch. 32.

8 Quoted in John Grigg, *1943: The Victory That Never Was*, 1980, p. 150. In general Grigg draws a highly critical picture.

9 The argument of support for the ally served as an excuse and a palliative for one's own conscience right up to the end, and so too for the attack on Dresden in February 1945. At the time the city had been 'a centre of communications of Germany's Eastern Front', writes Churchill (see *The Second World War*, vol VI, bk II, ch. 32). That, however, is nonsense. There were no longer any supplies worth mentioning which could have been directed to the Front. The Soviets therefore did not request the attack. But Dresden was filled to overflowing with wounded and refugees, with women and children and old people who had tried to save themselves before the advancing Red Army and had now landed in an even worse inferno.

A Community of Fate

1 *The Second World War*, vol. III, bk II, ch. 32.

2 Churchill speaks of madness and writes: 'A declaration of war by Japan could not be reconciled with reason. I felt sure she would be ruined for a generation by such a plunge, and this proved true. But Governments and peoples do not always take rational decisions. Sometimes they take mad decisions, or one set

of people get control who compel all others to obey and aid them in folly. I have not hesitated to record repeatedly my belief that Japan would go mad. However sincerely we try to put ourselves in another person's position, we cannot allow for processes of the human mind and imagination to which reason offers no key. Madness is however an affliction which in war carries with it the advantage of SURPRISE.' See *The Second World War*, vol. III, bk II, ch. 31.

3 *History of the English-Speaking Peoples*, vol. IV, p. 167. It is typical that in a reference work like Ploetz's *Auszug aus der Geschichte* (Excerpts from History) the American Civil War is dealt with in only a few lines. For the Americans on the other hand, this war has become a myth which occupies them far more than the two world wars of the twentieth century. For literature see Th. J. Pressly, *Americans Interpret Their Civil War*, Princeton, NJ, 1954; and B. Catton, *The Centennial History of the Civil War*, 3 vols, Garden City, NY, 1961–65. Since 1955 a periodical with the title *Civil War* had been published.

4 During the American Civil War a total of 2.5 million Union soldiers were mobilised against 1.2 million Confederates. Casualties were 360,000 Union killed and 260,000 Confederates.

5 *The Second World War*, vol. IV, bk I, ch. 22.

6 Edward Grey (1862–1933) was Foreign Secretary from 1905 to 1916.

7 The occasion was the formal leave-taking of Foreign Secretary Lord Halifax, who had been appointed as Ambassador to Washington to replace the recently deceased Lord Lothian. As already indicated, this was a political gambit by Churchill: the uncomfortable critic and possible rival Halifax was transferred to an apparently particularly important post which in reality was a sort of exile.

8 The complete speech is reproduced in *Blood, Sweat and Tears*, p. 447 *et seq.*

9 *Prince of Wales*, at the time the most modern British battleship, was sunk by Japanese torpedo planes on 10 December 1941 off the Malayan coast together with the battlecruiser *Repulse*. In his account of the voyage aboard *Prince of Wales* Churchill writes: 'I took a great liking to our captain, Leach, a charming and lovable man and all that a British sailor should be. Alas! within four months he and many of his comrades and his splendid ship were sunk for ever beneath the waves.' See *The Second World War*, vol. IV, bk I, ch. 23. Typical of Churchill's still unbroken lust for adventure is his reply to a message from his deputy Clement Attlee, who cabled from London his fear that on her return from Newfoundland *Prince of Wales* could be intercepted and attacked by *Tirpitz*. 'Concerning *Tirpitz*: I fear there will be no such luck.'

10 Since the Atlantic Charter does form this important point of departure but still gives cause for criticism to the present, here is the complete wording:

'The President of the United States of America and the Prime Minister, Mr. Churchill, representing His Majesty's Government in the United Kingdom, being met together, deem it right to make known certain common principles in the national policies of their respective countries on which they base their hopes for a better future for the world.

'First, their countries seek no aggrandisement, territorial or other.

'Second, they desire to see no territorial changes that do not accord with the freely expressed wishes of the people concerned.

'Third, they respect the rights of all peoples to choose the form of government under which they will live; and they wish to see sovereign rights and self-government restored to those who have been forcibly deprived of them.

'Fourth, they will endeavour, with due respect to their existing obligations, to further enjoyment by all States, great or small, victor or vanquished, of access, on equal terms, to the trade and to the raw materials of the world which are needed for their economic prosperity.

'Fifth, they desire to bring about the fullest collaboration between all nations in the economic field, with the object of securing for all improved labour standards, economic advancement, and social security.

'Sixth, after the final destruction of the Nazi tyranny they hope to see established a peace which will afford to all nations the means of dwelling in safety within their own boundaries, and which will afford assurance that all the men in all the lands may live out their lives in freedom from fear and want.

'Seventh, such a peace should enable all men to traverse the high seas and oceans without hindrance.

'Eighth, they believe that all the nations of the world, for realistic as well as spiritual reasons, must come to the abandonment of the use of force. Since no future peace can be maintained if land, sea, or air armaments continue to be employed by nations which threaten, or may threaten, aggression outside of their frontiers, they believe, pending the establishment of a wider and more permanent system of general security, that the disarmament of such nations is essential. They will likewise aid and encourage all other practicable measures which will lighten for peace-loving peoples the crushing burden of armaments.'

11 *The Second World War*, vol. III, bk II, ch. 33.

12 *Ibid.*, ch. 35.

13 *Ibid.*

14 *Ibid.*

15 A selection from the voluminous, often controversial literature on the Anglo-American alliance and the relationship between Roosevelt and Churchill – and because of the topical overlap, also books which include the Soviet Union and Stalin – would comprise Herbert Feis, *Churchill – Roosevelt – Stalin*, Oxford, 1957; Joseph P. Lash, *Roosevelt and Churchill, 1939–1941: The Partnership That Saved the West*, New York, 1976; Robin Edmonds, *The Big Three: Churchill, Roosevelt and Stalin in Peace and War*, London, 1991; Richard Lamb, *Churchill as War Leader: Right or Wrong?*, London, 1991; Keith Salisbury, *Churchill and Roosevelt at War: The War They Fought and the Peace They Hoped to Make*, Houndmills, 1994; Keith Alldritt, *The Greatest of Friends: Franklin D. Roosevelt and Winston Churchill, 1941–1945*, London, 1995; and John Charmley, *Churchill's Grand Alliance: The Anglo-American Special Relationship, 1940–1957*, London, 1995.

16 The Lend-Lease law was renewed in 1943 and remained in force until Septem-

ber 1946. On 6 November 1941 the Soviet Union was included, initially with a credit line of one billion dollars.

17 The basis for this is a sense of mission which Thomas Jefferson expressed almost exemplarily when he wrote: 'We feel we have been charged with duties which go beyond our own society. It is impossible that we do not feel how we act for all mankind, that by circumstances denied to others but granted to us we have been given the task to test in practice the degree of liberty and self-government a society may entrust to its members.' See letter to Dr Priestley of 19 June 1802. Otto Vossler was quite correct when he said: 'Jefferson was not the founder of American democracy. Its roots reach back further to England. But he was the founder of the consciousness of American democracy, its glorification, its pride and its humanitarian mission.' See *Die amerikanischen Revolutionsideale in ihrem Verhältnis zu den europäischen, untersucht an Thomas Jefferson* (The Relationship between the American Revolutionary Ideals and those of Europe using Thomas Jefferson as an Example), Munich, 1929, p. 187. This feeling of being a model leads to an ambivalence — either to missionary work or to isolationism in order to protect one's own good from a depraved world. But it leads, above all, to dividing the world at large into good and evil powers. During the Second World War Germany and Japan were evil; therefore the Soviet ally had to belong to the good powers. Later the situation changed completely, and as a consequence the Soviet Union became the 'Evil Empire'.

18 It was only thanks to refugees from Germany that a 'realistic' school of American foreign policy came about. One of particular importance and influence was the political scientist Hans J. Morgenthau — not to be confused with the Minister of Finance Henry M. Morgenthau Jr., the author of the so-called Morgenthau Plan — with his principal work *Politics Among Nations* (1963). The most important disciple of Morgenthau is Henry Kissinger.

19 *The Second World War*, vol. III, bk II, ch. 37. Because Churchill had enjoyed the adventure so much he eschewed battleships and for his second trip to Washington in June 1942 expressly ordered the Boeing flying boat with its Chief Pilot Kelly Rogers. The non-stop flight took 27 hours. Nevertheless, Churchill prepared a sort of last will and wrote to the King: 'In case I should die on the journey I am just embarking upon, I feel it would be useful with Your Majesty's kind permission to suggest that you charge Mr Anthony Eden with forming a new government . . . ' See *The Second World War*, vol. IV, bk I, ch. 22. Since Churchill did not die, Eden had to wait until 1955 before he could succeed him in office.

Between Bulls and Bears

1 *The Second World War*, vol. IV, bk I, ch. 6.
2 *Ibid.*, ch. 22.
3 Quoted in G. M. Thompson, *Vote of Censure*, 1968, p. 92.

4 *The Second World War*, vol. IV, bk I, ch. 4.

5 *Ibid.*, ch. 23.

6 When Tobruk surrendered Churchill had just arrived in Washington on his second visit and reported: 'There were no reproaches; not an unkind word was spoken. "What can we do to help?" said Roosevelt. I replied at once, "Give us as many Sherman tanks as you can spare, and ship them to the Middle East as quickly as possible." The President sent for General Marshall, who arrived in a few minutes, and told him of my request. Marshall replied, "Mr. President, the Shermans are only just coming into production. The first few hundred have been issued to our own armoured divisions, who have hitherto had to be content with obsolete equipment. It is a terrible thing to take the weapons out of a soldier's hands. Nevertheless, if the British need is so great they must have them; and we could let them have a hundred 105-mm. self-propelled guns in addition." To complete the story . . . the Americans were better than their word. Three hundred Sherman tanks with engines not yet installed and a hundred self-propelled guns were put into six of their fastest ships and sent off to the Suez Canal. The ship containing the engines for all the tanks was sunk by a submarine off Bermuda. Without a single word from us the President and Marshall put a further supply of engines into another fast ship and dispatched it to overtake the convoy. "A friend in need is a friend indeed."' See *The Second World War*, vol. III, bk II, ch. 22. The Sherman was the best tank the Western Allies had in the Second World War.

7 Göring had 'guaranteed' that the Luftwaffe could supply the Army, but poor weather, the lack of aircraft and the loss of air bases made his promise worthless. The dogged clinging to positions already lost marked Hitler's strategy more and more as the war went on. With this the German Army in the East was robbed of possibly the only advantage it still had: to be able to fight a defensive war of mobility. A commander who would have been suitable for this, Manstein, was not given supreme command but dismissed in March 1944. Two mistakes of particular importance should still be mentioned. After the Allied landings in Normandy in June 1944 the deployment of the divisions stationed on the Channel coast between Le Havre and Calais was delayed until it was too late. And the offensive in the Ardennes, which began on 16 December 1944, must be seen as a crime. Instead of holding the still combat-worthy armoured divisions behind the Eastern Front in readiness for the expected Russian offensive, they were senselessly squandered in the West. The almost completely unprotected German eastern provinces could therefore be overrun and the civilian population exposed to suffering and casualties which could have at least been reduced, given a slower advance by the Red Army and a faster one by the Americans and British.

8 *The Second World War*, vol. VI, bk I, ch. 16.

9 It was only after the collapse of the Soviet Union that the situation changed. Today even the Russian government has admitted that this was a Stalinist crime.

10 George Curzon (1859–1925) projected the 'line of 18 December 1919' which the

Western Powers saw as the eastern border of Poland and which they recommended to the Soviet Union at the conference in Spa on 11 July 1920 in order to settle the conflict with Poland. Thus the decisions taken at the conference in Teheran had precedents. Poland, however, lost her historic claims to Vilna and Lemberg. In 1920 the Curzon Line became redundant because the Polish Army drove the Red Army back in the Battle of Warsaw and then advanced victoriously eastwards. Accordingly, in the peace treaty of Riga on 18 March 1921 the Russian/Polish border was moved foward close to the city of Minsk and deep into the Ukraine.

11 See, for example, Nicolas Baciu, *Verraten und verkauft: Der tragische Fehler Churchills und Roosevelts in Osteuropa* (Betrayed and Sold Out: Churchill's and Roosevelt's Tragic Mistake in Eastern Europe), Tübingen, 1985; and also Remi Naneau, *Stalin, Churchill, and Roosevelt Divide Europe*, New York, 1990.

12 *The Second World War*, vol. V, bk II, ch. 19.

13 *Ibid.*, ch. 3. When Churchill put his memoirs of Teheran down on paper seven years had gone by, but one can still sense his anger about the uncouth son of the President. Elliott Roosevelt, it is claimed, had forced his way into the dinner party uninvited and intervened in a forward manner in the conversation. Later he then gave 'a very colourful and misleading report' about what he had heard.

14 Quoted in J. Wheeler-Bennet, *Action This Day: Working with Churchill*, 1968, p. 96.

15 Lord Moran, *op. cit.*, p. 159 *et seq.*

16 *The Second World War*, vol. V, bk II, ch. 24.

17 *Ibid.*, ch. 25.

The Military Finale

1 *The Second World War*, vol. IV, bk II, ch. 15.

2 See, for example, Erich Schwinge, *op. cit.*, p. 91 *et seq.* Schwinge cites allied authorities giving sources, for example Ambassador Bohlen: 'Hostilities would have ceased sooner and thousands of lives would have been spared if the President had not insisted on unconditional surrender.' Or General Wedemeyer: 'Instead of encouraging Hitler's German enemies, we forced all the Germans to fight to the end under a regime that most of them hated.' This is pure speculation, or is demonstrably wrong. Most Germans only discovered their aversion to tyranny after the unconditional surrender.

3 As late as the end of April 1945, shortly before his suicide, Hitler had Heinrich Himmler and Hermann Göring dismissed from office as traitors because they had offered to negotiate a surrender or asked for permission to act.

4 Fabian von Schlabrendorff, *Offiziere gegen Hitler* (Officers Against Hitler), Frankfurt-am-Main and Hamburg, 1959, p. 138.

5 *Ibid.*, p. 154. For information on Tresckow see Bodo Scheurig, *Henning von*

Tresckow: Eine Biographie (Henning von Tresckow: A Biography), Oldenburg and Hamburg, 1973.

6 *The Second World War*, vol. V, bk II, ch. 19.

7 Sebastian Haffner, *Winston Churchill mit Selbstzeugnissen und Bilddokumenten*, p. 140.

8 In Greece in 1944 the British became involved in a bitter civil war which could only be ended in 1949 by American aid against the Communists.

9 *The Second World War*, vol. V, bk II, ch. 19.

10 In his biography of Rommel David Irving gives us a colourful portrayal of the events on the German side which is, however, burdened by his polemics against Rommel's Chief of Staff General Speidel. See *Rommel: Eine Biography* (Rommel: A Biography), Hamburg, 1978, p. 554. It was typical that Hitler tried to avoid impending disaster by changing commanders. On 3 July he replaced the CinC West, Field Marshal von Rundstedt, by Field Marshal von Kluge. After Rommel was wounded, Kluge also took over command of the Army Group. Compromised by his knowledge of the conspiracy and the assassination attempt of 20 July, Kluge committed suicide and was again replaced by von Rundstedt.

11 *The Second World War*, vol. VI, bk I, ch. 1. When we read Churchill's portrayal we are almost reminded of a holiday idyll. It is interesting, therefore, to have a look at the official *Wehrmacht* reports. There we find for that very day, 10 July 1944: 'The violence of the battle in the southern sector of the Normandy bridgehead is increasing due to both sides having brought in new forces . . . In the Caen–Bayeux area [in other words, on Montgomery's front] heavy tank action continues. After bitter fighting the enemy has succeeded in pushing back our line of security behind which our reserves are deployed. There is bitter fighting in the Cherbourg Peninsula. Our troops are fighting gallantly against strong enemy forces and a superior air force. Along the whole front many pockets of resistance and strongpoints encircled by the enemy are holding out in tenacious fighting. During the first three days more than 200 enemy tanks have been hit and several thousand prisoners brought in. In addition the enemy, especially his airborne forces, suffered heavy bloody casualties.'

12 *The Second World War*, vol. VI, bk II, ch. 24. To quote again from the official *Wehrmacht* report of the same day: 'On the Rhine front between Rees and Dinslaken the defensive battle against the attacking British Second Army and parts of the American Ninth Army is raging. In isolated sectors the enemy was able to cross the Rhine under heavy losses and penetrate our main line of resistance. On both sides of Wesel, in whose streets heavy fighting is in progress, our troops were able to throw the enemy back to the Rhine.'

13 Official Biography,vol. II, p. 283.

14 *The Second World War*, vol. VI, bk II, ch. 25.

15 *Ibid.*

16 *Ibid.*

17 *Ibid.*, ch. 27.

18 Eisenhower was a diplomatic strategist, so to speak — which is precisely why he

had been selected for the difficult job of Allied Commander-in-Chief. Patton, on the other hand, was a brilliant tactician and a daredevil, whose wilfulness often provoked outrage. On Eisenhower see William Childs, *Eisenhower: Captive Hero*, 1958; and Stephen E. Ambrose, *The Supreme Commander: The War Years of General Dwight D. Eisenhower*, 1970. On Patton see B. G. Wallace, *Patton and his Third Army*, Washington, DC, 1946; and F. Ayer, *Before the Colors Fade*, Boston, 1964.

Triumph and Tragedy

1 Frederick had made an implacable enemy of Tsarina Elisabeth by his rashness when he called her, the Austrian Empress Maria Theresa and Madame Pompadour, the influential mistress of Louis XV, 'the three arch-whores of Europe'. Things like this create the ties that bind, and during the Seven Years' War Prussia was almost crushed by the alliance created by the three great powers. But the Tsarina died in 1762 and her nephew and successor Tsar Peter III admired Frederick almost to the point of adulation. He immediately concluded a peace and even changed alliances. While he was deposed and murdered after only a few months, the new Tsarina Catherina II, confirmed the peace treaty, if not the alliance. In 1841 Thomas Carlyle published his book *On Heroes, Hero-Worship, and the Heroic in History*. This was followed by a six-volume work published between 1858 and 1865 which portrays the exemplary hero—namely Frederick the Great.

2 *The Second World War*, vol. VI, bk II, ch. 28.

3 *Ibid.*, ch. 27.

4 In 1995, on the fiftieth anniversary, the young (now old) officers William Robertson and Alexander Silwashenko were invited to attend the festivities and were made honorary citizens of Torgau. In actual fact, the first handshake between Russians and Americans had occured further south near Strehla, and here the commander of the American patrol was named Kotzebue—like the German writer in the honorary pay of Russia who was assassinated as one of the first victims of fanatical nationalism in 1819.

5 The effectiveness of poison capsules was tested on the bitch and her puppies.

6 *Mein Kampf*, p. 693.

7 Harold Nicolson, *op. cit.*, p. 486 *et seq.*

8 *The Second World War*, vol. VI, bk II, ch. 323.

9 *Ibid.*, ch. 40.

10 *Ibid.*, ch. 34.

11 *Ibid.* Churchill coined the term 'Iron Curtain' and he first used it here and not, as is often claimed, in his famous speeches in the later post-war period.

12 The author can confirm this from his own experience. He still has his certificate of discharge from British captivity. The form foresaw not only a civilian registration with the residential community but also a military registration with the local (German!) 'garrison officer'. The author's discharge took place on 2

July and his civil registration on the 9th. Military registration—apparently after some hesitation—is entered for 21 July, officially countersigned by a sergeant, and stamped with an official German stamp from which the swastika had been cut out. In the British zone of occupation, therefore, there was still a network of German military offices two and a half months after the unconditional surrender.

13 For more details see Arthur Lee Smith, *Churchill's German Army: Wartime Strategy and Cold War Politics, 1943–1947*, Beverly Hills, Ca., 1977.

14 *The Second World War*, vol. VI, bk II, ch. 26.

15 *Ibid.*, ch. 29.

16 For such a portrayal see Christian Graf von Krockow, *Die Stunde der Frauen: Bericht aus Pommern 1944–1947* (The Hour of the Women: A Report from Pomerania 1944–1947), 9th edn, Stuttgart, 1993. There are also the several volumes of 'Documentation of the Expulsion of Germans from Central Eastern Europe' published by the Federal Ministry for Deportees, Refugees and War Victims. For a synopsis of this documentation see Gerhard Ziemer, *Deutscher Exodus: Vertreibung und Eingliederung von 15 Millionen Ostdeutschen* (German Exodus: Deportation and Integration of 15 Million East Germans), Stuttgart, 1973. For a vivid portrayal with pictorial documents see Frank Grube and Gerhard Richter, *Flucht und Vertreibung: Deutschland zwischen 1944 und 1947* (Flight and Deportation: Germany between 1944 and 1947), Hamburg, 1980. For the other side of the coin—German tyranny in Poland—see Martin Broszat, *Nationalsozialistische Polenpolitik 1939–1945* (National Socialist Policy towards Poland 1939–1945), revised edn, Frankfurt-am-Main and Hamburg, 1965.

October Sun and November Fog

1 *The Second World War*, vol. VI, bk II, ch. 21.

2 See *Churchill, Europe Unite: Speeches 1947 and 1948*, pub. by Randolph S. Churchill, London, 1950.

3 Quoted in Sebastian Haffner, *Winston Churchill mit Selbstzeugnissen und Bilddokumenten*, p. 163.

4 See *Churchill, The Unwritten Alliance: Speeches 1953 to 1959*, pub., by Randolph S. Churchill, London, 1961.

5 For the contradictory relationship between Adenauer and Churchill see Hans-Peter Schwarz, *Churchill and Adenauer*, Cambridge, 1994. In global politics Adenauer bet on the United States and in European politics on France, hardly on Great Britain. He basically agreed with Charles de Gaulle that Britain was not yet 'mature enough' for Europe. A comparison between the two old men in power suggests itself. Adenauer, born on 24 January 1876, was only a little more than a year younger than Churchill. The dates of death are also close: Churchill died on 24 January 1965, Adenauer on 19 April 1967. But Churchill had always been overly generous with his strength, whereas Adenauer had conserved his.

Churchill's great days ended in 1945, at a time when those of Adenauer were just beginning. Adenauer was therefore still able to perform, whereas Churchill had already exhausted himself.

6 Churchill is even alleged to have said: 'Dulles is just intelligent enough to be stupid to a large measure.' See Haffner, *op. cit.*

7 Quoted in Haffner, *op. cit.*, p. 165

8 On Churchill's health, illnesses and death see Lord Moran, *op. cit.*

Attempt at a Summary

1 Spencer's principal work, *A System of Synthetic Philosophy*, appeared between 1862 and 1896 in eleven volumes. Spencer had originally been a railway engineer, and for the rest of his life one can sense in him the optimism of the engineer—which is easy to uphold in the field of technical advancement.

2 This description of British society can be found in the works of the eccentric Prince Hermann von Pückler-Muskau (1785–1871), who was not only a famous landscape designer but also a precise observer and successful author of travelogues. The four volumes of his *Briefe eines Verstorbenen* (Letters from a Deceased) first appeared between 1830 and 1832. In letter No 22 he writes: 'From abroad one normally forms a more or less democratic view of British society. While this principle is quite remarkable in the public life of the nation, and becomes increasingly more so . . . in social relationships there is not the slightest trace of democratic elements to be found from the top down to the lowest level. To the greatest degree everything here is aristocratic; it is caste-like as in India.' See *Fürst Pückler reist nach England: Aus den Briefen eines Verstorbenen* (Prince Pückler Travels to England: From the Letters from a Deceased), pub. by Ch. M. Mettin, Stuttgart, 1958, p. 287 *et seq*. The reason for Pückler's trip to England was truly eccentric: in order to escape from his debts Pückler intended to marry a rich English lady. To be able to do so he had formally to separate from his existing wife, the daughter of Chancellor Prince Hardenberg, and he then lovingly reported all his adventures to her in the form of 'letters from a deceased'. Some time later, in 1845, and from the very much different point of view of a manufacturer in Manchester, Friedrich Engels was to describe *The Situation of the Working Class in England* and thereby provide Karl Marx with the material for his thesis that 'all history is the history of the class struggle'. See *The Communist Manifesto*, 1848.

3 In Britain the age of the social democratic reformers began with the founding of the Fabian Society by Sidney and Beatrice Webb in 1884. The Society later became the intellectual foundation of the Labour Party. While the Social Democratic Party in Germany had sworn itself to orthodox Marxism with its appropriate revolutionary rhetoric, also due to a large degree to Bismarck's persecution, in practice the SPD developed more and more into a reform party of the welfare state. This reformism found its expression in the writings of Eduard Bernstein,

who had spent formative years in England during the time of the persecution of socialism. His 'revisionist' principal work, *Die Voraussetzungen des Sozialismus und die Aufgaben der Sozialdemokratie* (The Preconditions of Socialism and the Tasks of Social Democracy), published in 1899, provoked passionate debates and was voted down by large majorities at all the party rallies. But in practice one did exactly what he had demanded – as Ignaz Auer, the Party Secretary of many years, confirmed to him in a letter: 'To act the way you demand, particularly on the part of the Party leadership, would simply mean breaking up the Party, throwing the work of many years to the dogs. My dear Ede, what you demand is not something one decides, not something one says, it is something one simply does. All of our work – even under the Shameful Law [Bismarck's law against Socialism] – was the work of a social democratic reform party. A Party which counts on the masses can hardly be anything else.' – quoted in Helga Grebing, *Der Revisionismus: Von Bernstein bis zum 'Prager Frühling'* (Revisionism: From Bernstein to the 'Prague Spring'), Munich, 1977, p. 36. See also Helmut Hirsch, *Der 'Fabier' Eduard Bernstein: Zur Entwicklungsgeschichte des evolutionären Sozialismus* (The 'Fabian' Eduard Bernstein: On the History of the Development of Evolutionary Socialism), Berlin and Bonn-Bad Godesberg, 1977; and Thomas Meyer, *Bernsteins konstruktiver Sozialismus: Eduard Bernsteins Beitrag zur Theorie des Sozialismus* (Bernstein's Constructive Socialism: Eduard Bernstein's Contribution to the Theory of Socialism), Berlin and Bonn-Bad Godesberg, 1977. The dichotomy between theory and practice, however, demanded a high price: on the one hand it was easy for the opponents to take the revolutionary rhetoric at face value and to generate fear by painting the 'red danger' on the wall, while on the other hand their practical contributions to the development of the welfare state had not prepared the Social Democrats for taking over total political responsibility as was demanded of them from 1918.

4 The term was primarily made popular by Ralf (now Lord) Dahrendorf. The beginning of the 'Thatcher Revolution' in 1979 marked a turning-point for Great Britain.

5 The most important work on this subject, J. A. Hobson's *Imperialism*, appeared in 1902 and provoked a plethora of further studies. Lenin wrote his pamphlet *Imperialism as the Newest Stage of Capitalism* in 1917.

6 One example is the Congo Conference initiated by Bismarck and held in Berlin from 15 November 1884 to 26 February 1885. The Fashoda Crisis in 1898 involving Great Britain and France and the Moroccan Crises in 1905–06 and again in 1911 between Germany and France were also settled by diplomatic means. The peaceful carving up of Africa by agreement had mostly been completed before the start of the First World War.

7 To repeat once more, in 1913 the respective shares in world trade were: Great Britain 15 per cent, Germany 13 per cent, the United States 11 per cent and France 8 per cent. This resulted in a trade deficit of 0.6 billion dollars for Great Britain, 0.3 billion for France, and 0.2 billion for Germany, whereas the United States achieved a surplus of 0.6 billion dollars. Britain had foreign investments

of 18, France of 9 and Germany of 5.8 billion dollars. The United States still belonged to the debtor countries. The accounts were largely balanced by interest transfers and the gold standard to which the leading nations had tied their currrencies made an uncomplicated foreign exchange possible.

8 When Churchill as First Lord of the Admiralty described British naval might as beneficial for the whole world, this may appear somewhat naïve in retrospect, and we can understand the outrage it caused in a Germany just in the process of arming in order to challenge this naval might. But it was completely in line with the spirit of an age which came to its end immediately thereafter.

9 See also Churchill's speech of 18 June 1940 in the chapter 'His Finest Hour', in which he says: 'If we can stand up to him [Hitler], all Europe may be free and the life of the world may move forward into broad, sunlit uplands.'

10 Ever since Thomas Morus's *Utopia* was published in 1516 it has been the outcome of positive utopias that they end in boredom, because for the human being who is only good there are no more evil desires, no more lust for fame and adventure, no more tragedies. At the same time the utopia itself falls into the evils of a dictatorship of re-education which, because it is against human nature, constantly discovers traitors and enemies who have to be re-educated, or, if re-education fails, to be exterminated so that the goal may be reached.

11 Max Scheler, 'Versuche einer Philosophie des Lebens' (Essays of a Philosophy of Life) in *Vom Umsturz der Werte: Abhandlungen und Aufsätze* (On the Upheaval of Values: Treatises and Essays), 2nd revised edn, Leipzig, 1919, vol. II, p. 189. The essays stem from the period 1912–14. During the war Scheler wrote a paean entitled *Der Genius des Krieges und der deutsche Krieg* (The Genius of War and the German War), Leipzig, 1915. At the end of the book, on p. 442 *et seq.*, there is a table of categories which confronts the decadence of British civilisation with the heights or depths of true — in other words German — culture.

12 *The Second World War*, vol. I, bk I, ch. 1.

13 *Ibid.* Thinking along the same lines as Foch, Churchill begins his history of the Second World War with the end of the First World War.

14 In the Weimar Republic there were many Republicans from rationale, but few democrats from the heart. Among those who had only come round to the support of the Republic by a deliberate act of willpower was Thomas Mann, who had nevertheless written late in the war: 'From deep conviction I avow that the German nation will never be able to love democracy for the simple reason that it is not able to love politics, and that the much vilified "authoritarian state" is the form of government which is appropriate for the Germans, which agrees with them, and which they basically wanted and still do . . . The difference between spirit and politics includes the differences between culture and civilisation, between the soul and society, between liberty and the franchise, between art and literature; and being German means culture, soul, liberty, art, and not civilisation, society, the franchise, literature.' See Thomas Mann, *Betrachtungen eines Unpolitischen* (Reflections of a Non-Political), 19th/24th edns, Berlin, 1922, pp. XXXIV and XXXVI. The conversion of Thomas Mann, however, remains

more the exception than the rule. In general, the dominating currents in the Weimar Republic were anti-Western and anti-liberal. One of the still fundamental studies on this topic is Kurt Sontheimer, *Antidemokratisches Denken in der Weimarer Republik* (Anti-Democratic Thinking in the Weimar Republic), Munich, 1962. See also Christian Graf von Krockow, *Die Entscheidung: Eine Untersuchung über Ernst Jünger, Carl Schmitt, Martin Heidegger* (The Decision: A Study on Ernst Jünger, Carl Schmitt, Martin Heidegger), new edn, Frankfurt-am-Main and New York, 1990.

15 This is normally referred to as the conservative revolution. See Stefan Breuer, *Anatomie der Konservativen Revolution* (Anatomy of the Conservative Revolution), Darmstadt, 1993.

16 We should recall Balfour's malicious comment: 'They tell me Winston has written a thick book about himself and called it *The World Crisis*.' But when we consider that Churchill felt himself personally affected by the crisis of war because it caused and destroyed a possibility inherent in his nature, the malice suddenly gains a deeper meaning.

17 One can only understand Bismarck's statesmanlike application of war when we take this for granted. His subsequent conversion to a defender of peace may also have to do with the fact that the possibilities of the degeneration of war frightened him. This was indicated in the second phase of the Franco-Prussian war of 1870–71 when — not without Bismarck's complicity — the extension of the war due to the demand for the cession of Alsace-Lorraine took place, giving the conflict a totally different character from the first, still professional phase, so to speak.

18 It is a deep question whether the destruction of war does not turn the lust for violence into a commonplace occurrence, all the way to the escape into fantasies of the future. It is hardly a coincidence that television series about space flights are normally portrayed as 'star wars'. What is no longer possible on earth should again be successful in space.

19 Erich Schwinge, *op. cit.*, p. 21. Schwinge quotes Hugh Dalton, *The Fateful Years: Memoirs*, 1957, p. 335.

20 As a model for such quarrelsome portrayals see John Charmley, *op. cit.*

Winston Churchill and His Age: A Chronology

Data concerning Churchill personally is set in italics

1871	Proclamation of the German Kaiser in Versailles and foundation of the German Reich.
1874	Benjamin Disraeli becomes Prime Minister. *Churchill born on 30 November in Blenheim Palace*
1876	Queen Victoria crowned Empress of India.
1876–79	*Childhood in Dublin.*
1880	Disraeli resigns; William Gladstone becomes Prime Minister.
1881–92	*School at Ascot, Brighton, and Harrow.*
1886	Defeat of the Irish Home Rule Bill. Gladstone resigns. Lord Salisbury forms a Conservative government.
1888	'Three-Emperor Year' in Germany; Willhelm II succeeds to the throne.
1890	Bismarck is dismissed.
1892	Salisbury resigns and Gladstone becomes Prime Minister for the second time.
1893–94	*Cadet at Sandhurst*
1895	*In January death of father Lord Randolph Churchill. From March Lieutenant with the 4th Hussars. Reporter in Cuba.* Lord Salisbury forms his second Conservative government
1896–97	*Officer in India. Takes part in border warfare,*
1898	*Takes part in the campaign in Sudan and Battle of Omdurman. Appears for the first time as an author with 'The Story of the Malakand Field Force'.* Beginning of German battlefleet construction.
1899	Start of Boer War. *Churchill leaves the Army. First unsuccessful candidacy for House of Commons. Goes to South Africa as war correspondent in Boer War. Capture and escape.*
1900	*Takes part in the war as a reactivated officer. Elected to House of Commons.*
1901	Death of Queen Victoria. Edward VII succeeds to the throne and reigns until 1910.

1902	Lord Salisbury resigns.
1904	Anglo-French 'Entente Cordiale'. *Churchill crosses the floor from the Tories to the Whigs.*
1906	*Churchill appointed Under-Secretary in the Colonial Office. Publishes his Biography of Lord Randolph Churchill.*
1907	Anglo-Russian Alliance.
1908	Asquith becomes Prime Minister. *Churchill appointed Minister of Economic Affairs. Marries Clementine Hozier.*
1910	Death of Edward VII. George V succeeds to the throne. *Churchill appointed Home Secretary.*
1911	*Churchill becomes First Lord of the Admiralty.*
1912	Failure of the 'Haldane Mission', the attempt to reach an Anglo-German agreement on limitations of naval strength.
1914	Start of the First World War.
1915	Failure of the Dardanelles operation. *Churchill resigns. From November is battalion commander in France.*
1916	David Lloyd George becomes Prime Minister. *Churchill returns to the House of Commons.*
1917	Germany declares unrestricted submarine warfare. The United States joins the war. Revolution in Russia. *Churchill appointed Minister of Munitions.*
1918	On 9 November revolution in Germany and proclamation of the republic. Armistice on 11 November ends the First World War.
1919	Peace treaty of Versailles. *Churchill appointed Minister of War and Aviation.*
1920	*Churchill becomes Colonial Secretary.*
1922	The government falls in October. *Churchill is defeated in the November elections.*
1924	*Churchill crosses the floor to the Conservatives. Appointed Chancellor of the the Exchequer.*
1929	Fall of the government. *Churchill out of office until 1939. Intensive work as journalist and author.*
1933	Adolf Hitler becomes German Chancellor.
1935	Re-introduction of conscription in Germany. Anglo-German Naval Treaty.
1936	Death of George V. Resignation of Edward VIII; his brother succeeds as King George VI. Germany renounces Locarno Pact and occupies the demilitarised Rhineland. Olympic Games in Berlin.
1937	Baldwin resigns; Neville Chamberlain becomes Prime Minister.
1938	13 March: annexation of Austria by Germany. September: Sudetenland Crisis. Threatening war is avoided by the Munich Accord.
1939	15 March: German troops enter Prague. Slovakia split off from the 'Reich Protectorate of Bohemia and Moravia'. Change in British foreign policy: independence of Poland is guaranteed. 23 August: treaty of non-aggression between Germany and the Soviet Union. 1 September: German attack

on Poland. 3 September: France and Great Britain declare war on Germany. *Churchill appointed First Lord of the Admiralty again.*

1940   April: German campaign against Norway. 10 May: German attack against the Low Countries, Belgium and France; *Churchill becomes Prime Minister the same day.* Italy joins the war. France surrenders on 22 June. Battle of Britain, with high point in August and September

1941   22 June: Germany attacks the Soviet Union. 14 August: Roosevelt and Churchill announce the Atlantic Charter. December: reversals of the German Army in the Russian winter. Japanese attack on Pearl Harbor. The United States join the war.

1942   15 February: Singapore surrenders. 21 June: Tobruk surrenders. Turn of the war in Africa in October and November: Battle of El Alamein and Allied landings in Morocco and Algeria.

1943   Turn of the war in Russia: in January destruction of German Sixth Army in Stalingrad, in July German defeat in the tank Battle of Kursk. Allied landings in Italy lead to fall of Mussolini and Italy quitting the war. 28 November to 1 December: conference of the 'Big Three' in Teheran

1944   6 June: Allied landings in Normandy lead to liberation of France. Between June and August the Red Army destroys the German eastern front.

1945   12 January: start of the Russian offensive against eastern Germany. 4–11 February: summit meeting of the 'Big Three' in Yalta. March: Allies cross the Rhine and by May will have occupied western, southern, northern and central Germany. 12 April: death of President Roosevelt. 30 April: Hitler commits suicide. 4–9 May: Germany surrenders. 17 July–2 August: summit meeting of the 'Big Three' in Potsdam. *Churchill resigns on 26 July after the Conservative defeat in the General Election.*

1947   European Recovery Programme (Marshal Plan). Start of the Cold War.

1948–49 Partitioning of Germany. Berlin Blockade. Foundation of the Federal Republic and the German Democratic Republic. September 1949: Konrad Adenauer becomes the first Chancellor of the Federal Republic.

1948–54 *Churchill publishes his history of the Second World War.*

1949   North Atlantic Treaty Organisation (NATO) is founded.

1950   Start of the Korean War.

1951   *Churchill becomes Prime Minister for the second time.*

1952   George VI dies. Elizabeth II succeeds to the throne.

1953   Stalin dies on 5 March. *Churchill suffers a stroke. He is awarded the Nobel Prize for Literature.*

1955   *5 April: Churchill resigns as Prime Minister.*

1956   *Churchill awarded the* Karlspreis *of the city of Aix-la-Chapelle for his efforts on behalf of European unification.*

1963   *Churchill is awarded honorary citizenship of the United States of America.*

1965   *24 January: Winston Churchill dies in London.*

Select Bibliography

Books by Winston Churchill

The Story of the Malakand Field Force: An Episode of Frontier War, London, 1898.
The River War: An Historical Account of the Reconquest of the Soudan, 2 vols, London, 1899.
Savrola: A Tale of the Revolution in Laurania, New York, 1900.
London to Ladysmith via Pretoria, London, 1900.
Ian Hamilton's March, London, 1900.
Mr. Brodrick's Army, London, 1903.
Lord Randolph Churchill, 2 vols, London, 1906.
My African Journey, London, 1906.
Liberalism and the Social Problem, London, 1909.
The World Crisis, 5 vols, London, 1923–31.
Parliamentary Government and the Economic Problem, Oxford, 1930.
My Early Life: A Roving Commission, London, 1930.
The World Crisis 1911–1918, abbreviated and edited edition with an additional chapter on the Battle of the Marne, London, 1931.
Thoughts and Adventures, London, 1932.
Marlborough: His Life and Times, 4 vols, London, 1933–38
Great Contemporaries, London, 1937.
Step by Step, 1936–1939, London, 1939.
On Human Rights, Melbourne, 1942.
United Europe, Newsletters of the United Europe Movement, No 1, London, 1946.
A United Europe: One Way to Stop a New War, London, 1947.
Painting as a Pastime, London, 1948.
The Second World War, 6 vols, London, 1948–54.
A History of the English-Speaking Peoples, 4 vols, London, 1956–58.
The Second World War, abridged with an Epilogue on the Years 1945–1957, London, 1959.
The Collected Works of Sir Winston Churchill, pub. by Frederick Woods, 34 vols, London, 1973-1976.

A Selection of Churchill's Speeches

For Free Trade: A Collection of Speeches, London, 1906.

For Liberalism and Free Trade: The Principal Speeches, Dundee, 1908.

The People's Rights: Selected from his Lancashire and Other Recent Speeches, London, 1910.

India: Speeches and an Introduction, London, 1931.

Arms and the Covenant, pub. by Randolph Churchill, London, 1938.

Blood, Sweat, and Tears, New York, 1941.

Into Battle, pub. by Randolph Churchill, London, 1941.

The Unrelenting Struggle: War Speeches, pub. by Charles Eade, London, 1942.

The End of the Beginning: War Speeches 1942, pub. by Charles Eade, London, 1943.

Onwards to Victory: War Speeches 1943, pub. by Charles Eade, London, 1944.

The Dawn of Liberation: War Speeches 1944, pub. by Charles Eade, London, 1945.

Victory: War Speeches 1945, pub. by Charles Eade, London, 1946.

Europe Unite: Speeches 1947–1948, pub. by Randolph Churchill, London, 1950.

In the Balance: Speeches 1949–1950, pub. by Randolph Churchill, London, 1951.

Stemming the Tide: Speeches 1951–1952, pub. by Randolph Churchill, London, 1953.

The Unwritten Alliance: Speeches 1953–1959, pub. by Randolph Churchill, London, 1961.

The War Speeches, pub. by Charles Eade, 3 vols, London, 1952.

Blood, Toil, Tears, and Sweat: Churchill's Famous Speeches, pub. by David Cannadine, London, 1989.

Winston S. Churchill: His Complete Speeches, 1897–1963, pub. by Robert Rhodes James, 8 vols, New York. 1974.

Churchill's Historically Important Correspondence

Stalin's Correspondence with Churchill, Attlee, Roosevelt and Truman, 1941–1945, 2 vols, London, 1958.

Roosevelt and Churchill: Their Secret Wartime Correspondence, pub. by Francis L. Loewenheim, London, 1975.

Churchill and Roosevelt: The Complete Correspondence, 3 vols, pub. by Warren F. Kimball, Princeton, NJ, 1984.

The Churchill–Eisenhower Correspondence 1953–1955, pub. by Peter G. Boyle, Chapel Hill, NC, 1990.

A Selection of Books About Churchill and His Times

Adé, Annemarie, *Winston Churchill und die Palästina-Frage 1917–1948* (Winston Churchill and the Palestine Question 1917-1948), Zürich, 1973.

Addison, Paul, *Churchill on the Home Front, 1900–1955*, London, 1992.

Aigner, Dieter, *Winston Churchill: Ruhm und Legende* (Winston Churchill: Fame and Legend), Göttingen, 1974.

Alldritt, Keith, *Churchill the Writer: His Life as a Man of Letters*, London, 1992.

———, *The Greatest of Friends: Franklin D. Roosevelt and Winston Churchill, 1941–1945*, London, 1995.

Améry, Jean, *Winston Churchill: Ein Jahrhundert Zeitgeschichte* (Winston Churchill: A Century of Contemporary History), Lucerne, 1965.

Amery, Julian, *What Was Churchill's Political Philosophy?*, Zürich, 1976.

Arthur, George C. A., *Concerning Winston S. Churchill*, London, 1940.

Baciu, Nicolas, *Verraten und verkauft: Der tragische Fehler Churchills und Roosevelts in Osteuropa* (Betrayed and Sold Out: The Tragic Mistake of Churchill and Roosevelt in Eastern Europe), Tübingen, 1985.

Boadle, Donald Graeme, *Winston Churchill and the German Question in British Foreign Policy 1918–1922*, The Hague, 1973.

Böttger, Peter, *Winston Churchill und die 'Zweite Front', 1941–1943* (Winston Churchill and the 'Second Front', 1941–1943), Frankfurt-am-Main, 1984.

Brendon, Piers, *Churchill*, Munich, 1984.

Broad, Lewis, *The War that Churchill Waged*, London 1960.

Brown, Anthony Montague, *Long Sunset: Memoirs of Churchill's Last Private Secretary*, London 1995.

Callahan, Raymond, *Churchill: Retreat from Empire*, Wilmington, 1984.

Caplin, E. D. W., *Winston Churchill and Harrow: Memoirs of the Prime Minister's Schooldays, 1888–1892*, Harrow, 1941.

Captain X, *With Winston Churchill at the Front*, Glasgow, 1924.

Charmley, John, *Churchill's Grand Alliance: The Anglo-American Special Relationship, 1940–1957*, London, 1995.

———, *Churchill, the End of Glory: A Political Biography*, London 1993.

Charter, V. B., *Winston Churchill: An Intimate Portrait*, New York, 1965.

Churchill, Randolph S., (pub.), *et al.*, *Churchill: His Life in Photographs*, London, 1955.

Churchill, Randolph S., *Winston S. Churchill*, 8 vols with 13 supp. vols (from vol. 3 on by Martin Gilbert), London, 1966–88.

Colville, John, *The Churchillians*, London, 1981.

———, *The Fringes of Power: Downing Street Diaries, 1939–1955*, Berlin, 1988.

———, *Winston Churchill and his Inner Circle*, New York, 1981.

Cowles, Virginia, *Winston Churchill: The Era and the Man*, London, 1953.

Davis, Richard H., *The Young Winston Churchill*, New York, 1941.

Dawson, Robert M., *Winston Churchill at the Admiralty, 1911–1915*, Oxford, 1940.

Deakin, Frederick William Dampier, *Churchill the Historian*, Zürich, 1969.

Denniston, Robin, *Churchill's Secret War*, Stroud, 1996.

Dunkirk to Berlin, June 1940–July 1945: A Map of the Journeys Undertaken by the Rt. Hon. Winston Churchill, London, 1947.

Edmonds, Robin, *The Big Three: Churchill, Roosevelt, and Stalin in Peace and War*, London, 1991.

Feis, Herbert, *Churchill – Roosevelt – Stalin*, Oxford, 1957.

Germains, H. V., *The Tragedy of Winston Churchill*, London, 1931.

Gilbert, Martin, *Churchill*, Garden City, NY, 1980.

———, *Churchill: A Photographic Portrait*, London, 1974.

———, *In Search of Churchill: A Historian's Journey*, London, 1994.

———, *Prophet of Truth: Winston S. Churchill 1922–1939*, London, 1990.

Graubard, Stephen R., *Burke, Disraeli, and Churchill: The Politics of Perseverance*, Cambridge, Mass., 1961.

Gretton, Peter, *Winston Churchill and the Royal Navy*, New York, 1969.

Haffner, Sebastian, *Winston Churchill mit Selbstzeugnissen und Bilddokumenten* (Winston Churchill with Self-Avowals and Pictorial Documents), 14th edn, Reinbek bei Hamburg, 1997

———, 'Winston Churchill: Vom Krieger aus Leidenschaft zum Friedenspolitiker' (Winston Churchill: From Warrior of Passion to Politician of Peace) in Haffner, *Im Schatten der Geschichte: Historisch-politische Variationen aus zwanzig Jahren* (In the Shadow of History: Historical-Political Variations from Twenty Years), Stuttgart, 1985.

Hagberg, Knut, *Kings, Churchills, and Statesmen: A Foreigner's View*, London, 1929.

———, *Winston Churchill*, Stockholm, 1944.

Hawthorne, Hildegard, *Long Adventure: The Story of Winston Churchill*, New York, 1942.

Higgins, Trumbull, *Winston Churchill and the Second Front*, Oxford, 1957

Holley, Darrell, *Churchill's Literary Allusions: An Index to the Education of a Soldier, Statesman and Litterateur*, Jefferson, Ohio, 1987.

Hughes, Emrys, *Churchill: Ein Mann in seinem Widerspruch* (Churchill: A Man in His Contradictions), Kiel, 1986.

Jablonsky, David, *Churchill and Hitler: Essays on the Political-Military Direction of Total War*, Portland 1994.

———, *Churchill, the Great Game and Total War*, London, 1990.

James, Robert Rhodes, *Churchill: A Study in Failure, 1900–1939*, London, 1970.

Jog, Narayan Gopal, *Churchill's Blind-Spot: India*, Bombay, 1944.

Keynes, John Maynard, *The Economic Consequences of Mr. Churchill*, London, 1925.

Lamb, Richard, *Churchill as a War Leader: Right or Wrong?*, London, 1991.

Lambakis, Steven James, *Winston Churchill, Architect of Peace: A Study of Statesmanship and the Cold War*, Westport, 1993.

Larres, Klaus, *Politik der Illusionen: Churchill, Eisenhower und die deutsche Frage* (Politics of Illusion: Churchill, Eisenhower and the German Question), Göttingen, 1995.

Lash, Joseph P., *Roosevelt and Churchill, 1939–1941. The Partnership that Saved the West*, New York, 1976.

Lee, Michael John, *The Churchill Coalition, 1940–1945*, London, 1980.

Lehnhoff, Franz, *Winston Churchill: Engländer und Europäer* (Winston Churchill: Englishman and European), Cologne, 1949.

Lewin, Ronald, *Churchill as Warlord*, New York, 1973.

Lukacs, John, *The Duel 10 May–31 July 1940. The Eighty-Day Struggle Between Churchill and Hitler*, New York and London, 1990.

Manchester, William, *Winston Spencer Churchill*, 2 vols, Boston, 1983.

Manning, Paul and Brunner, M., *Mr. England: The Life Story of Winston Churchill*, Toronto, 1941.

Marder, Arthur Jacob, *Winston is Back: Churchill at the Admiralty, 1939–1940*, London, 1972.

Marsh, John, *The Young Winston Churchill*, London, 1955.

Mayer, Frank A., *The Opposition Years: Winston S. Churchill and the Conservative Party, 1945–1951*, New York, 1992.

Mendelssohn, Peter de, *Churchill: Sein Weg und seine Welt* (Churchill: His Way and his World), vol. I: *Erbe und Abenteuer: Die Jugend Winston Churchills 1874–1914* (Heritage and Adventure: The Youth of Winston Churchill 1874–1914), Freiburg im Breisgau, 1957. Only this volume has been published.

Miner, Steven Merritt, *Between Churchill and Stalin: The Soviet Union, Great Britain, and the Origins of the Grand Alliance*, Chapel Hill, NC, 1988.

Moran, Charles Macmoran Wilson, *Churchill: Der Kampf ums Überleben. Aus dem Tagebuch seines Leibarztes Lord Moran* (Churchill: The Fight for Survival. From the Diary of his Personal Physician Lord Moran), Zürich 1967.

Morgan, Ted, *Churchill: Young Man in a Hurry, 1874–1915*, New York 1982.

Nadeau, Remi, *Stalin, Churchill, and Roosevelt Divide Europe*, New York, 1990.

Nelson, Francis, *The Churchill Legend*, New York, 1954.

Neville, Peter, *Winston Churchill: Statesman or Opportunist?*, London, 1996.

Nott, Stanley, *The Young Churchill*, New York, 1941.

Paneth, Philip, *The Prime Minister Winston Churchill: As Seen by his Enemies and Friends*, London, 1943.

Pearson, John, *The Private Lives of Winston Churchill*, New York, 1991.

Pilpel, Robert H., *Churchill in America, 1895–1961: An Affectionate Portrait*, New York, 1976.

Pitt, Barrie, *Churchill and the Generals*, London, 1981.

Ponting, Clive, *Churchill*, London, 1994.

Prior, Robin, *Churchill's 'World Crisis' as History*, London, 1983.

Rabinowicz, Oskar L., *Winston Churchill on Jewish Problems*, Westport, 1974.

Rose, Norman, *Churchill: An Unruly Life, London*, 1994.

Roskill, Stephen, *Churchill and the Admirals*, London, 1977.

Salisbury, Keith, *Churchill and Roosevelt at War: The War They Fought and the Peace They Hoped to Make*, Houndmills 1994.

Schneider, Robert W., *Novelist to a Generation: The Life and Thought of Winston Churchill*, Bowling Green, Ohio, 1976.

Schmidt, Alex P., *Churchills privater Krieg: Intervention und Konterrevolution im russischen Bürgerkrieg, November 1918–März 1920* (Churchill's Private War: Intervention and Counter-Revolution in the Russian Civil War, November 1918–March 1920), Zürich, 1975.

Schoenfeld, Maxwell Philip, *Sir Winston Churchill: His Life and Times*, Hinsdale, Ill., 1973.

———, *The War Ministry of Winston Churchill*, Ames, Iowa, 1972.

Schwarz, Hans-Peter, *Churchill and Adenauer*, Cambridge, 1994.

Schwinge, Erich, *Churchill und Roosevelt aus kontinentaleuropäischer Sicht* (Churchill and Roosevelt from a Continental European Point of View), 4th edn, Marburg, 1986.

Scott, A. McCallum, *Winston Churchill in War and Peace*, London, 1916.

———, *Winston Spencer Churchill*, London, 1905.

Seldon, Anthony, *Churchill's Indian Summer, 1951–1955*, London, 1981.

Seth, Hira Lal, *Churchill on India*, Lahore, 1942.

Smith, Arthur Lee, *Churchill's German Army: Wartime Strategy and Cold War Politics, 1943–1947*, Beverly Hills, Ca., 1977.

Soames, Mary, *A Churchill Family Album*, London, 1982.

———, *Clementine Churchill*, London, 1979.

———, *Winston Churchill: His Life as a Painter. A Memoir by his Daughter*, London, 1990.

Taylor, Robert Lewis, *Winston Churchill*, New York, 1952.

Thomas, David A., *Churchill: A Member for Woodford*, Ilford, 1994.

Thompson, Carlos, *Die Verleumdung des Winston Churchill* (The Slander against Winston Churchill), Munich, 1980.

Thompson, W. H., *I Was Churchill's Shadow*, London, 1951.

Tucker, Ben, *Winston Churchill: His Life in Pictures*, London, 1945.

Venkataramani, M. S., *Roosevelt, Gandhi, Churchill*, New Delhi, 1983.

Vogt, Werner, *Winston Churchill: Mahnung, Hoffnung und Vision, 1938–1946* (Winston Churchill: Admonition, Hope and Vision, 1938–1946). The Image of Churchill in the Reporting by the *Neue Zürcher Zeitung* and its Entrepreneurial-Historical Background, Zürich, 1996.

Waszak, Leon J., *Agreement in Principle: The Wartime Partnership of General Wladislaw Sikorski and Winston Churchill*, New York, 1996.

Weidhorn, Manfred, *Sir Winston Churchill*, Boston, 1979.

———, *Sword and Pen: A Survey of the Writings of Sir Winston Churchill*, Albuquerque, 1974.

Winston S. Churchill: Chronik eines glorreichen Lebens. Ein Bildband (Winston S. Churchill: Chronicle of a Glorious Life. A Volume of Illustrations), Zürich, 1966.

Woods, Frederick, *Artillery of Words: The Writings of Sir Winston Churchill*, London, 1992.

Young, John W. (pub.), *The Foreign Policy of Churchill's Peacetime Administration, 1951–1955*, Leicester, 1988.

———, *Winston Churchill's Last Campaign: Britain and the Cold War, 1951/5*, Oxford 1996.

Index of Names